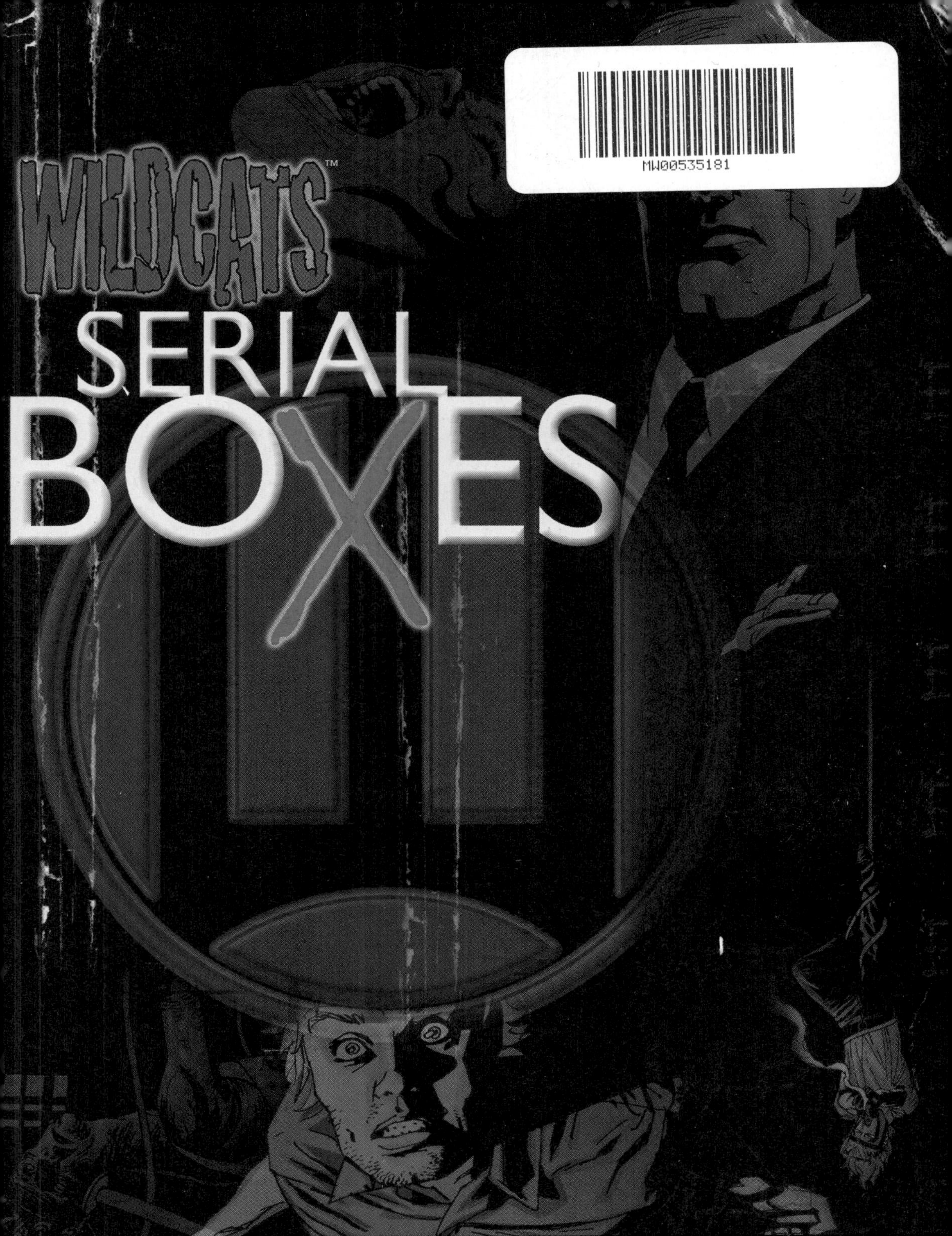
WILDCATS™
SERIAL BOXES

WILDCATS: SERIAL BOXES. Published by WildStorm Productions, 7910 Ivanhoe Ave # 438, La Jolla, CA 92037.

Originally published in single magazine form as WILDCATS v2 # 14-19 ©2000 WildStorm Productions, an imprint of DC Comics. WILDCATS and all related characters and indicia are trademarks of DC Comics. The stories, characters and incidents mentioned in this magazine are entirely fictional. Printed on recyclable paper. Printed in Canada. DC Comics. A division of Warner Bros. -an AOL Time Warner Company.
ISBN : 1-56389-766-0

story tellers
JOE CASEY
SEAN PHILLIPS

colors
DAN BROWN
BRIAN HABERLIN
&
WILDSTORM FX

letters
RICHARD STARKINGS
&
COMICRAFT'S
SAIDA
TEMOFONT

collection
design
LARRY BERRY

WildCats created by JIM LEE & BRANDON CHOI

JENETTE KAHN, President & Editor-in-Chief
PAUL LEVITZ, Executive VP & Publisher
JIM LEE, Editorial Director - WildStorm
JOHN NEE, VP & General Manager - WildStorm
SCOTT DUNBIER, Group Editor
SCOTT DUNBIER & ERIC DESANTIS, Original Series Editors
ALEX SINCLAIR, Art Director
RICHARD BRUNING, VP - Creative Director
PATRICK CALDON, Senior VP - Finance & Operations
DOROTHY CROUCH, VP - Licensed Publishing
TERRI CUNNINGHAM, VP - Managing Editor
JOEL EHRLICH, Senior VP - Advertising & Promotions
ALISON GILL, Executive Director - Manufacturing
LILLIAN LASERSON, VP & General Counsel
CHERYL RUBIN, VP - Licensing & Merchandising
BOB WAYNE, VP - Sales & Marketing

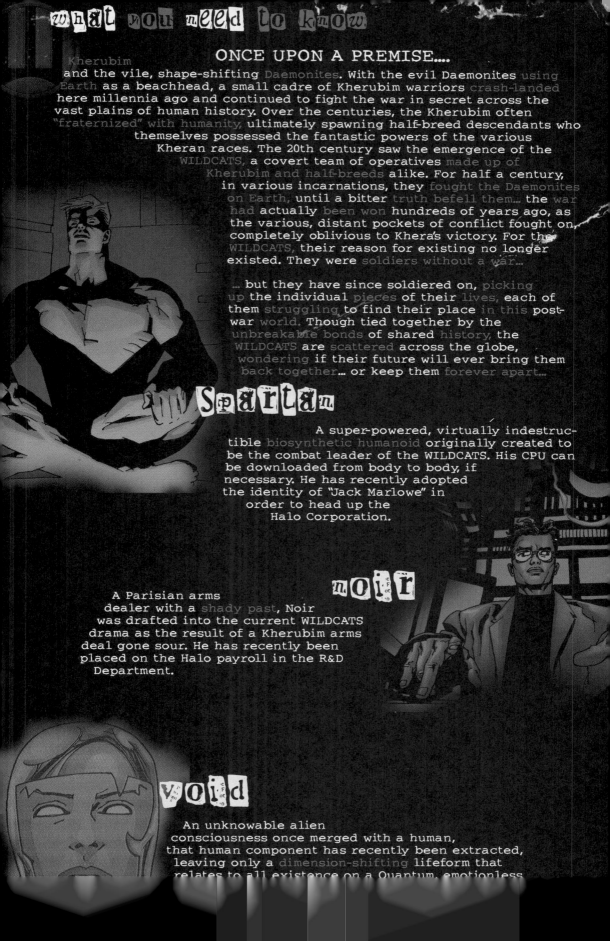

ONCE UPON A PREMISE....

Kherubim and the vile, shape-shifting Daemonites. With the evil Daemonites using Earth as a beachhead, a small cadre of Kherubim warriors crash-landed here millennia ago and continued to fight the war in secret across the vast plains of human history. Over the centuries, the Kherubim often "fraternized" with humanity, ultimately spawning half-breed descendants who themselves possessed the fantastic powers of the various Kheran races. The 20th century saw the emergence of the WILDCATS, a covert team of operatives made up of Kherubim and half-breeds alike. For half a century, in various incarnations, they fought the Daemonites on Earth, until a bitter truth befell them... the war had actually been won hundreds of years ago, as the various, distant pockets of conflict fought on, completely oblivious to Khera's victory. For the WILDCATS, their reason for existing no longer existed. They were soldiers without a war...

... but they have since soldiered on, picking up the individual pieces of their lives, each of them struggling to find their place in this post-war world. Though tied together by the unbreakable bonds of shared history, the WILDCATS are scattered across the globe, wondering if their future will ever bring them back together... or keep them forever apart...

Spartan

A super-powered, virtually indestruc-tible biosynthetic humanoid originally created to be the combat leader of the WILDCATS. His CPU can be downloaded from body to body, if necessary. He has recently adopted the identity of "Jack Marlowe" in order to head up the Halo Corporation.

noir

A Parisian arms dealer with a shady past, Noir was drafted into the current WILDCATS drama as the result of a Kherubim arms deal gone sour. He has recently been placed on the Halo payroll in the R&D Department.

void

An unknowable alien consciousness once merged with a human, that human component has recently been extracted, leaving only a dimension-shifting lifeform that relates to all existence on a Quantum, emotionless

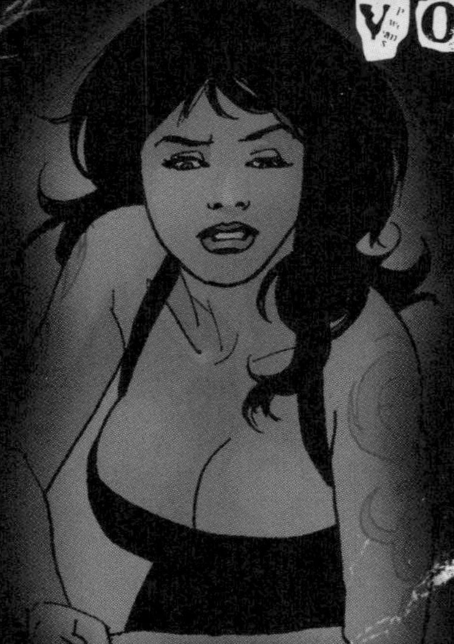

Voodoo

Priscilla Kitaen was living a simple life as an exotic dancer when she was "recruited" by the WILDCATS. Unlike the rest of the original team, she is a Daemonite half-breed (allowing her low- grade shape-shifting abilities). Post-war, Pris is currently crashing at the Miami home of a former teammate...

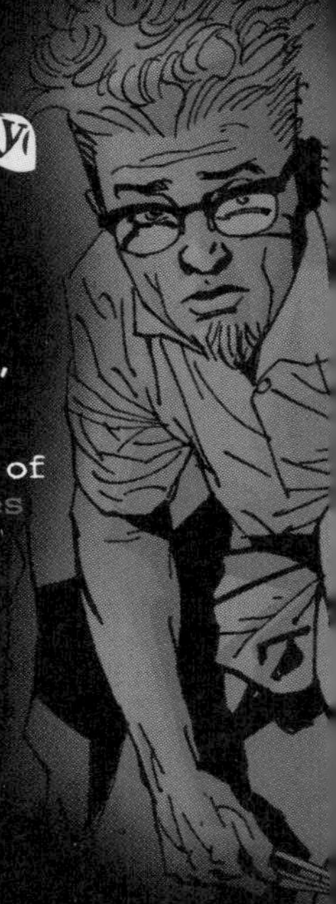

Jeremy Stone

Dr. Jeremy Stone's Kherubim DNA allows him to control his body mass, increasing or decreasing it at will. While increasing it (to increase his strength) causes a corresponding loss of intellect, decreasing it actually magnifies his intelligence, allowing him to engage in scientific research on a much higher level than your typical genius.

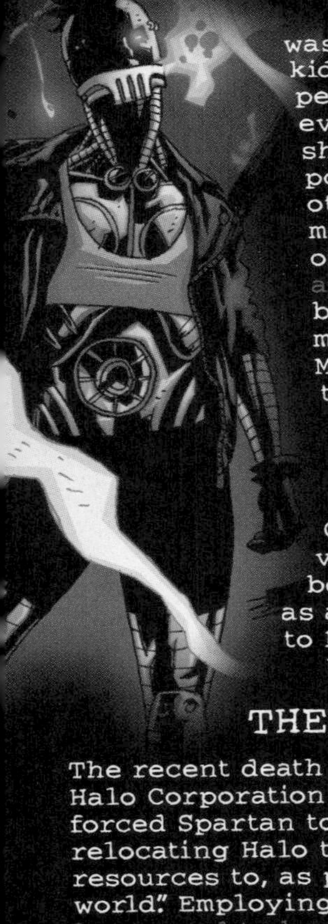

Ladytron

Maxine Manchester was a bad seed from day one. A kid with an acidic attitude and a penchant for chaos, her lifestyle eventually caught up with her and she ended up on the losing end of a police shootout. Emerging from the other end of the meat grinder with most of her flesh replaced with cyber-organic parts, this only fueled her appetite for destruction. After a brief affiliation with the mecha-maniacal Church of Gort, Maxine has been returned to her former teammates.

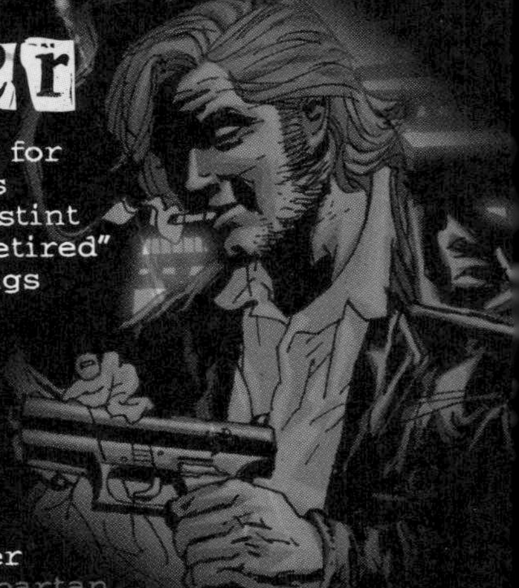

Grifter

Cole Cash began his career working for various covert intelligence agencies before joining the WILDCATS. After a stint as a freelance mercenary, Cash has "retired" to New York City, far away from all things WILDCATS-related.

THE STORY SO FAR....

The recent death of Lord Emp (founder of both the Halo Corporation and the original WILDCATS) has forced Spartan to take command of his estate, relocating Halo to Los Angeles and using its resources to, as per Emp's final wishes, "make a better world." Employing several of his former teammates, Spartan has vowed to break with the past and seek out a new future. Such is the case with all of the WILDCATS. But, as Lord Emp before them has learned, their colorful -- and often violent -- past can continue to haunt them in impossib unpredictable ways...

New York City.
Park Avenue.

GOING DOWN?

OF COURSE. ALL THE WAY.

1EEP MEEP MEEP MEEP

SIR...? SIR, IT'S ME. IT'S RUDDOCK.

CAN YOU HEAR ME, SIR...?

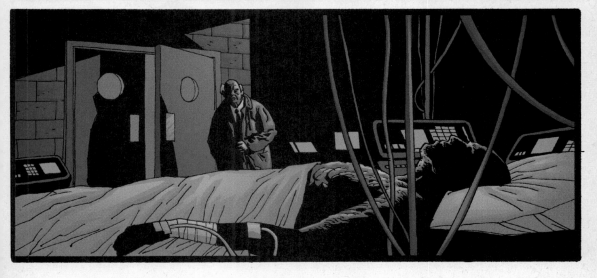

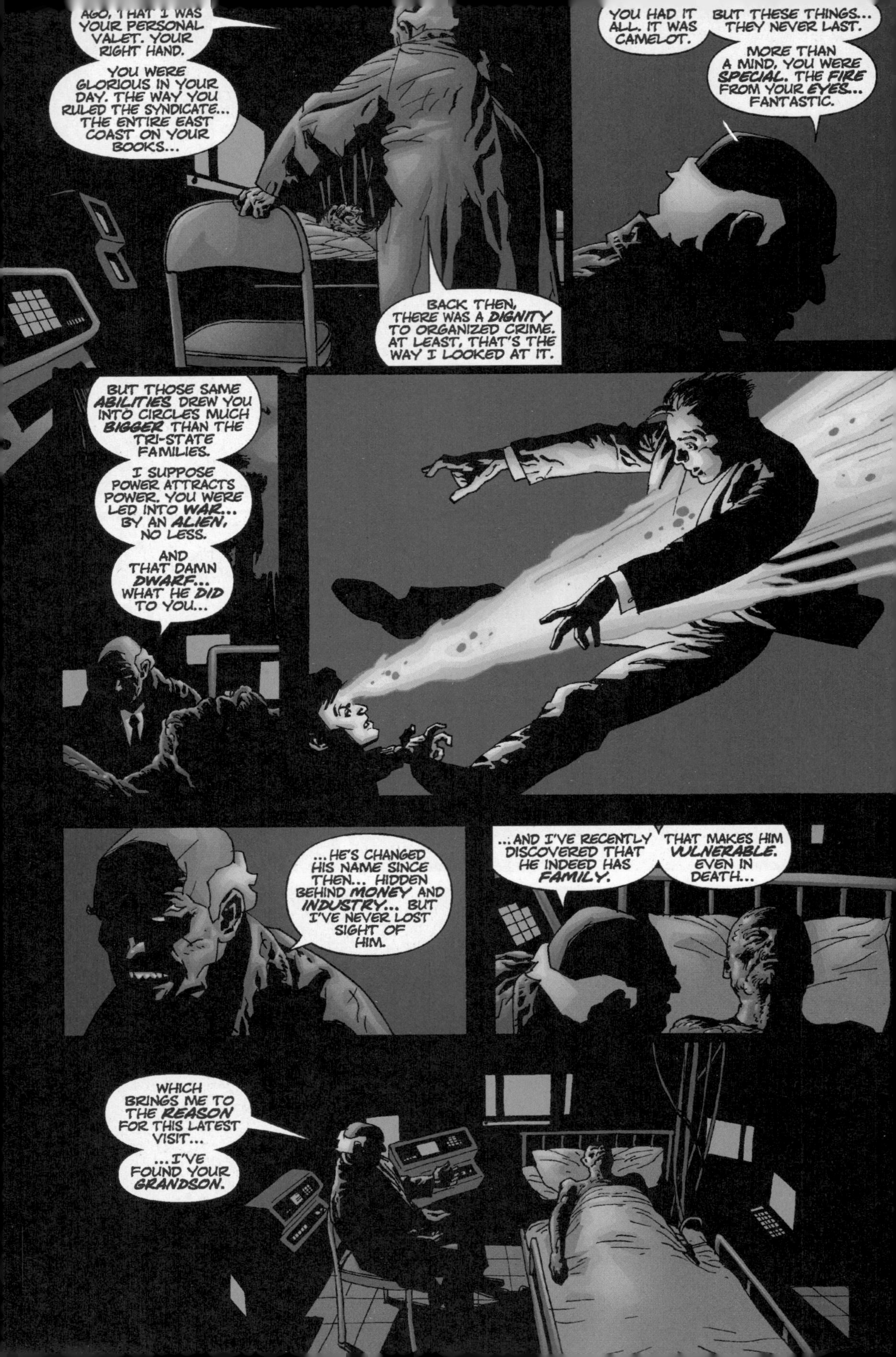
AGO, THAT I WAS YOUR PERSONAL VALET. YOUR RIGHT HAND.
YOU WERE GLORIOUS IN YOUR DAY. THE WAY YOU RULED THE SYNDICATE... THE ENTIRE EAST COAST ON YOUR BOOKS...
BACK THEN, THERE WAS A DIGNITY TO ORGANIZED CRIME. AT LEAST, THAT'S THE WAY I LOOKED AT IT.
YOU HAD IT ALL. IT WAS CAMELOT.
BUT THESE THINGS... THEY NEVER LAST.
MORE THAN A MIND, YOU WERE SPECIAL. THE FIRE FROM YOUR EYES... FANTASTIC.
BUT THOSE SAME ABILITIES DREW YOU INTO CIRCLES MUCH BIGGER THAN THE TRI-STATE FAMILIES.
I SUPPOSE POWER ATTRACTS POWER. YOU WERE LED INTO WAR... BY AN ALIEN, NO LESS.
AND THAT DAMN DWARF... WHAT HE DID TO YOU...
...HE'S CHANGED HIS NAME SINCE THEN... HIDDEN BEHIND MONEY AND INDUSTRY... BUT I'VE NEVER LOST SIGHT OF HIM.
...AND I'VE RECENTLY DISCOVERED THAT HE INDEED HAS FAMILY.
THAT MAKES HIM VULNERABLE. EVEN IN DEATH...
WHICH BRINGS ME TO THE REASON FOR THIS LATEST VISIT...
...I'VE FOUND YOUR GRANDSON.

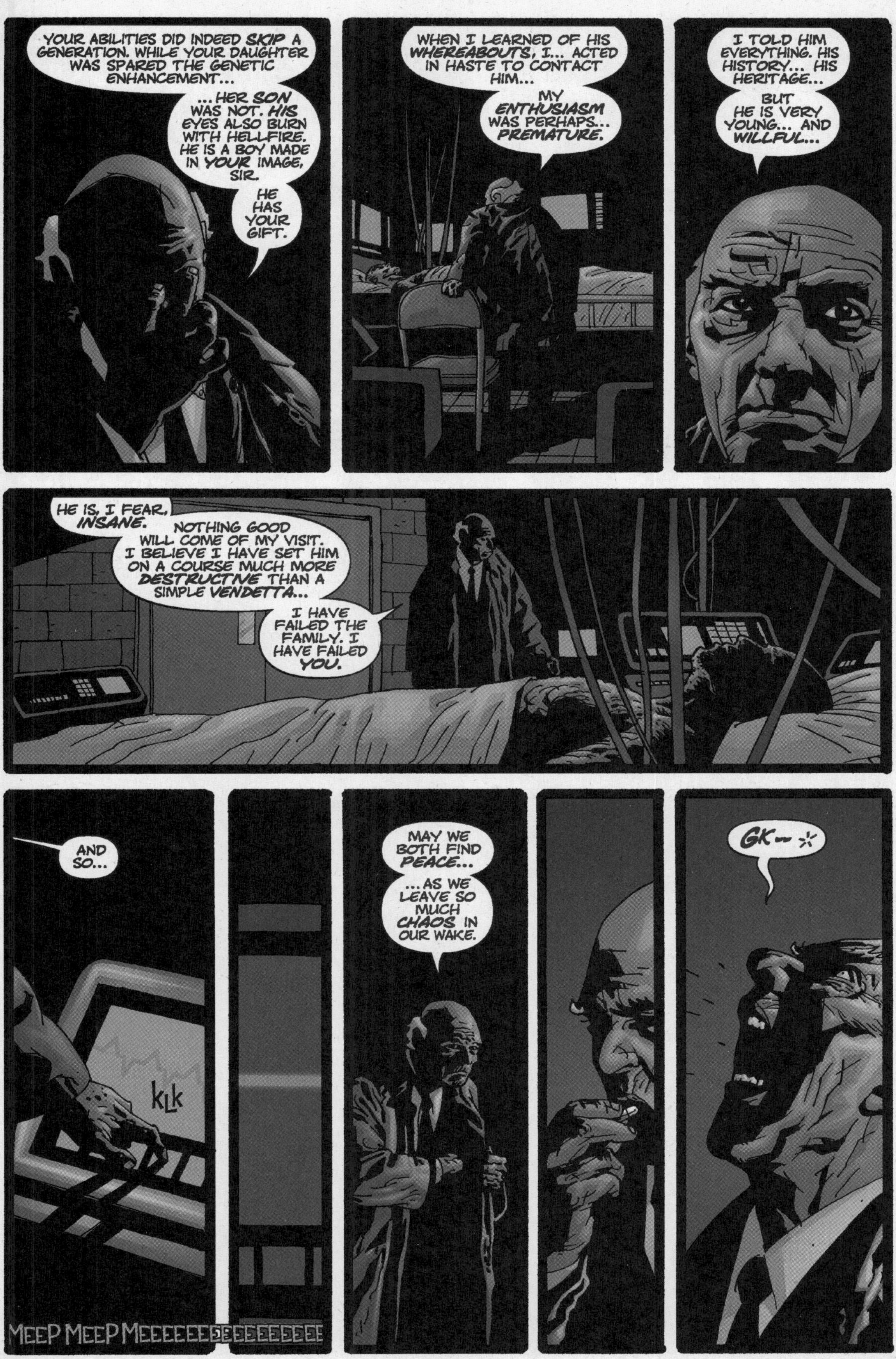

YOUR ABILITIES DID INDEED SKIP A GENERATION. WHILE YOUR DAUGHTER WAS SPARED THE GENETIC ENHANCEMENT...
...HER SON WAS NOT. HIS EYES ALSO BURN WITH HELLFIRE. HE IS A BOY MADE IN YOUR IMAGE, SIR.
HE HAS YOUR GIFT.
WHEN I LEARNED OF HIS WHEREABOUTS, I... ACTED IN HASTE TO CONTACT HIM...
MY ENTHUSIASM WAS PERHAPS... PREMATURE.
I TOLD HIM EVERYTHING. HIS HISTORY... HIS HERITAGE...
BUT HE IS VERY YOUNG... AND WILLFUL...
HE IS, I FEAR, INSANE.
NOTHING GOOD WILL COME OF MY VISIT. I BELIEVE I HAVE SET HIM ON A COURSE MUCH MORE DESTRUCTIVE THAN A SIMPLE VENDETTA...
I HAVE FAILED THE FAMILY. I HAVE FAILED YOU.
AND SO...
KLK
MEEP MEEP MEEEEEEEEEEEEEEEEEE
MAY WE BOTH FIND PEACE...
...AS WE LEAVE SO MUCH CHAOS IN OUR WAKE.
GK--

BLACK ACTION FALL$

BY JØE CASEY
SE&N PHILLIPS
BRIAÑ HABERLIÑ
C%L%RS
RICH^RD ST&RKINGS
CØM'CRAFT'S
S^ID^ TEMØ4ONTE
L*TT*RS
ÆRIC DÆSANTIS
ÆDITOR

W'LD©AT$ CREATED BY J'M LEE BR&NDØN CHØI

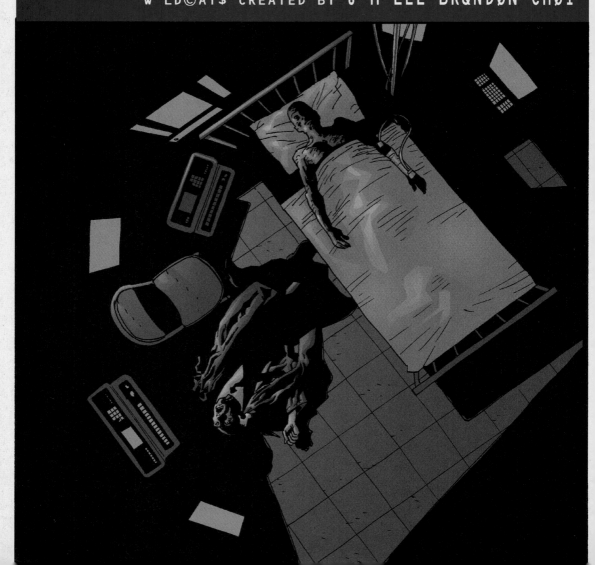

Downtown L.A.
The Halo Building.

ALERT:
INTERNAL ENERGY
WAVE DETECTED.
ANOMALOUS
FREQUENCY.
INITIATE SEARCH:
LOCATING...

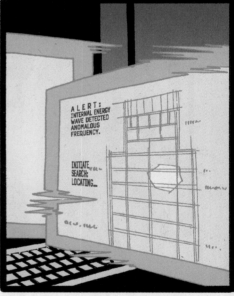

ALERT:
INTERNAL ENERGY
WAVE DETECTED
ANOMALOUS
FREQUENCY.

INITIATE
SEARCH:
LOCATING...

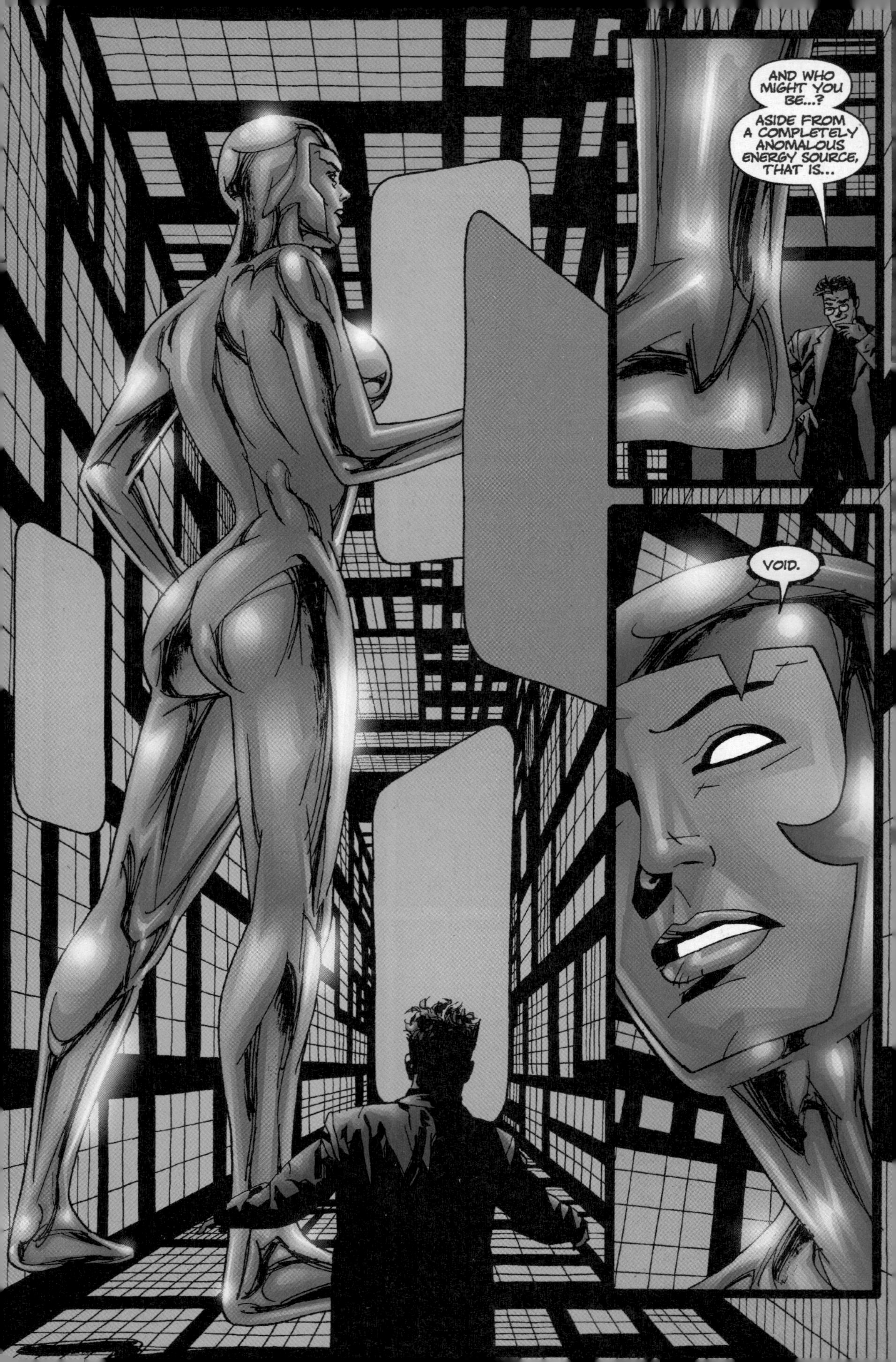
AND WHO MIGHT YOU BE...?
ASIDE FROM A COMPLETELY ANOMALOUS ENERGY SOURCE, THAT IS...
VOID.

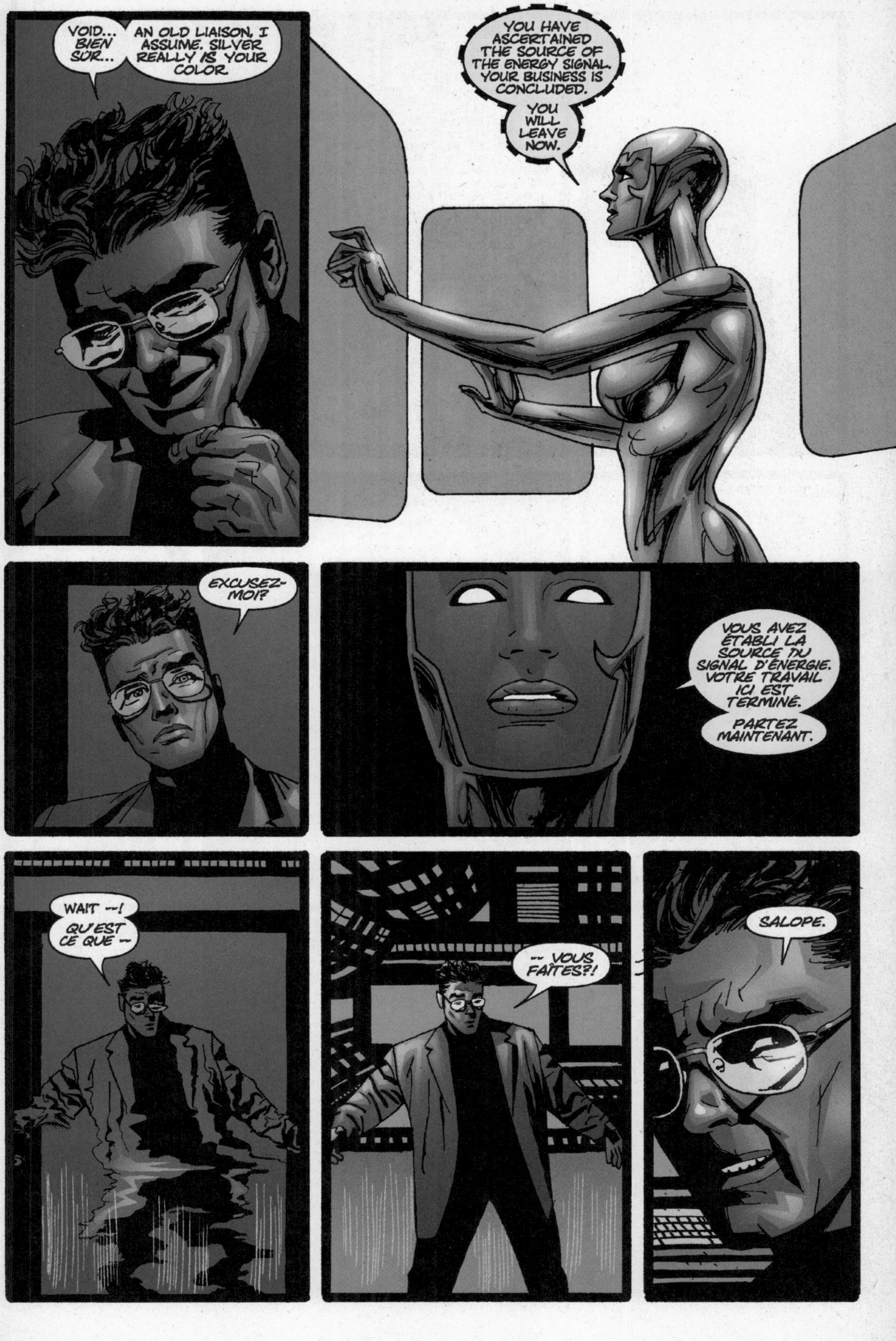

VOID... BIEN SÛR...
AN OLD LIAISON, I ASSUME. SILVER REALLY IS YOUR COLOR
YOU HAVE ASCERTAINED THE SOURCE OF THE ENERGY SIGNAL. YOUR BUSINESS IS CONCLUDED.
YOU WILL LEAVE NOW.
EXCUSEZ-MOI?
VOUS AVEZ ÉTABLI LA SOURCE DU SIGNAL D'ÉNERGIE. VOTRE TRAVAIL ICI EST TERMINÉ.
PARTEZ MAINTENANT.
WAIT --! QU'EST CE QUE --
-- VOUS FAÎTES?!
SALOPE.

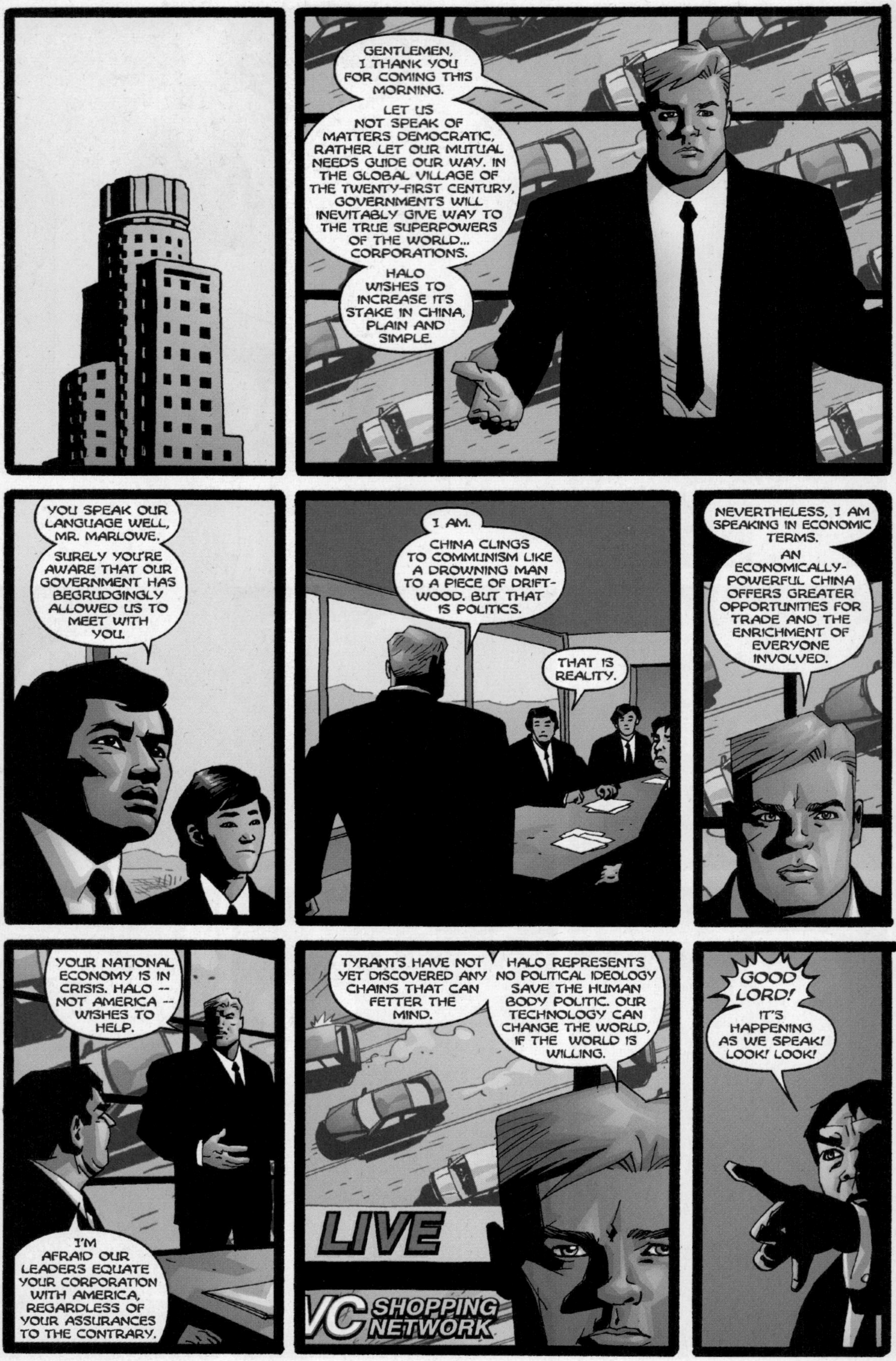
GENTLEMEN, I THANK YOU FOR COMING THIS MORNING.
LET US NOT SPEAK OF MATTERS DEMOCRATIC, RATHER LET OUR MUTUAL NEEDS GUIDE OUR WAY. IN THE GLOBAL VILLAGE OF THE TWENTY-FIRST CENTURY, GOVERNMENTS WILL INEVITABLY GIVE WAY TO THE TRUE SUPERPOWERS OF THE WORLD... CORPORATIONS.
HALO WISHES TO INCREASE IT'S STAKE IN CHINA, PLAIN AND SIMPLE.
YOU SPEAK OUR LANGUAGE WELL, MR. MARLOWE.
SURELY YOU'RE AWARE THAT OUR GOVERNMENT HAS BEGRUDGINGLY ALLOWED US TO MEET WITH YOU.
I AM.
CHINA CLINGS TO COMMUNISM LIKE A DROWNING MAN TO A PIECE OF DRIFT-WOOD. BUT THAT IS POLITICS.
THAT IS REALITY.
NEVERTHELESS, I AM SPEAKING IN ECONOMIC TERMS.
AN ECONOMICALLY-POWERFUL CHINA OFFERS GREATER OPPORTUNITIES FOR TRADE AND THE ENRICHMENT OF EVERYONE INVOLVED.
YOUR NATIONAL ECONOMY IS IN CRISIS. HALO -- NOT AMERICA -- WISHES TO HELP.
I'M AFRAID OUR LEADERS EQUATE YOUR CORPORATION WITH AMERICA, REGARDLESS OF YOUR ASSURANCES TO THE CONTRARY.
TYRANTS HAVE NOT YET DISCOVERED ANY CHAINS THAT CAN FETTER THE MIND.
HALO REPRESENTS NO POLITICAL IDEOLOGY SAVE THE HUMAN BODY POLITIC. OUR TECHNOLOGY CAN CHANGE THE WORLD, IF THE WORLD IS WILLING.
LIVE
VC SHOPPING NETWORK
GOOD LORD!
IT'S HAPPENING AS WE SPEAK! LOOK! LOOK!

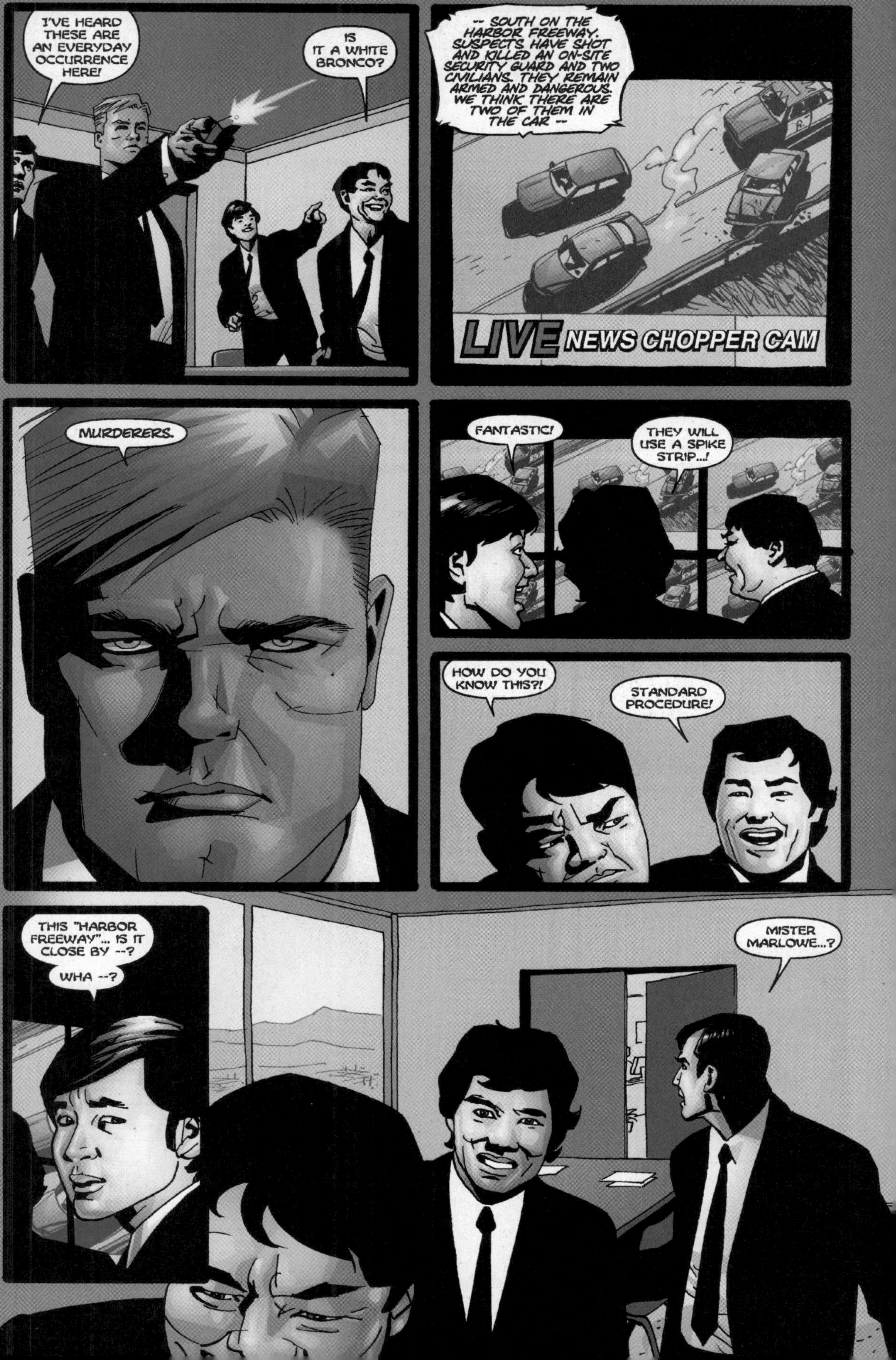
I'VE HEARD THESE ARE AN EVERYDAY OCCURRENCE HERE!
IS IT A WHITE BRONCO?
-- SOUTH ON THE HARBOR FREEWAY. SUSPECTS HAVE SHOT AND KILLED AN ON-SITE SECURITY GUARD AND TWO CIVILIANS. THEY REMAIN ARMED AND DANGEROUS. WE THINK THERE ARE TWO OF THEM IN THE CAR --
LIVE NEWS CHOPPER CAM
MURDERERS.
FANTASTIC!
THEY WILL USE A SPIKE STRIP...!
HOW DO YOU KNOW THIS?!
STANDARD PROCEDURE!
THIS "HARBOR FREEWAY"... IS IT CLOSE BY --?
WHA --?
MISTER MARLOWE...?

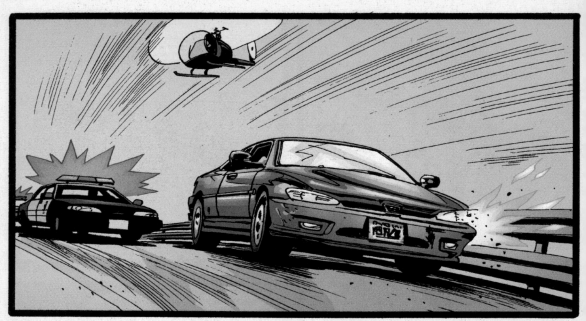

I'M STAYING RIGHT *WITH* HIM! THEY'RE GONNA GO *NATIONAL* WITH THIS FOOTAGE!

CARL! KEEP THE CAMERA ON THE *CROOKS!*

CARL! WHAT THE HELL ARE YOU *DOING?!*

WHAT'RE *YOU* LOOKIN' AT ---?!

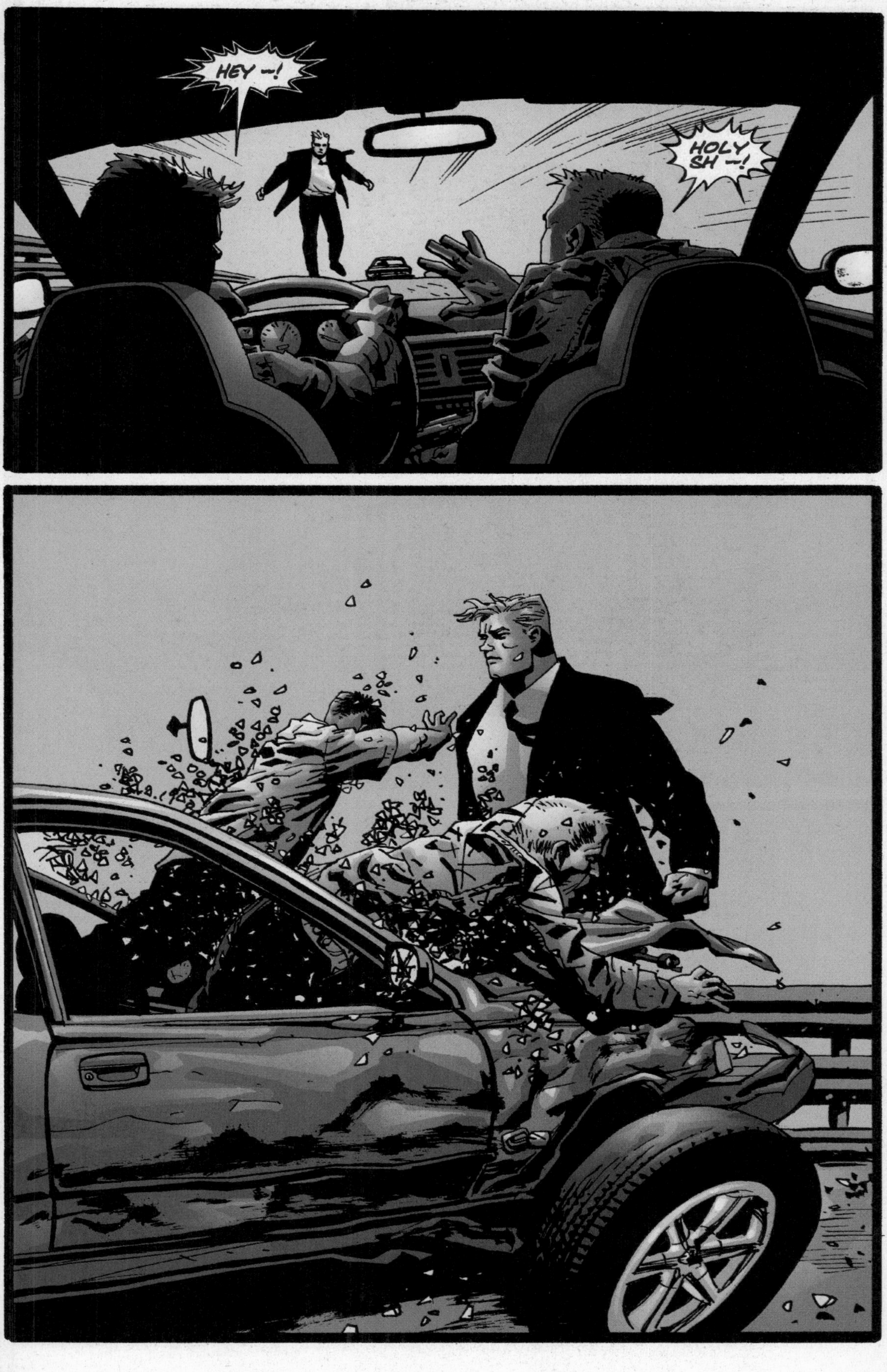
HEY --!
HOLY SH --!

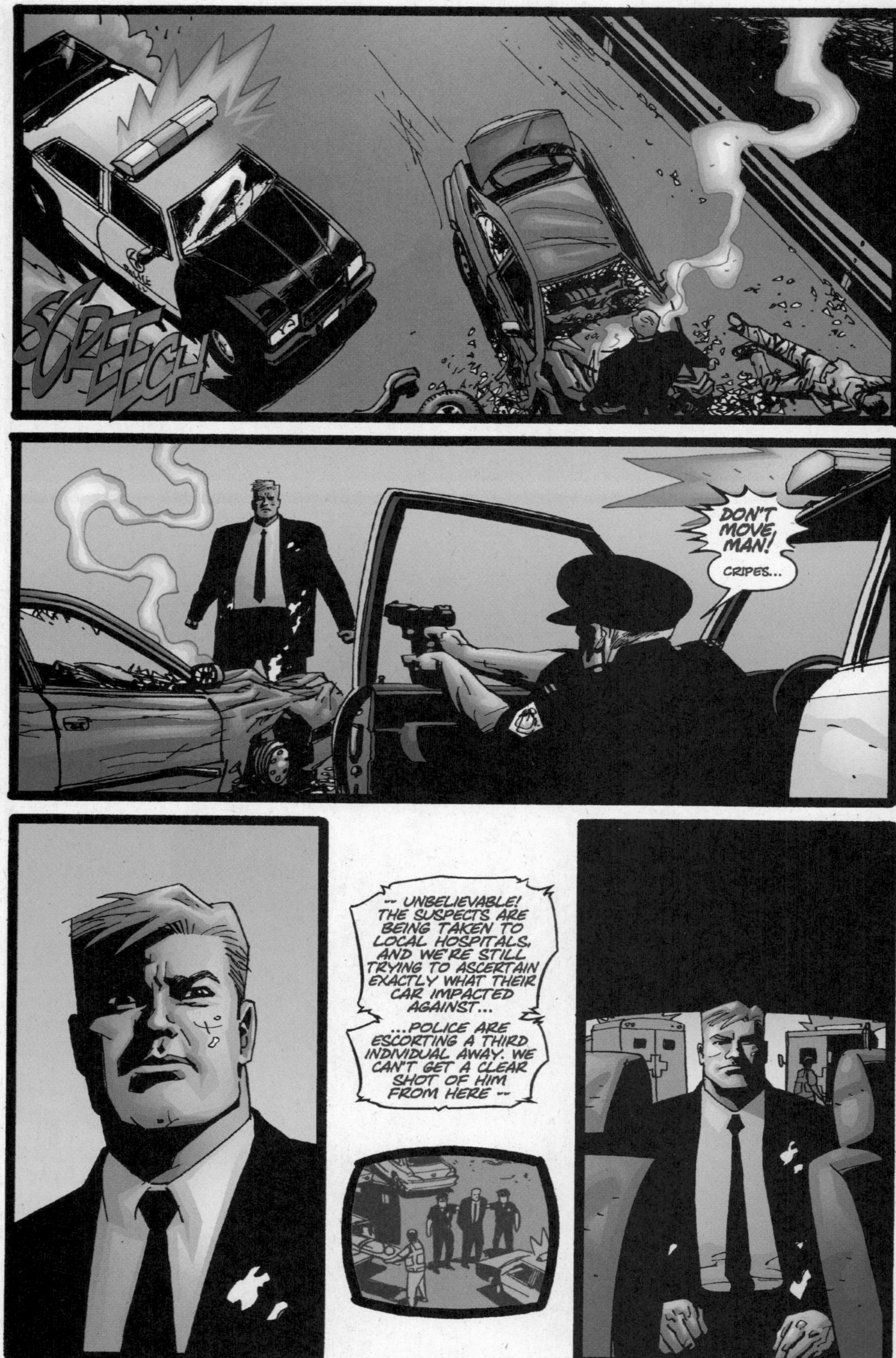
SCREECH
DON'T MOVE, MAN!
CRIPES...
-- UNBELIEVABLE! THE SUSPECTS ARE BEING TAKEN TO LOCAL HOSPITALS, AND WE'RE STILL TRYING TO ASCERTAIN EXACTLY WHAT THEIR CAR IMPACTED AGAINST...
...POLICE ARE ESCORTING A THIRD INDIVIDUAL AWAY. WE CAN'T GET A CLEAR SHOT OF HIM FROM HERE --

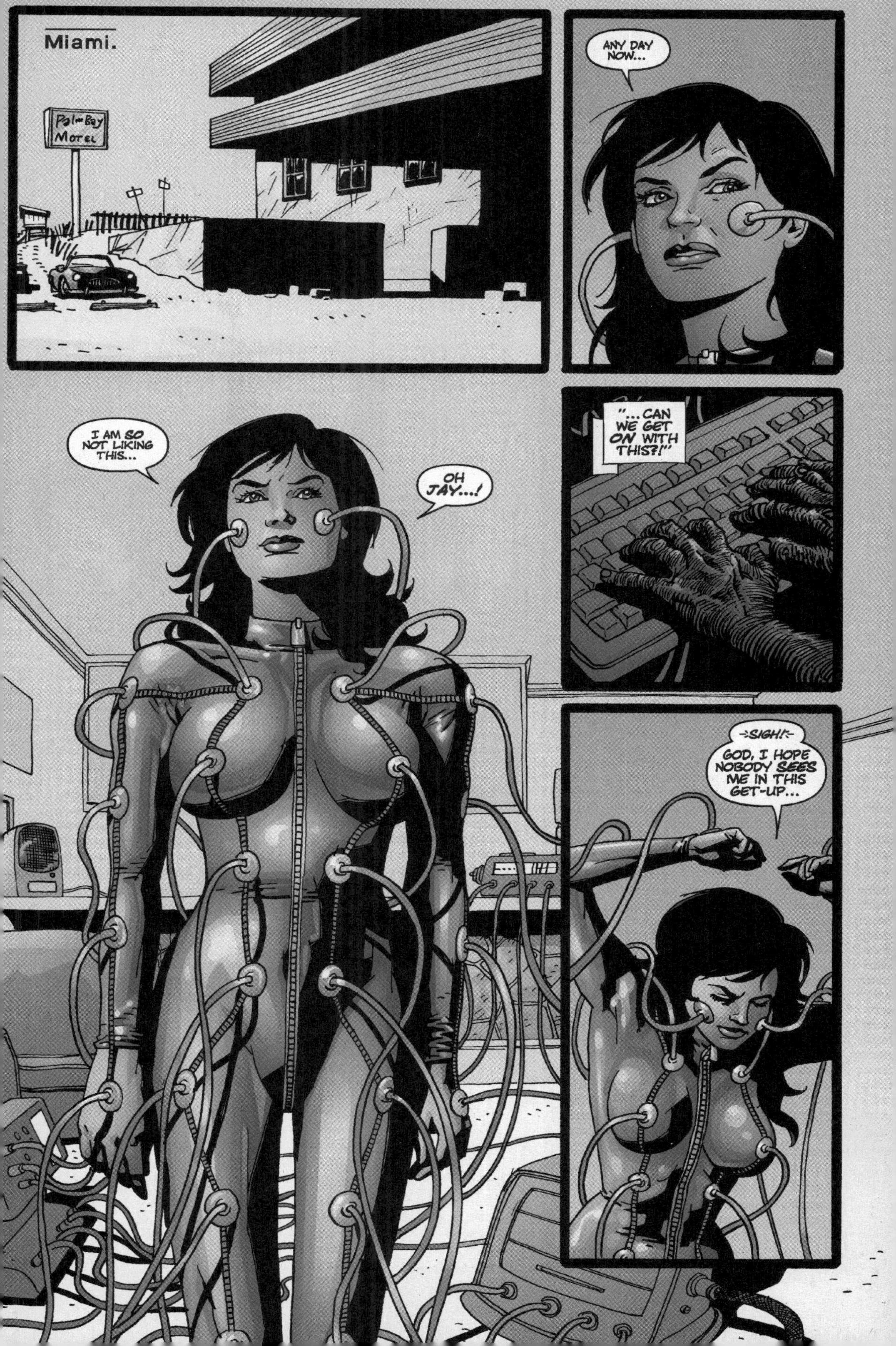
Miami.
Pal-Bay Motel
ANY DAY NOW...
I AM SO NOT LIKING THIS...
OH JAY...!
"...CAN WE GET ON WITH THIS?!"
-SIGH!-
GOD, I HOPE NOBODY SEES ME IN THIS GET-UP...

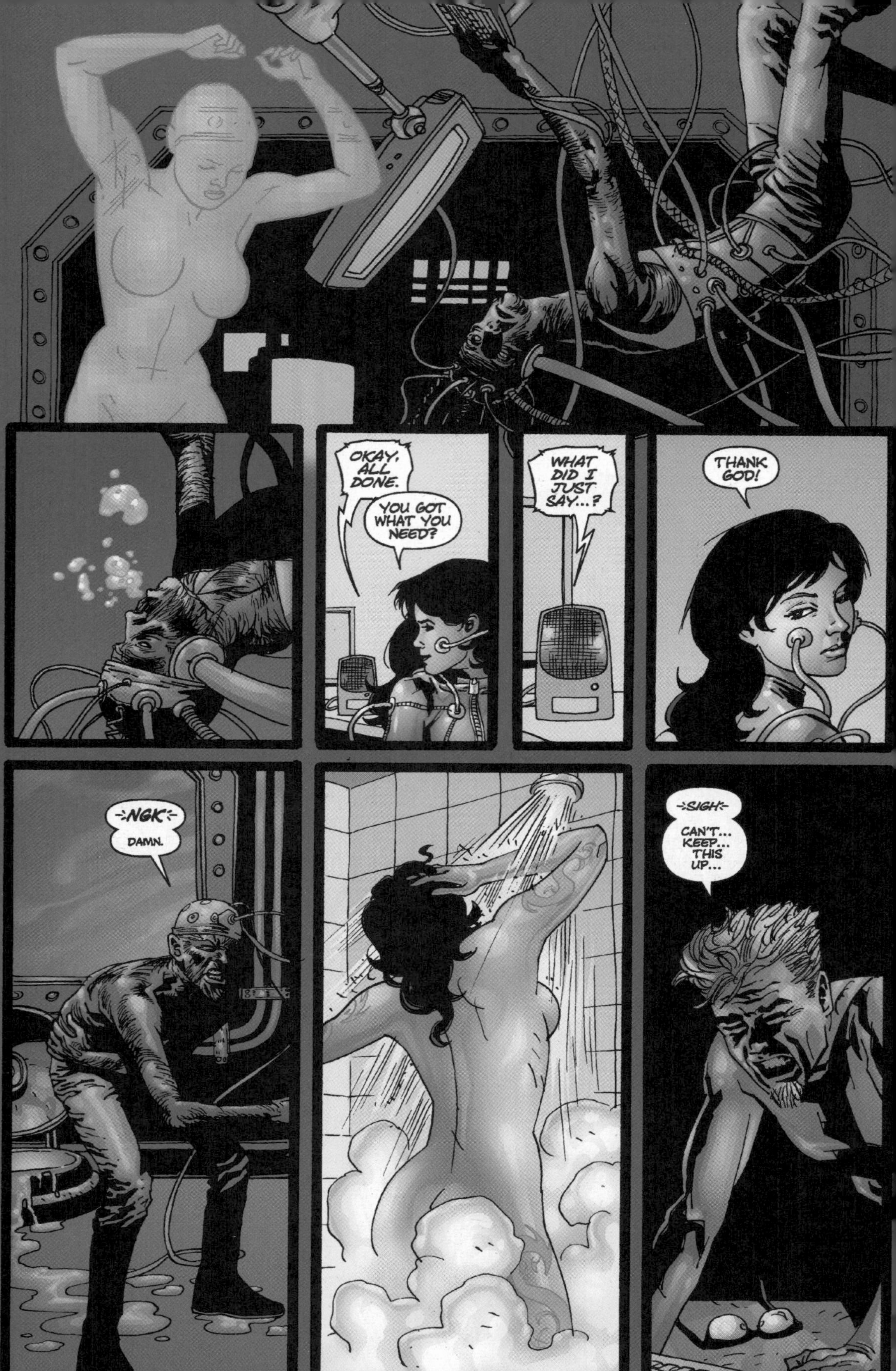
OKAY, ALL DONE.
YOU GOT WHAT YOU NEED?
WHAT DID I JUST SAY...?
THANK GOD!
-NGK-
DAMN.
-SIGH-
CAN'T... KEEP... THIS UP...

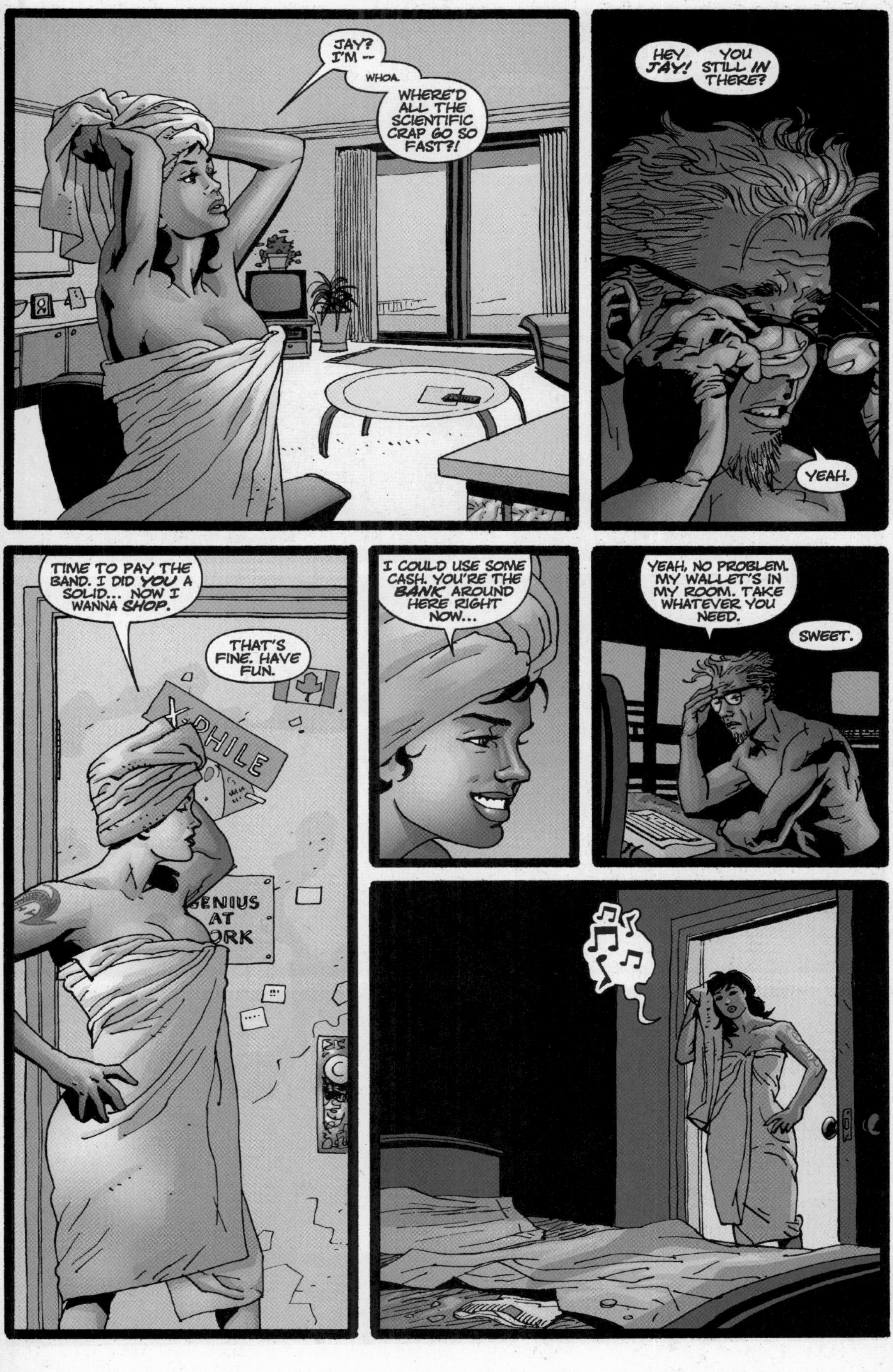
JAY? I'M --
WHOA.
WHERE'D ALL THE SCIENTIFIC CRAP GO SO FAST?!
HEY JAY!
YOU STILL IN THERE?
YEAH.
TIME TO PAY THE BAND. I DID YOU A SOLID... NOW I WANNA SHOP.
THAT'S FINE. HAVE FUN.
X-PHILE
GENIUS AT WORK
I COULD USE SOME CASH. YOU'RE THE BANK AROUND HERE RIGHT NOW...
YEAH, NO PROBLEM. MY WALLET'S IN MY ROOM. TAKE WHATEVER YOU NEED.
SWEET.

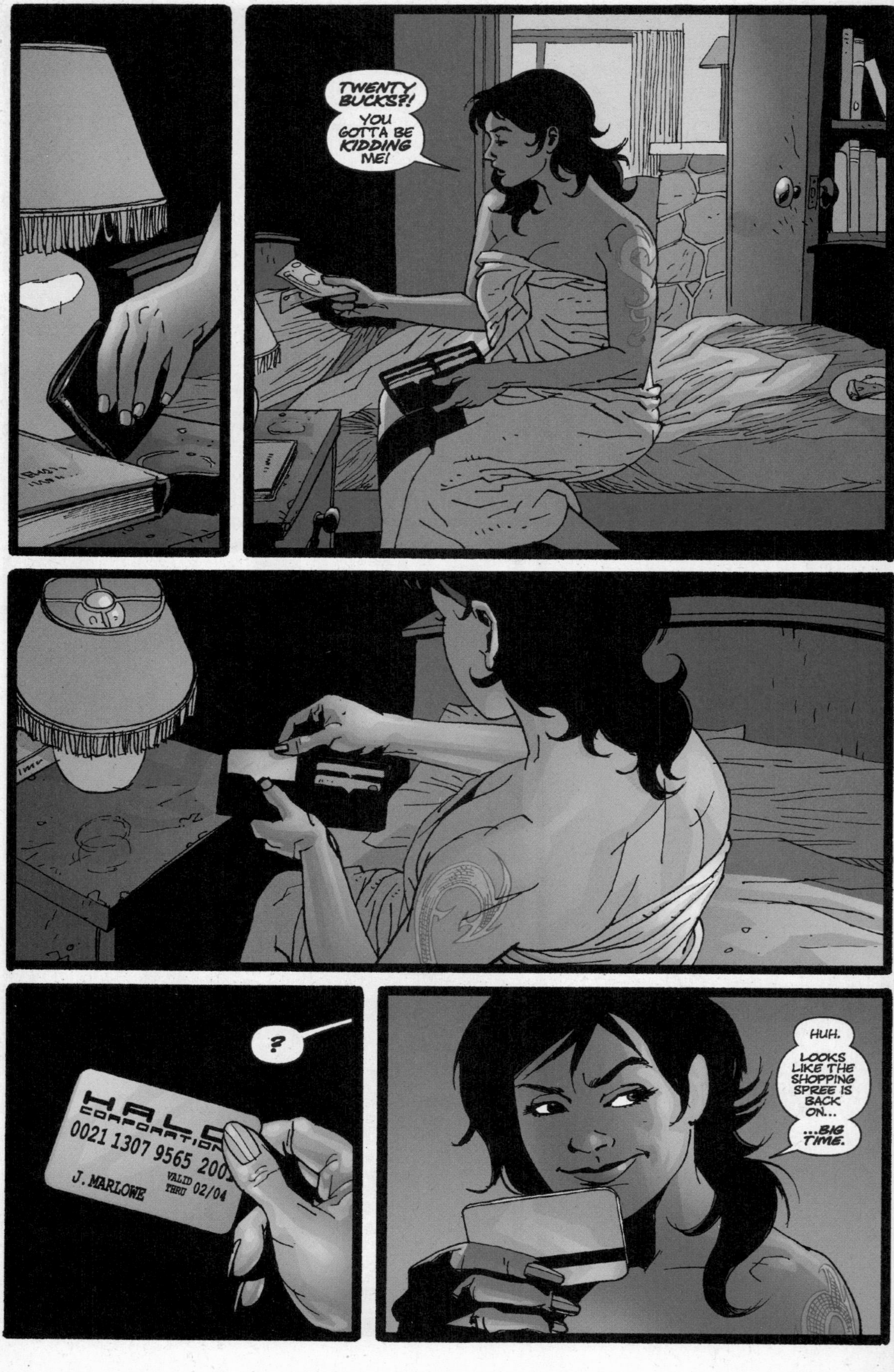
TWENTY BUCKS?! YOU GOTTA BE KIDDING ME!
?
HALO CORPORATION
0021 1307 9565 2001
J. MARLOWE
VALID THRU 02/04
HUH.
LOOKS LIKE THE SHOPPING SPREE IS BACK ON...
...BIG TIME.

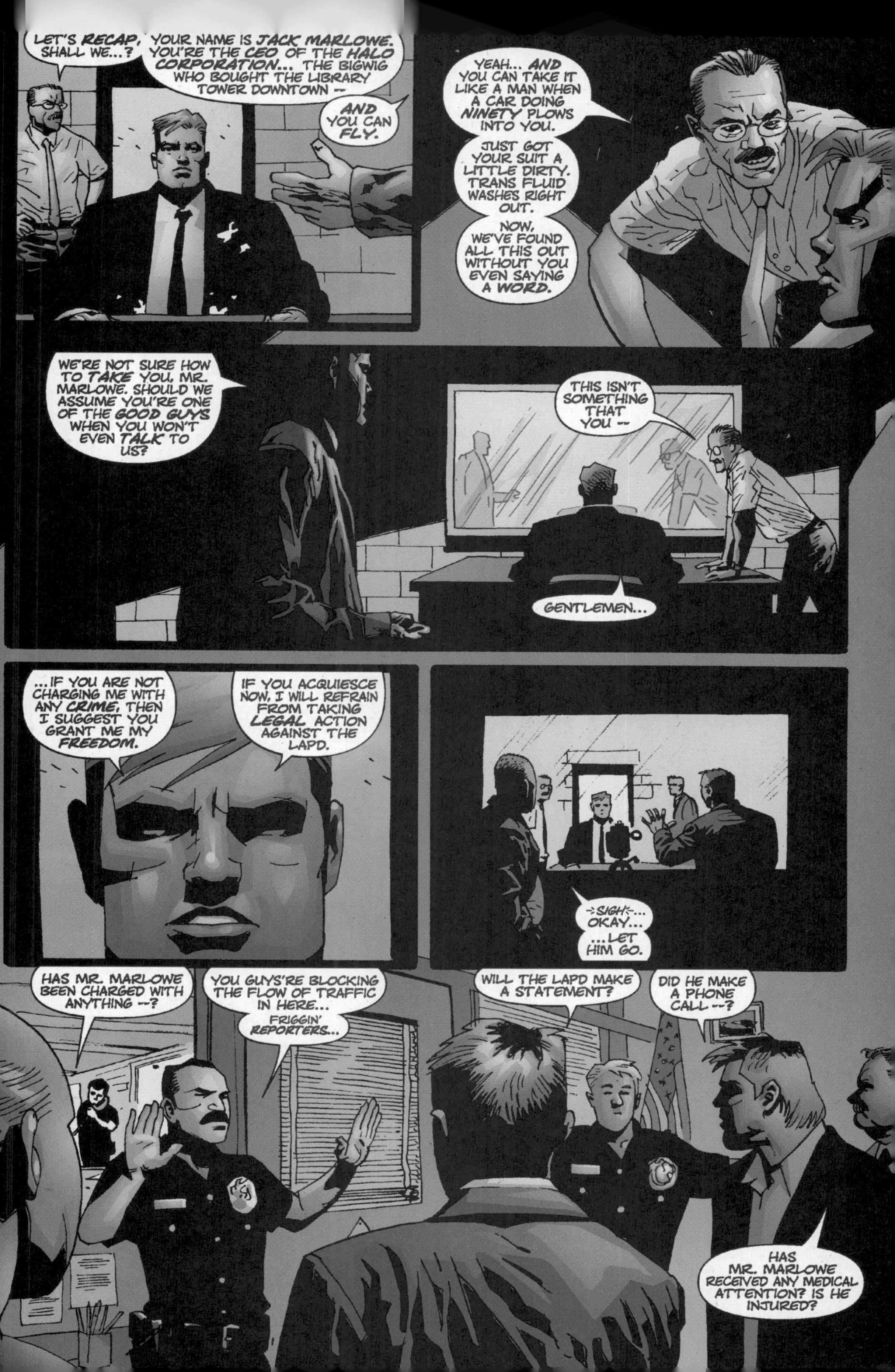
LET'S RECAP, SHALL WE...?
YOUR NAME IS JACK MARLOWE. YOU'RE THE CEO OF THE HALO CORPORATION... THE BIGWIG WHO BOUGHT THE LIBRARY TOWER DOWNTOWN --
AND YOU CAN FLY.
YEAH... AND YOU CAN TAKE IT LIKE A MAN WHEN A CAR DOING NINETY PLOWS INTO YOU.
JUST GOT YOUR SUIT A LITTLE DIRTY. TRANS FLUID WASHES RIGHT OUT.
NOW, WE'VE FOUND ALL THIS OUT WITHOUT YOU EVEN SAYING A WORD.
WE'RE NOT SURE HOW TO TAKE YOU, MR. MARLOWE. SHOULD WE ASSUME YOU'RE ONE OF THE GOOD GUYS WHEN YOU WON'T EVEN TALK TO US?
THIS ISN'T SOMETHING THAT YOU --
GENTLEMEN...
...IF YOU ARE NOT CHARGING ME WITH ANY CRIME, THEN I SUGGEST YOU GRANT ME MY FREEDOM.
IF YOU ACQUIESCE NOW, I WILL REFRAIN FROM TAKING LEGAL ACTION AGAINST THE LAPD.
-SIGH-... OKAY... ...LET HIM GO.
HAS MR. MARLOWE BEEN CHARGED WITH ANYTHING --?
YOU GUYS'RE BLOCKING THE FLOW OF TRAFFIC IN HERE... FRIGGIN' REPORTERS...
WILL THE LAPD MAKE A STATEMENT?
DID HE MAKE A PHONE CALL --?
HAS MR. MARLOWE RECEIVED ANY MEDICAL ATTENTION? IS HE INJURED?

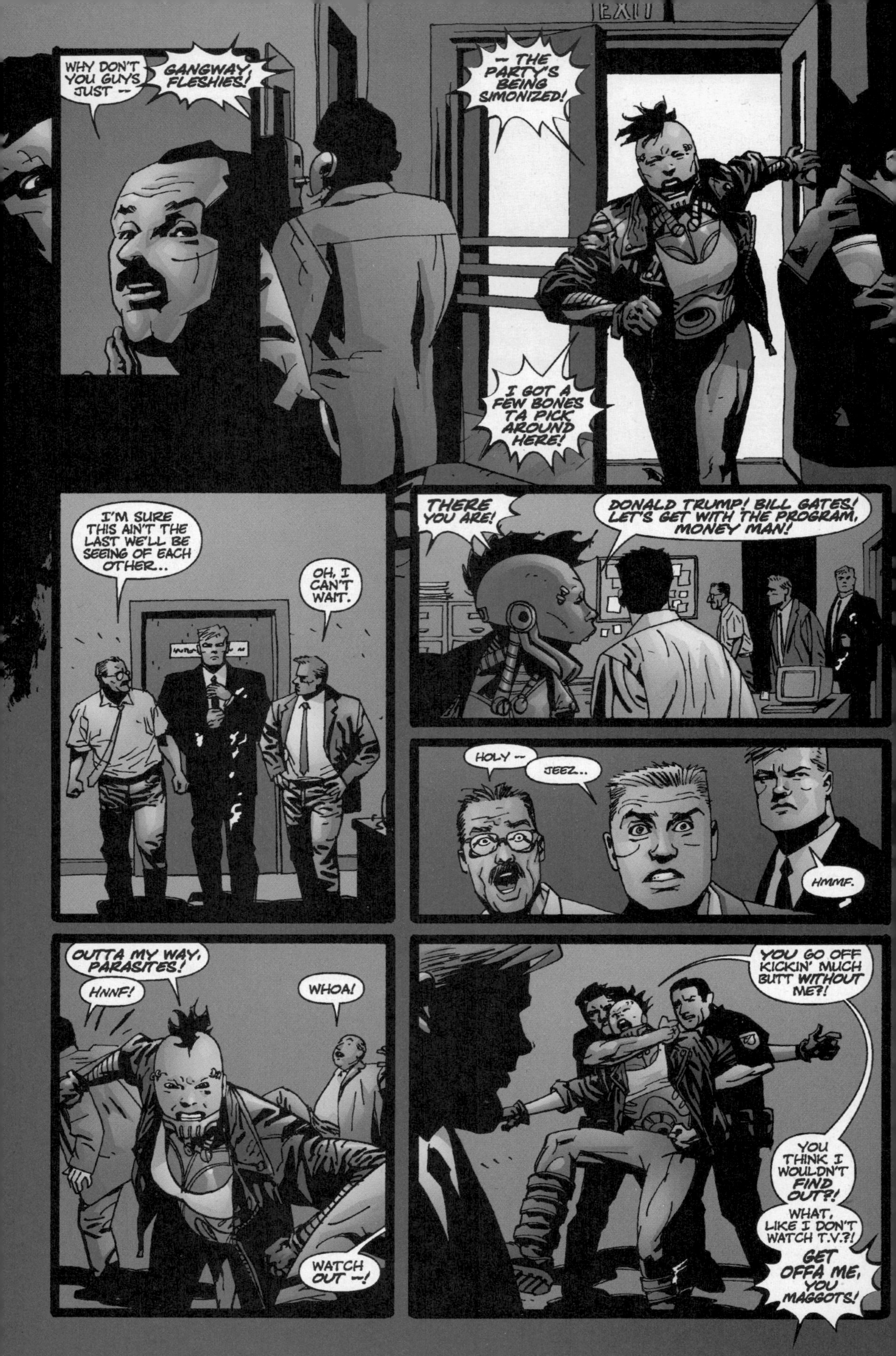
EXIT
WHY DON'T YOU GUYS JUST --
GANGWAY, FLESHIES!
-- THE PARTY'S BEING SIMONIZED!
I GOT A FEW BONES TA PICK AROUND HERE!
I'M SURE THIS AIN'T THE LAST WE'LL BE SEEING OF EACH OTHER...
OH, I CAN'T WAIT.
THERE YOU ARE!
DONALD TRUMP! BILL GATES! LET'S GET WITH THE PROGRAM, MONEY MAN!
HOLY --
JEEZ...
HMMF.
OUTTA MY WAY, PARASITES!
HNNF!
WHOA!
WATCH OUT --!
YOU GO OFF KICKIN' MUCH BUTT WITHOUT ME?!
YOU THINK I WOULDN'T FIND OUT?!
WHAT, LIKE I DON'T WATCH T.V.?!
GET OFFA ME, YOU MAGGOTS!

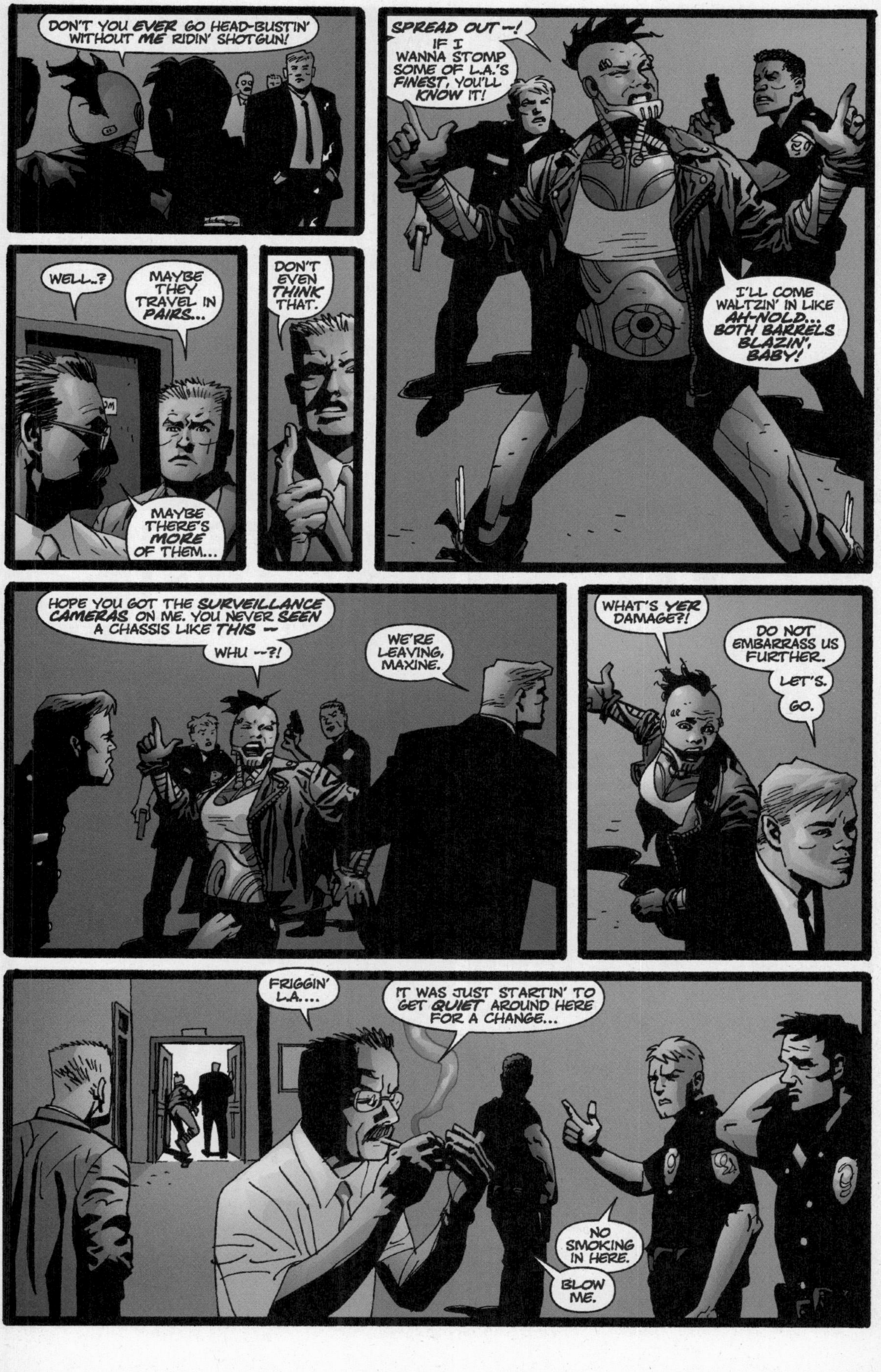
DON'T YOU EVER GO HEAD-BUSTIN' WITHOUT ME RIDIN' SHOTGUN!
SPREAD OUT --!
IF I WANNA STOMP SOME OF L.A.'S FINEST, YOU'LL KNOW IT!
I'LL COME WALTZIN' IN LIKE AH-NOLD... BOTH BARRELS BLAZIN', BABY!
WELL..?
MAYBE THEY TRAVEL IN PAIRS...
MAYBE THERE'S MORE OF THEM...
DON'T EVEN THINK THAT.
HOPE YOU GOT THE SURVEILLANCE CAMERAS ON ME. YOU NEVER SEEN A CHASSIS LIKE THIS --
WHU --?!
WE'RE LEAVING, MAXINE.
WHAT'S YER DAMAGE?!
DO NOT EMBARRASS US FURTHER.
LET'S.
GO.
FRIGGIN' L.A....
IT WAS JUST STARTIN' TO GET QUIET AROUND HERE FOR A CHANGE...
NO SMOKING IN HERE.
BLOW ME.

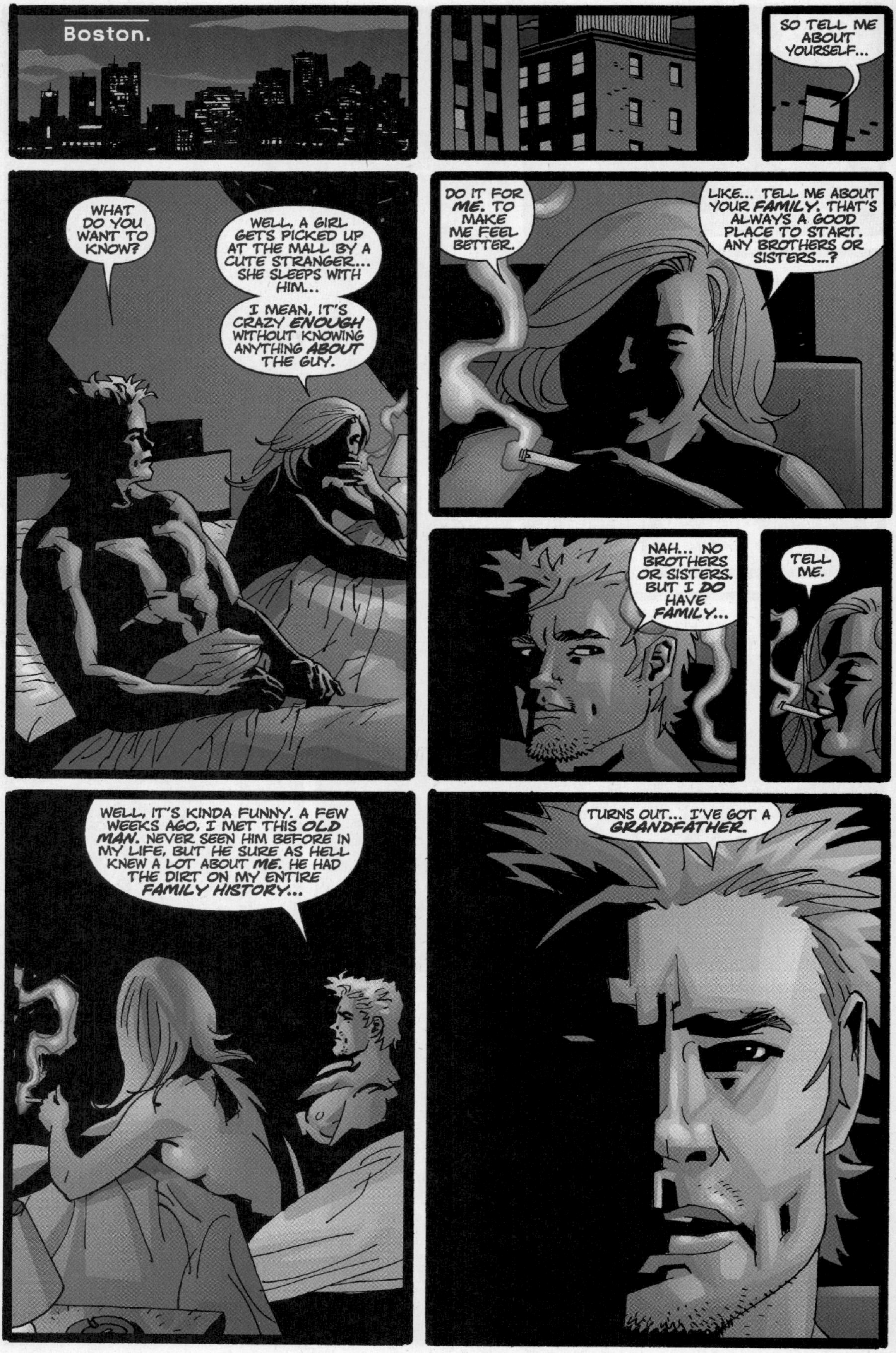

Boston.
SO TELL ME ABOUT YOURSELF...
WHAT DO YOU WANT TO KNOW?
WELL, A GIRL GETS PICKED UP AT THE MALL BY A CUTE STRANGER... SHE SLEEPS WITH HIM...
I MEAN, IT'S CRAZY ENOUGH WITHOUT KNOWING ANYTHING ABOUT THE GUY.
DO IT FOR ME. TO MAKE ME FEEL BETTER.
LIKE... TELL ME ABOUT YOUR FAMILY. THAT'S ALWAYS A GOOD PLACE TO START. ANY BROTHERS OR SISTERS...?
NAH... NO BROTHERS OR SISTERS. BUT I DO HAVE FAMILY...
TELL ME.
WELL, IT'S KINDA FUNNY. A FEW WEEKS AGO, I MET THIS OLD MAN. NEVER SEEN HIM BEFORE IN MY LIFE, BUT HE SURE AS HELL KNEW A LOT ABOUT ME. HE HAD THE DIRT ON MY ENTIRE FAMILY HISTORY...
TURNS OUT... I'VE GOT A GRANDFATHER.

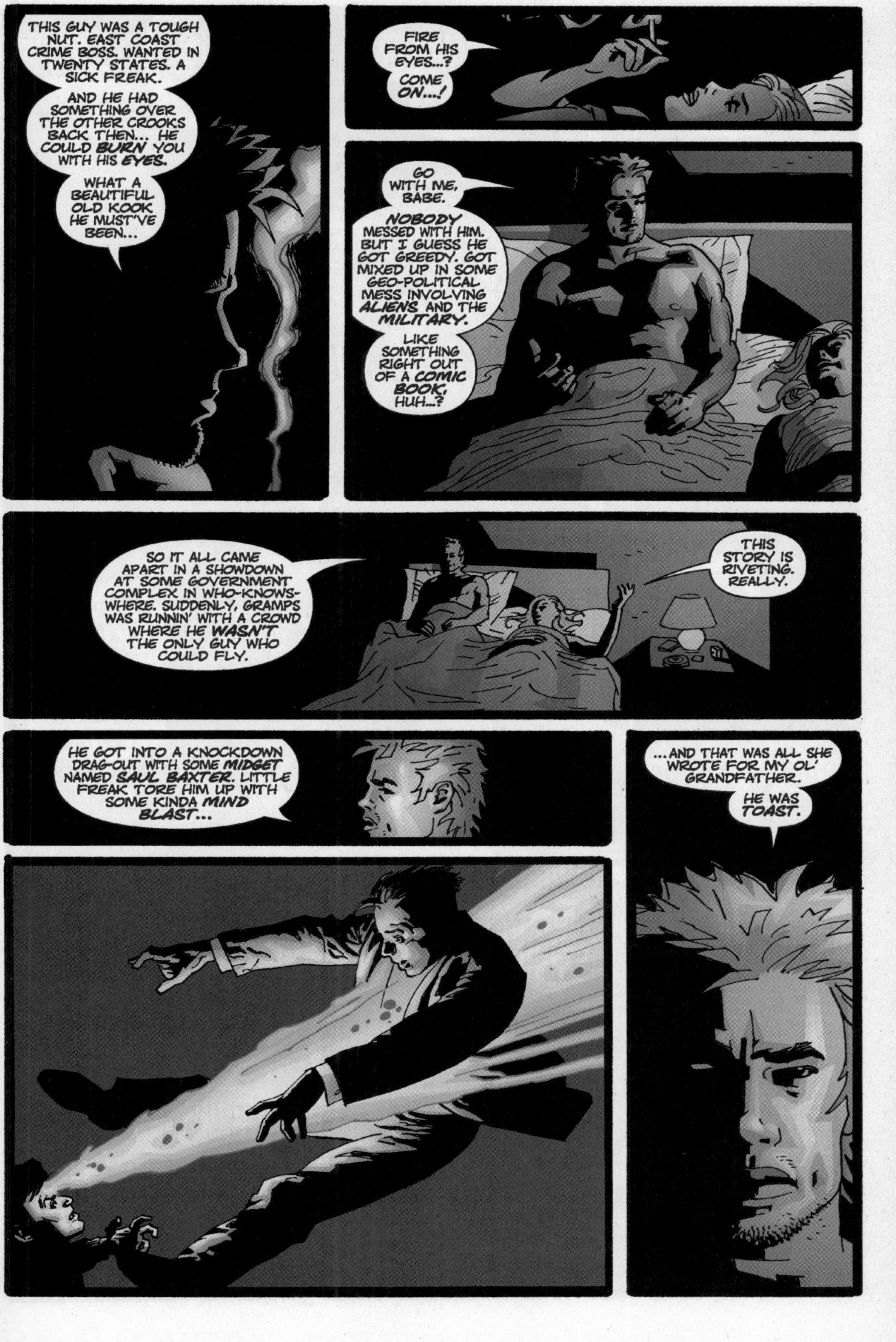
THIS GUY WAS A TOUGH NUT. EAST COAST CRIME BOSS. WANTED IN TWENTY STATES. A SICK FREAK.
AND HE HAD SOMETHING OVER THE OTHER CROOKS BACK THEN... HE COULD BURN YOU WITH HIS EYES.
WHAT A BEAUTIFUL OLD KOOK HE MUST'VE BEEN...
FIRE FROM HIS EYES...?
COME ON...!
GO WITH ME, BABE.
NOBODY MESSED WITH HIM. BUT I GUESS HE GOT GREEDY. GOT MIXED UP IN SOME GEO-POLITICAL MESS INVOLVING ALIENS AND THE MILITARY.
LIKE SOMETHING RIGHT OUT OF A COMIC BOOK, HUH...?
SO IT ALL CAME APART IN A SHOWDOWN AT SOME GOVERNMENT COMPLEX IN WHO-KNOWS-WHERE. SUDDENLY, GRAMPS WAS RUNNIN' WITH A CROWD WHERE HE WASN'T THE ONLY GUY WHO COULD FLY.
THIS STORY IS RIVETING. REALLY.
HE GOT INTO A KNOCKDOWN DRAG-OUT WITH SOME MIDGET NAMED SAUL BAXTER. LITTLE FREAK TORE HIM UP WITH SOME KINDA MIND BLAST...
...AND THAT WAS ALL SHE WROTE FOR MY OL' GRANDFATHER.
HE WAS TOAST.

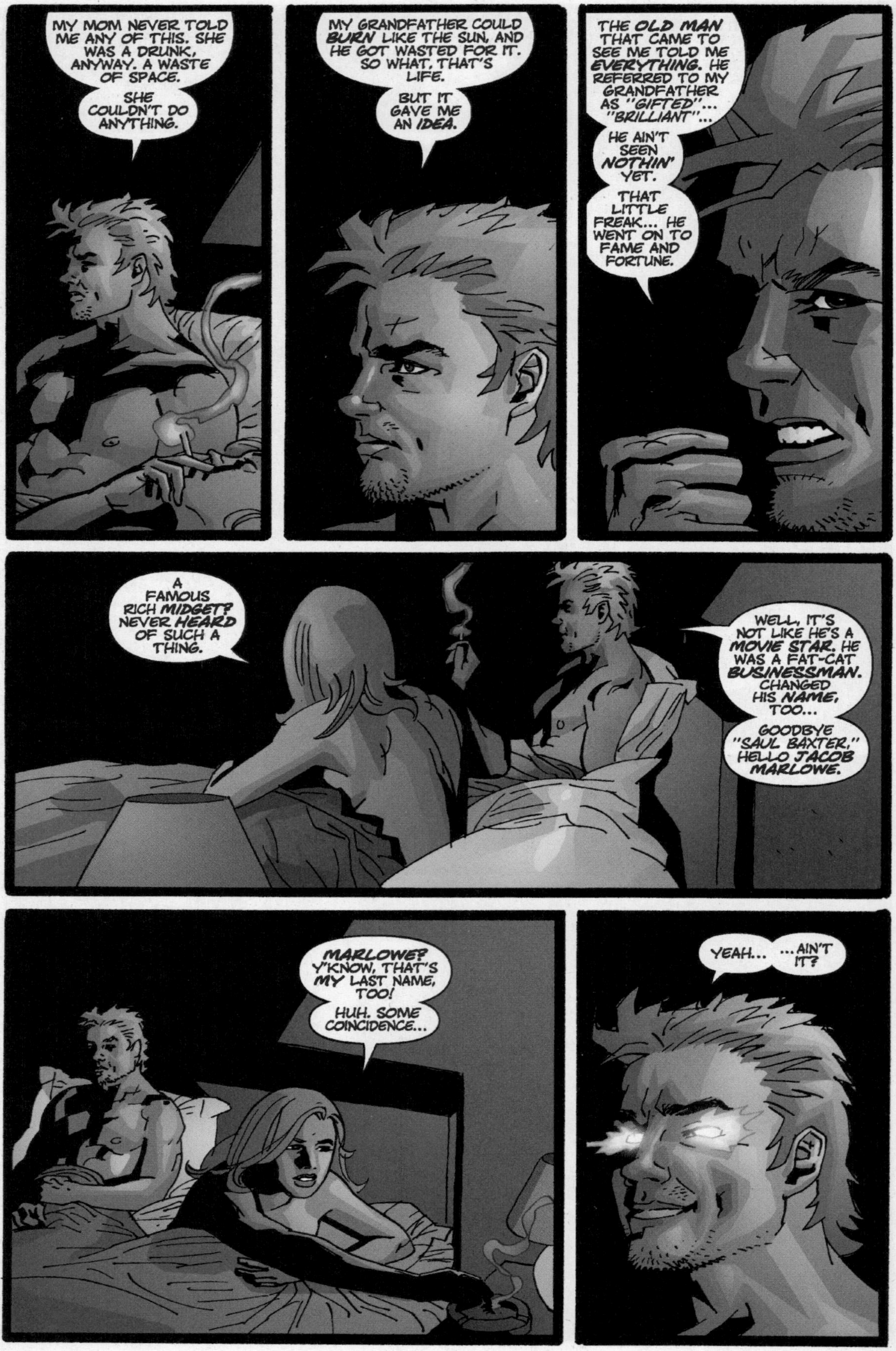

MY MOM NEVER TOLD ME ANY OF THIS. SHE WAS A DRUNK, ANYWAY. A WASTE OF SPACE.
SHE COULDN'T DO ANYTHING.
MY GRANDFATHER COULD BURN LIKE THE SUN, AND HE GOT WASTED FOR IT. SO WHAT, THAT'S LIFE.
BUT IT GAVE ME AN IDEA.
THE OLD MAN THAT CAME TO SEE ME TOLD ME EVERYTHING. HE REFERRED TO MY GRANDFATHER AS "GIFTED"... "BRILLIANT"...
HE AIN'T SEEN NOTHIN' YET.
THAT LITTLE FREAK... HE WENT ON TO FAME AND FORTUNE.
A FAMOUS RICH MIDGET? NEVER HEARD OF SUCH A THING.
WELL, IT'S NOT LIKE HE'S A MOVIE STAR. HE WAS A FAT-CAT BUSINESSMAN. CHANGED HIS NAME, TOO...
GOODBYE "SAUL BAXTER," HELLO JACOB MARLOWE.
MARLOWE? Y'KNOW, THAT'S MY LAST NAME, TOO!
HUH. SOME COINCIDENCE...
YEAH...
...AIN'T IT?

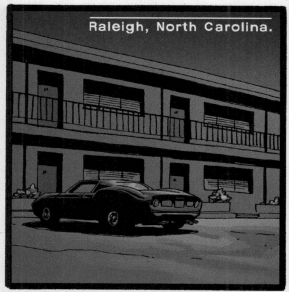

Raleigh, North Carolina.

SEPTEMBER 6
2:48 A.M.

SEPTEMBER 9
3:07 P.M.

3:28 P.M.

RALEIGH SPRINGS GALLERIA

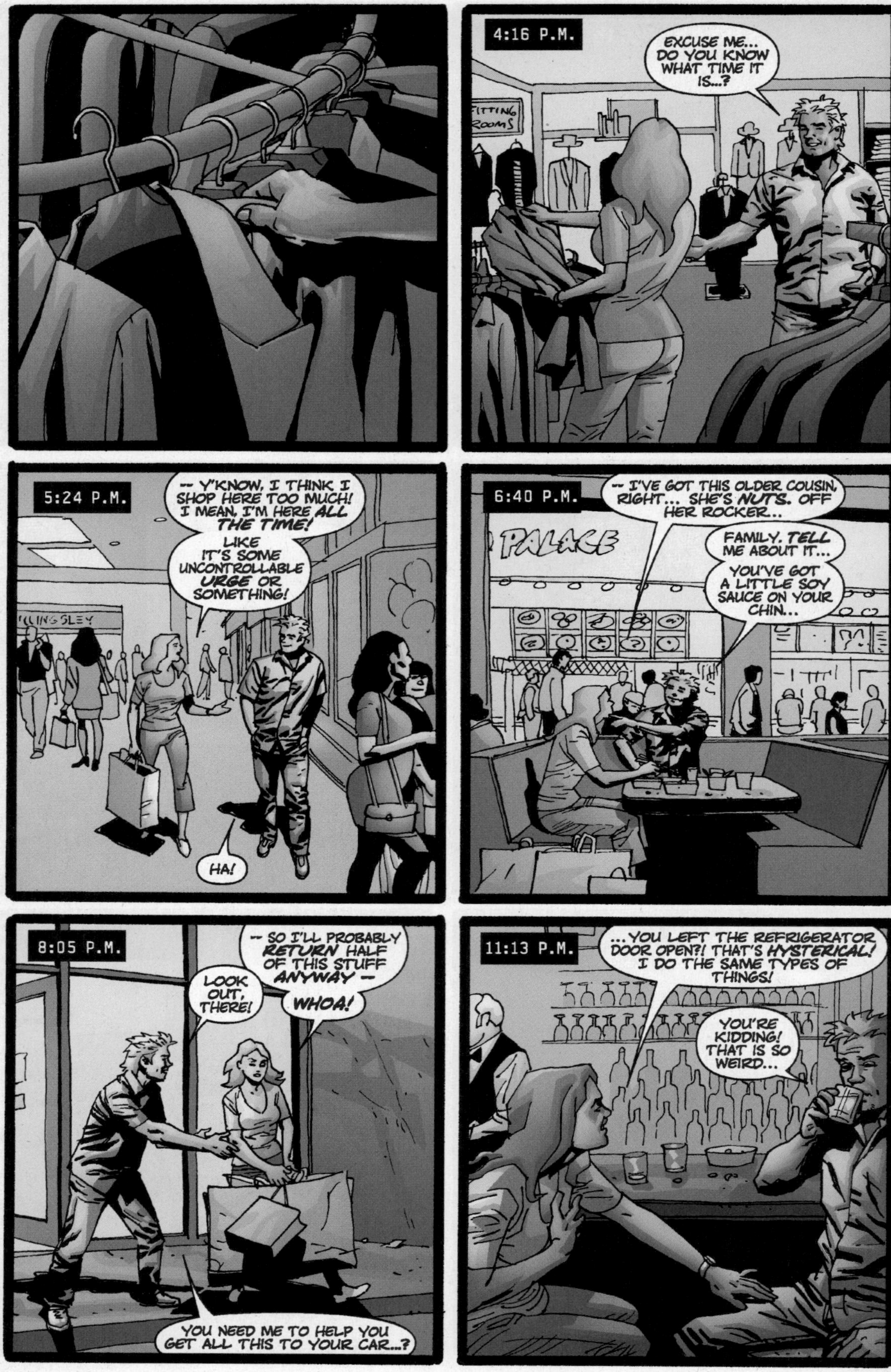
4:16 P.M.
FITTING ROOMS
EXCUSE ME... DO YOU KNOW WHAT TIME IT IS...?
5:24 P.M.
-- Y'KNOW, I THINK I SHOP HERE TOO MUCH! I MEAN, I'M HERE ***ALL THE TIME!***
LIKE IT'S SOME UNCONTROLLABLE ***URGE*** OR SOMETHING!
HA!
6:40 P.M.
PALACE
-- I'VE GOT THIS OLDER COUSIN, RIGHT... SHE'S ***NUTS.*** OFF HER ROCKER...
FAMILY. ***TELL*** ME ABOUT IT...
YOU'VE GOT A LITTLE SOY SAUCE ON YOUR CHIN...
8:05 P.M.
-- SO I'LL PROBABLY ***RETURN*** HALF OF THIS STUFF ***ANYWAY*** --
LOOK OUT, THERE!
WHOA!
YOU NEED ME TO HELP YOU GET ALL THIS TO YOUR CAR...?
11:13 P.M.
...YOU LEFT THE REFRIGERATOR DOOR OPEN?! THAT'S ***HYSTERICAL!*** I DO THE SAME TYPES OF THINGS!
YOU'RE KIDDING! THAT IS SO WEIRD...

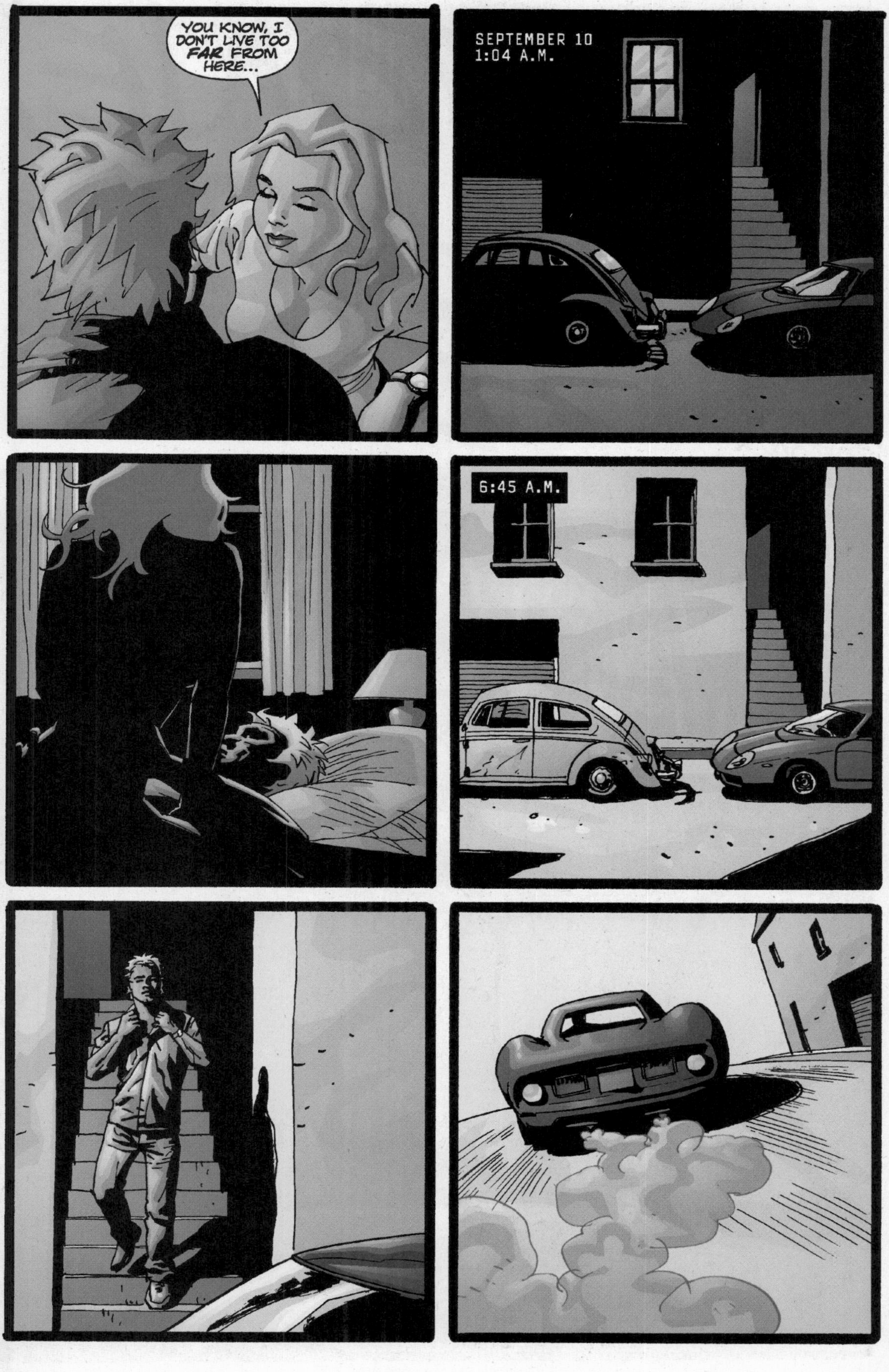
YOU KNOW, I DON'T LIVE TOO FAR FROM HERE...
SEPTEMBER 10
1:04 A.M.
6:45 A.M.

STONE, BLOOD, BURN

JOE CASEY
SEAN PHILLIPS
STORYTELLERS
DAN BROWN
COLORS
RICHARD STARKINGS & COMICRAFT'S SAIDA TEMOFONTE
LETTERS
DESANTIS & DUNBIER
EDITORS
WILDCATS CREATED BY JIM LEE & BRANDON CHOI

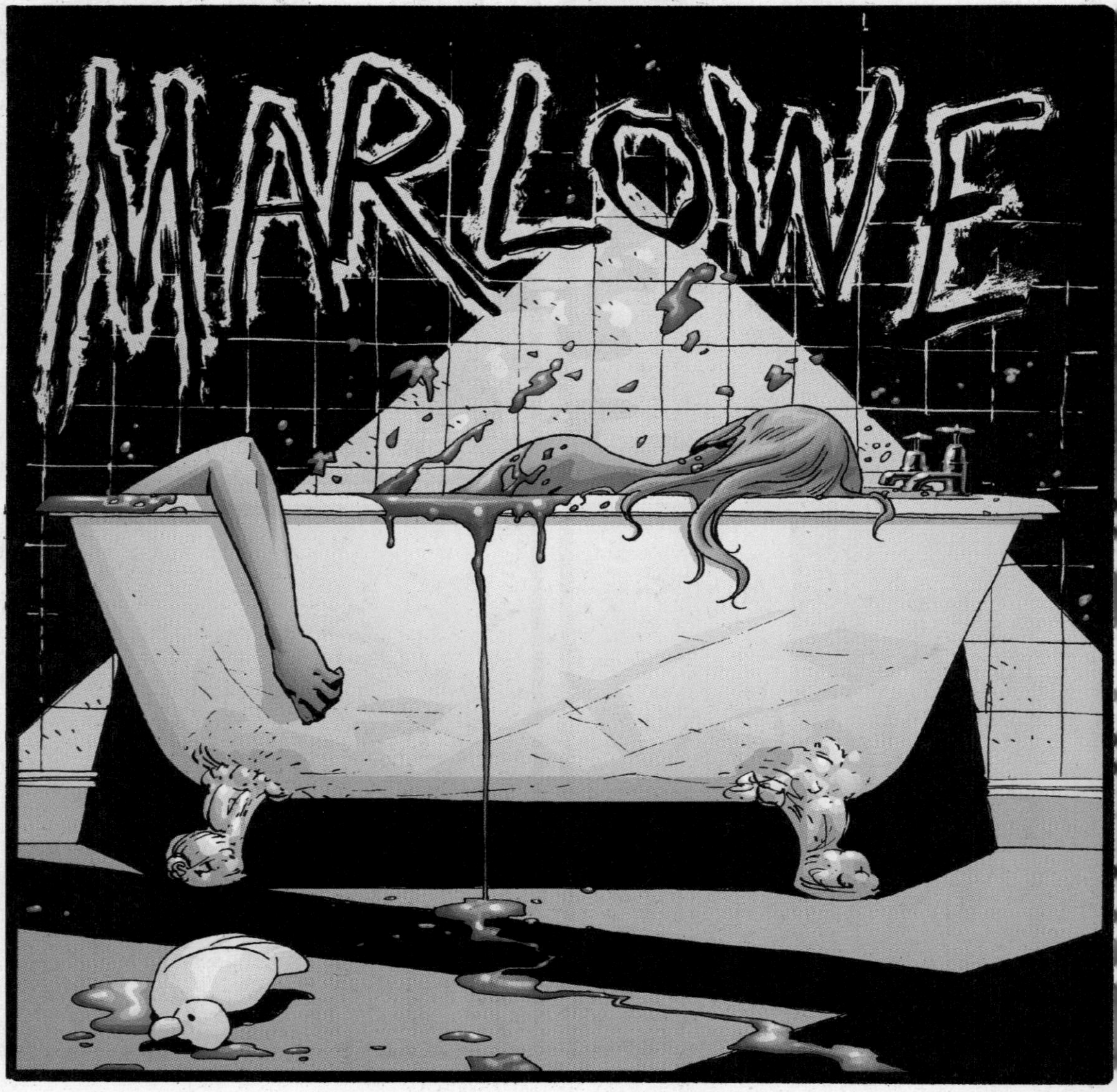
MARLOWE

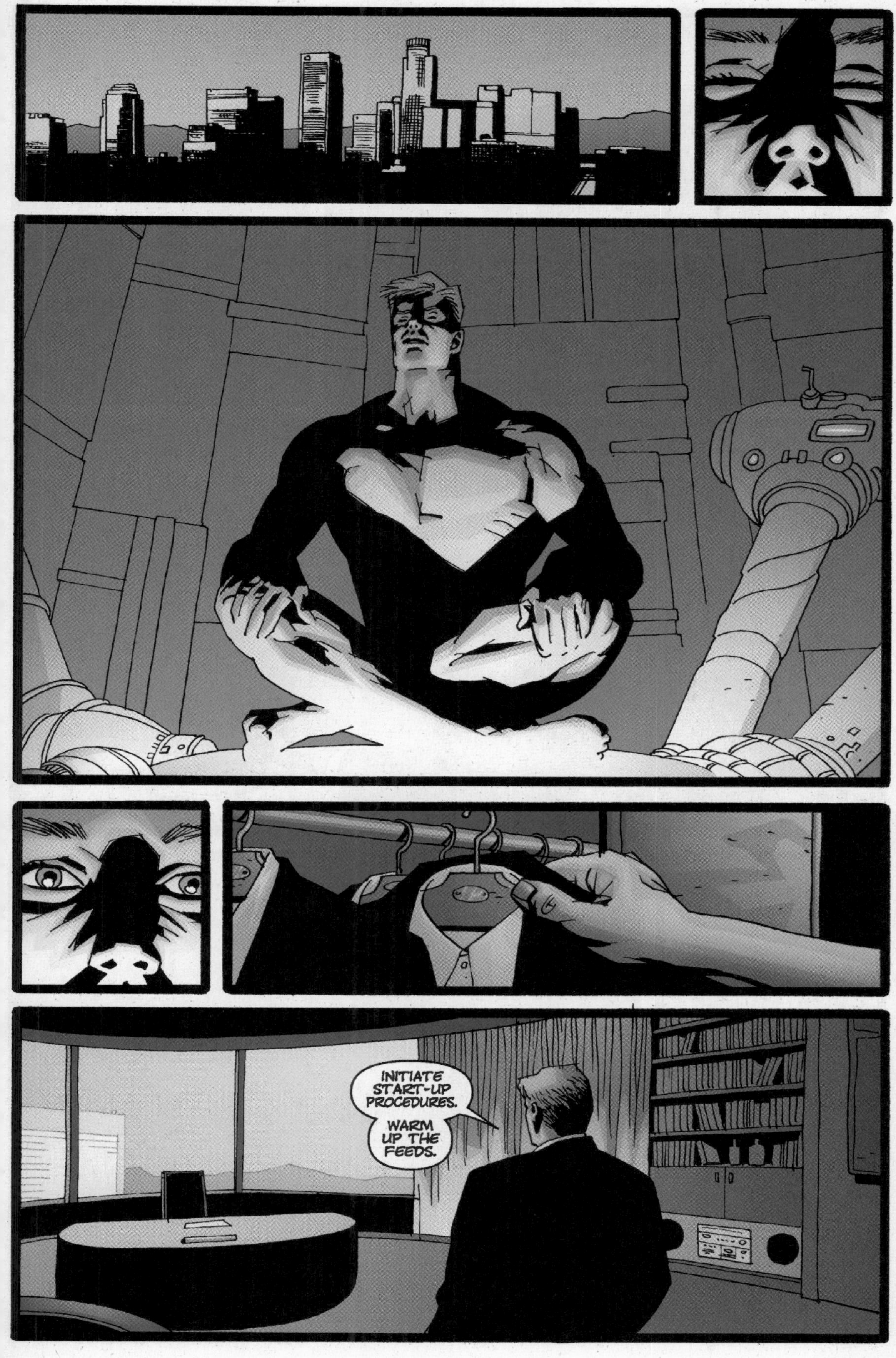
INITIATE START-UP PROCEDURES.
WARM UP THE FEEDS.

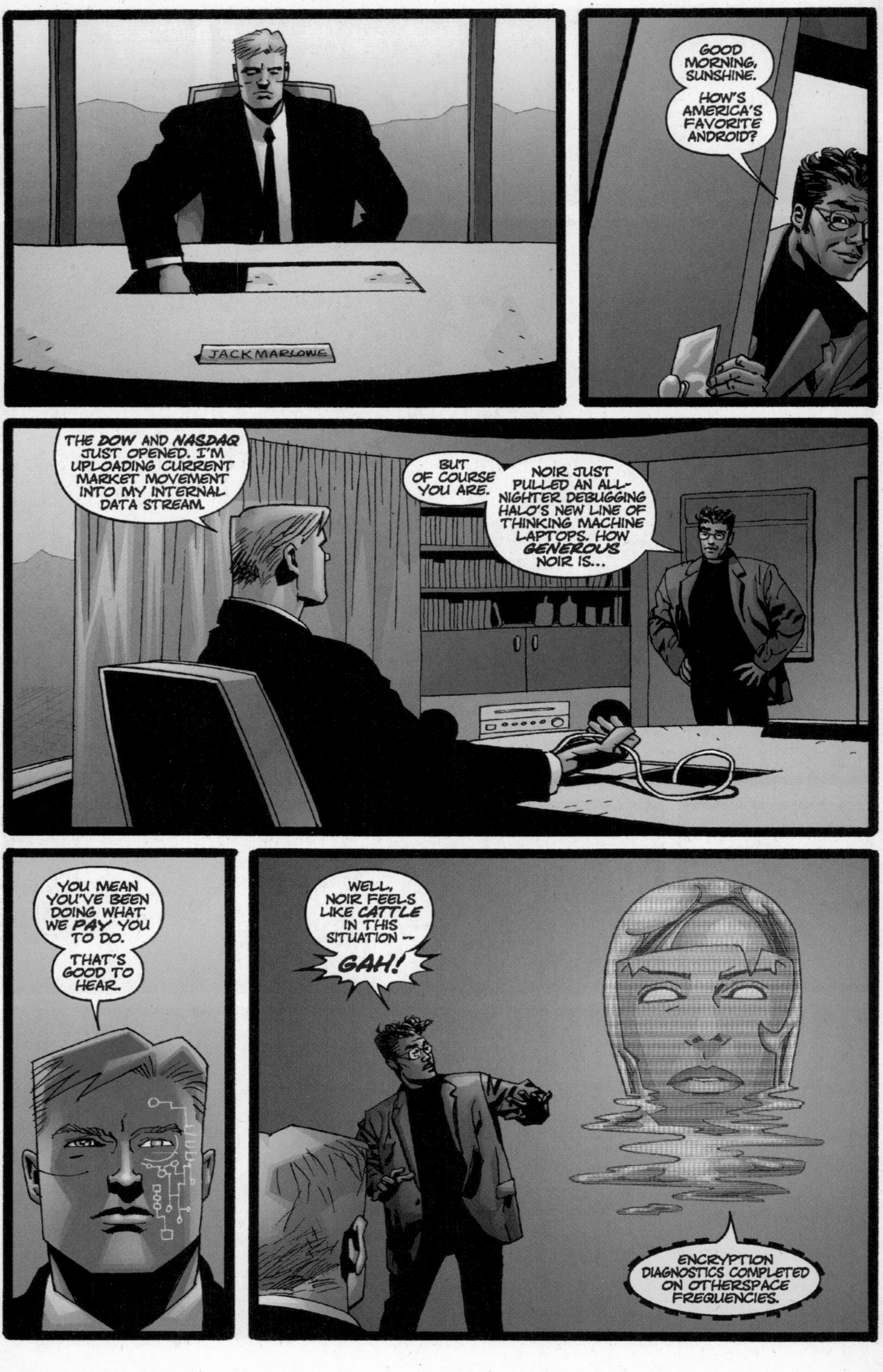
JACK MARLOWE
GOOD MORNING, SUNSHINE.
HOW'S AMERICA'S FAVORITE ANDROID?
THE DOW AND NASDAQ JUST OPENED. I'M UPLOADING CURRENT MARKET MOVEMENT INTO MY INTERNAL DATA STREAM.
BUT OF COURSE YOU ARE.
NOIR JUST PULLED AN ALL-NIGHTER DEBUGGING HALO'S NEW LINE OF THINKING MACHINE LAPTOPS. HOW GENEROUS NOIR IS...
YOU MEAN YOU'VE BEEN DOING WHAT WE PAY YOU TO DO.
THAT'S GOOD TO HEAR.
WELL, NOIR FEELS LIKE CATTLE IN THIS SITUATION --
GAH!
ENCRYPTION DIAGNOSTICS COMPLETED ON OTHERSPACE FREQUENCIES.

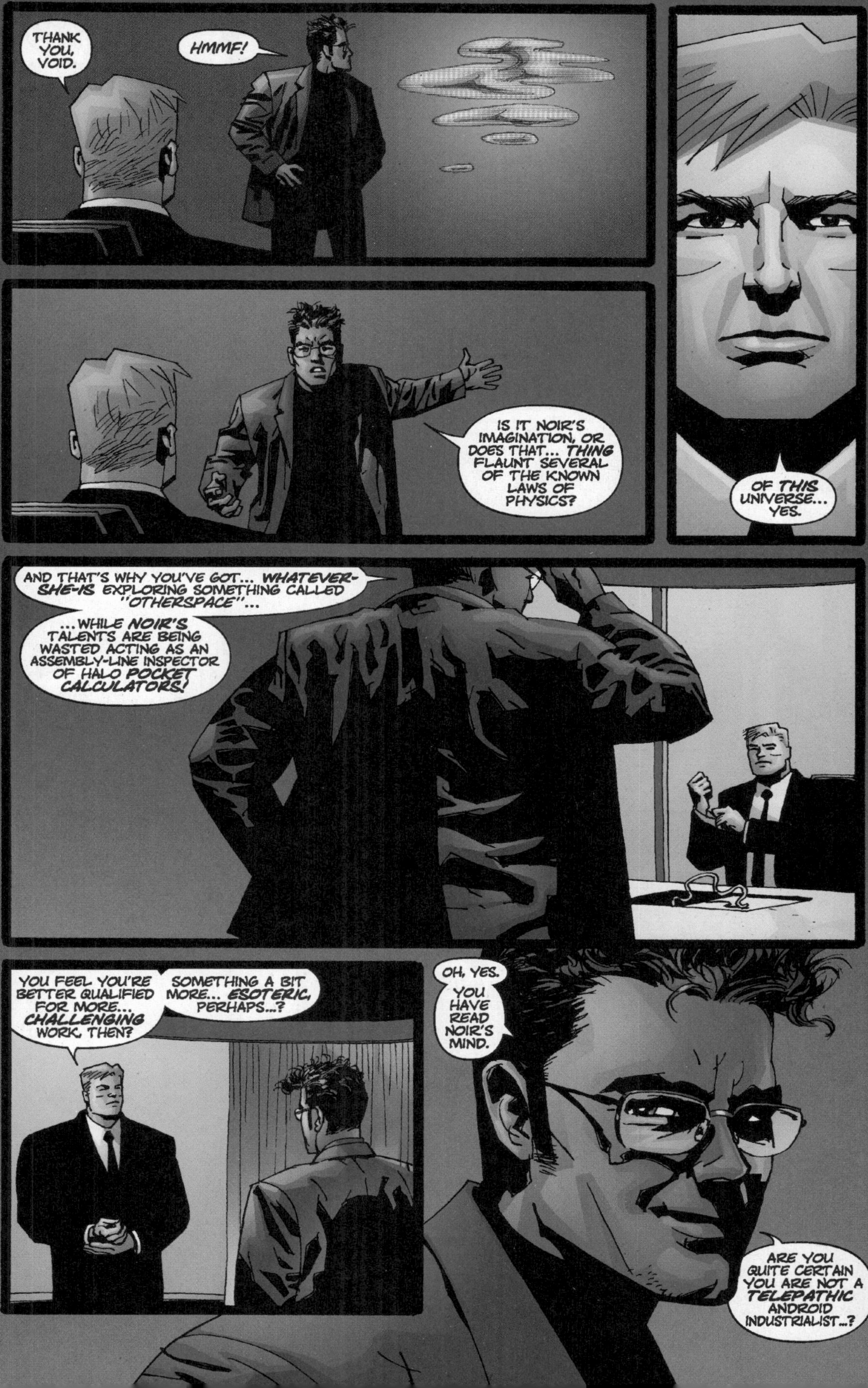

THANK YOU, VOID.
HMMF!
IS IT NOIR'S IMAGINATION, OR DOES THAT... THING FLAUNT SEVERAL OF THE KNOWN LAWS OF PHYSICS?
OF THIS UNIVERSE... YES.
AND THAT'S WHY YOU'VE GOT... WHATEVER-SHE-IS EXPLORING SOMETHING CALLED "OTHERSPACE"...
...WHILE NOIR'S TALENTS ARE BEING WASTED ACTING AS AN ASSEMBLY-LINE INSPECTOR OF HALO POCKET CALCULATORS!
YOU FEEL YOU'RE BETTER QUALIFIED FOR MORE... CHALLENGING WORK, THEN?
SOMETHING A BIT MORE... ESOTERIC, PERHAPS...?
OH, YES.
YOU HAVE READ NOIR'S MIND.
ARE YOU QUITE CERTAIN YOU ARE NOT A TELEPATHIC ANDROID INDUSTRIALIST...?

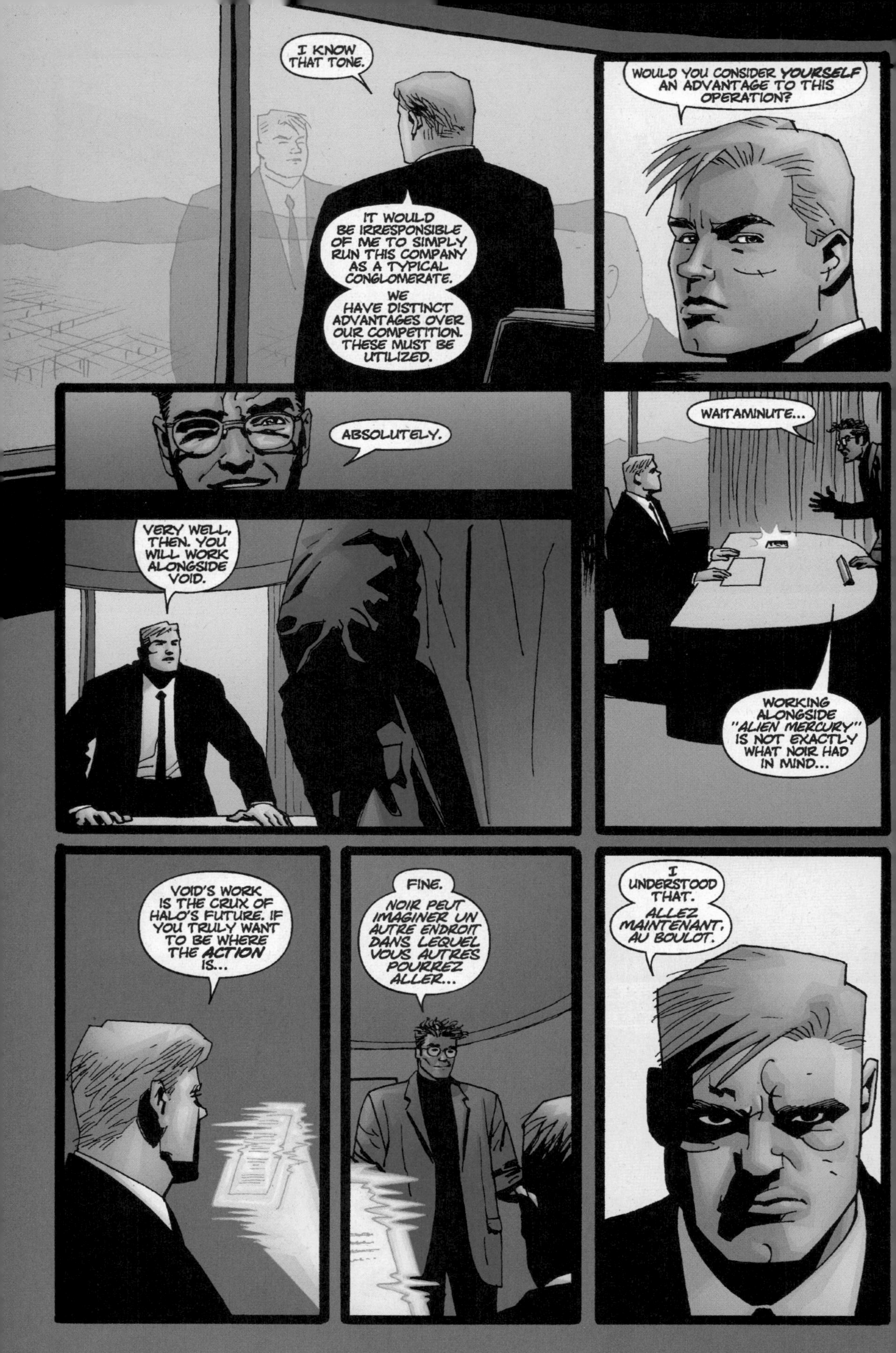

I KNOW THAT TONE.
IT WOULD BE IRRESPONSIBLE OF ME TO SIMPLY RUN THIS COMPANY AS A TYPICAL CONGLOMERATE.
WE HAVE DISTINCT ADVANTAGES OVER OUR COMPETITION. THESE MUST BE UTILIZED.
WOULD YOU CONSIDER YOURSELF AN ADVANTAGE TO THIS OPERATION?
ABSOLUTELY.
VERY WELL, THEN. YOU WILL WORK ALONGSIDE VOID.
WAITAMINUTE...
WORKING ALONGSIDE "ALIEN MERCURY" IS NOT EXACTLY WHAT NOIR HAD IN MIND...
VOID'S WORK IS THE CRUX OF HALO'S FUTURE. IF YOU TRULY WANT TO BE WHERE THE ACTION IS...
FINE.
NOIR PEUT IMAGINER UN AUTRE ENDROIT DANS LEQUEL VOUS AUTRES POURREZ ALLER...
I UNDERSTOOD THAT.
ALLEZ MAINTENANT, AU BOULOT.

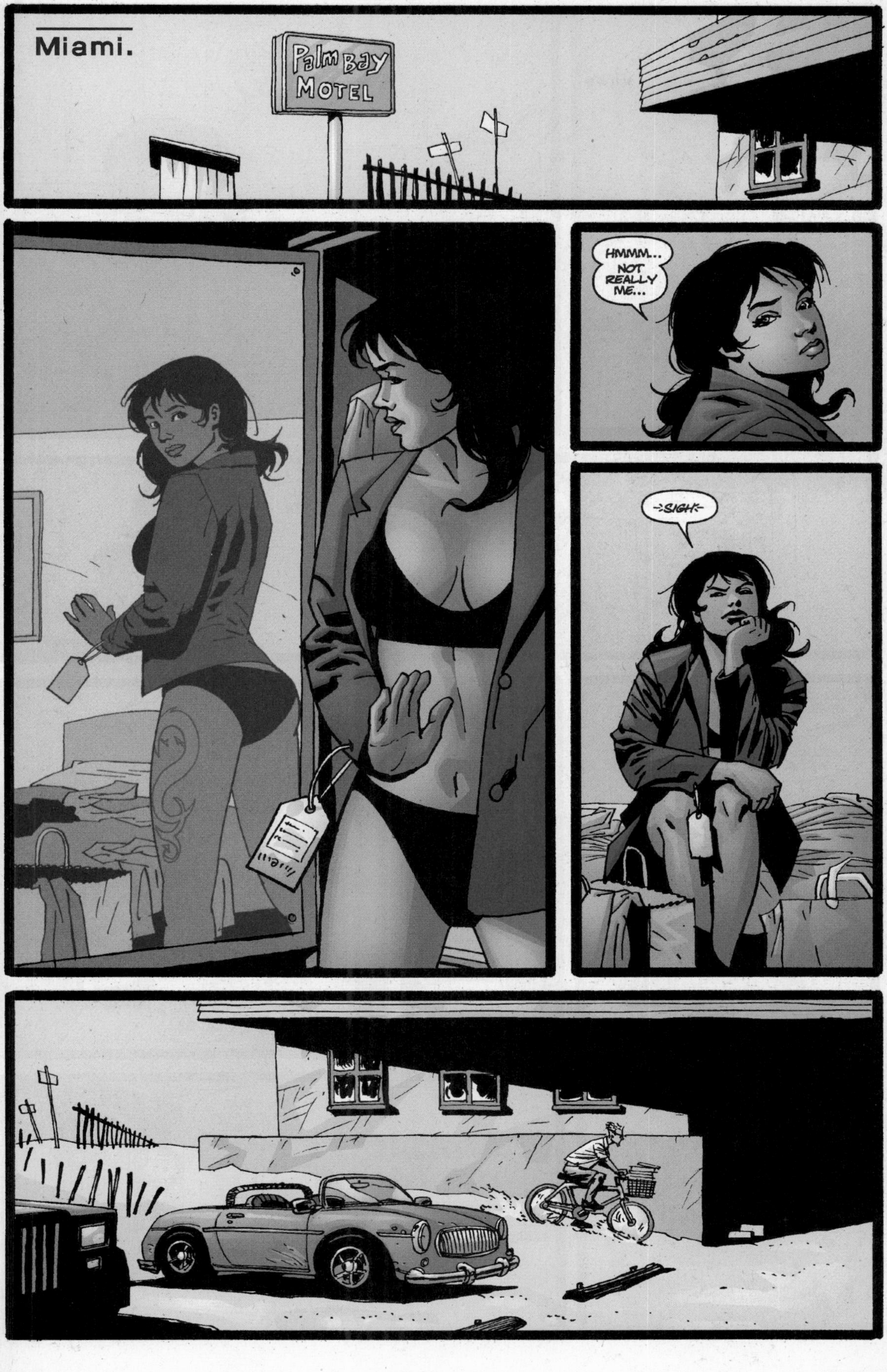
Miami.
Palm Bay
MOTEL
HMMM... NOT REALLY ME...
-SIGH-

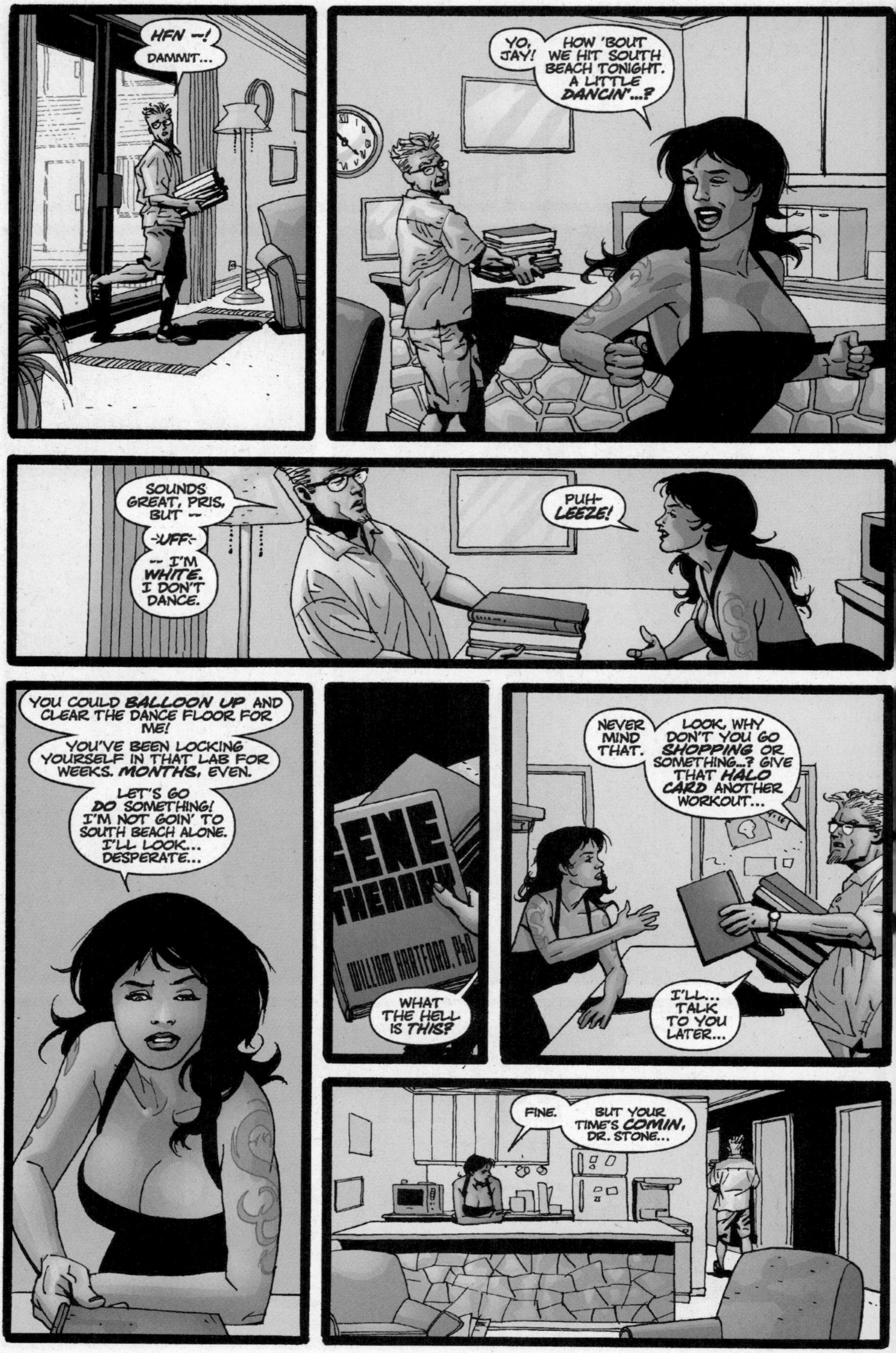
HFN --!
DAMMIT...
YO, JAY!
HOW 'BOUT WE HIT SOUTH BEACH TONIGHT. A LITTLE DANCIN'...?
SOUNDS GREAT, PRIS, BUT --
-UFF-
-- I'M WHITE. I DON'T DANCE.
PUH-LEEZE!
YOU COULD BALLOON UP AND CLEAR THE DANCE FLOOR FOR ME!
YOU'VE BEEN LOCKING YOURSELF IN THAT LAB FOR WEEKS. MONTHS, EVEN.
LET'S GO DO SOMETHING! I'M NOT GOIN' TO SOUTH BEACH ALONE. I'LL LOOK... DESPERATE...
GENE THERAPY
WILLIAM HARTFORD, PhD
WHAT THE HELL IS THIS?
NEVER MIND THAT.
LOOK, WHY DON'T YOU GO SHOPPING OR SOMETHING...? GIVE THAT HALO CARD ANOTHER WORKOUT...
I'LL... TALK TO YOU LATER...
FINE.
BUT YOUR TIME'S COMIN, DR. STONE...

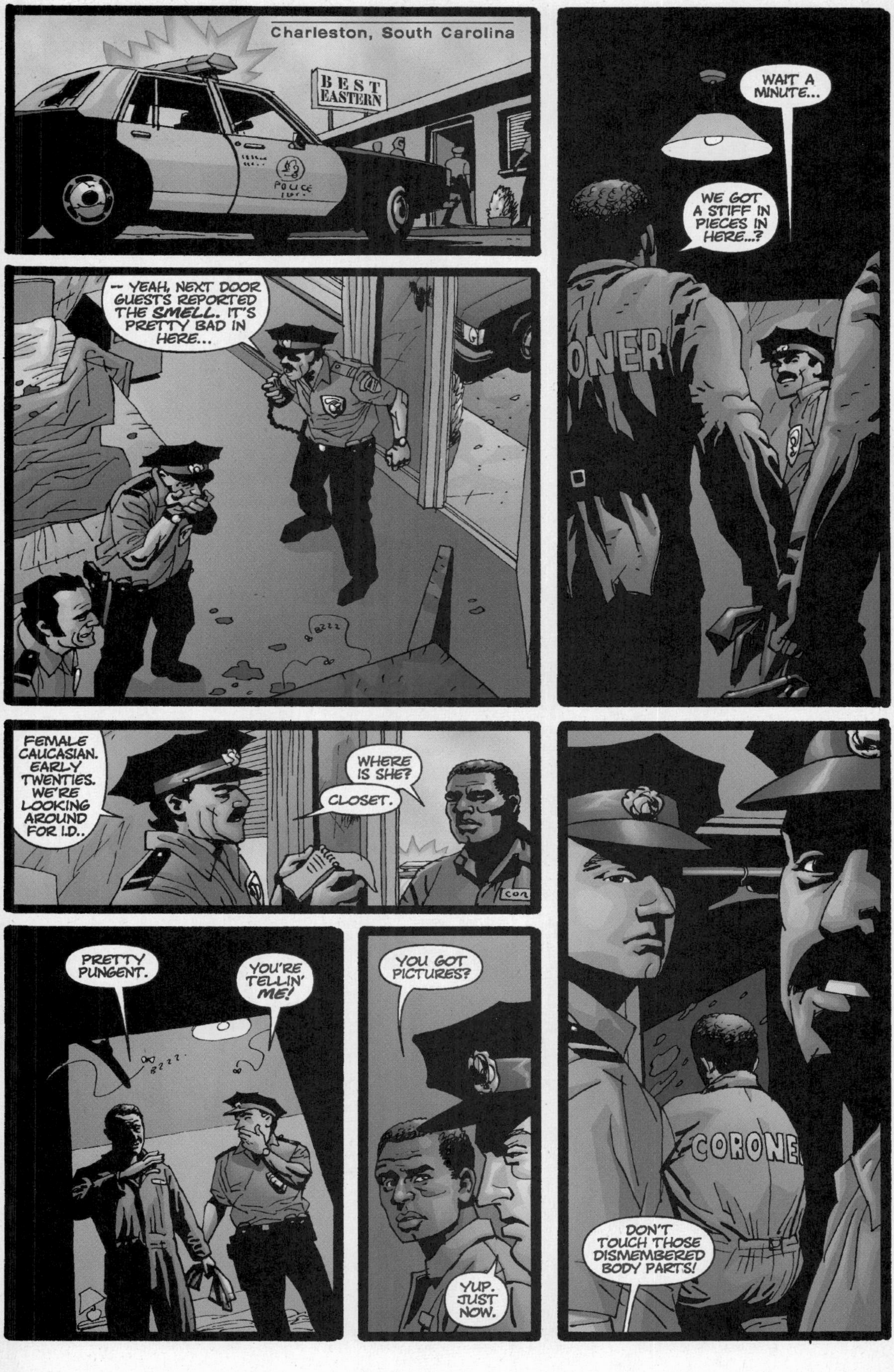
Charleston, South Carolina
BEST EASTERN
POLICE
-- YEAH, NEXT DOOR GUESTS REPORTED THE SMELL. IT'S PRETTY BAD IN HERE...
FEMALE CAUCASIAN. EARLY TWENTIES. WE'RE LOOKING AROUND FOR I.D..
WHERE IS SHE?
CLOSET.
PRETTY PUNGENT.
YOU'RE TELLIN' ME!
YOU GOT PICTURES?
YUP. JUST NOW.
WAIT A MINUTE...
WE GOT A STIFF IN PIECES IN HERE...?
ONER
CORONE
DON'T TOUCH THOSE DISMEMBERED BODY PARTS!

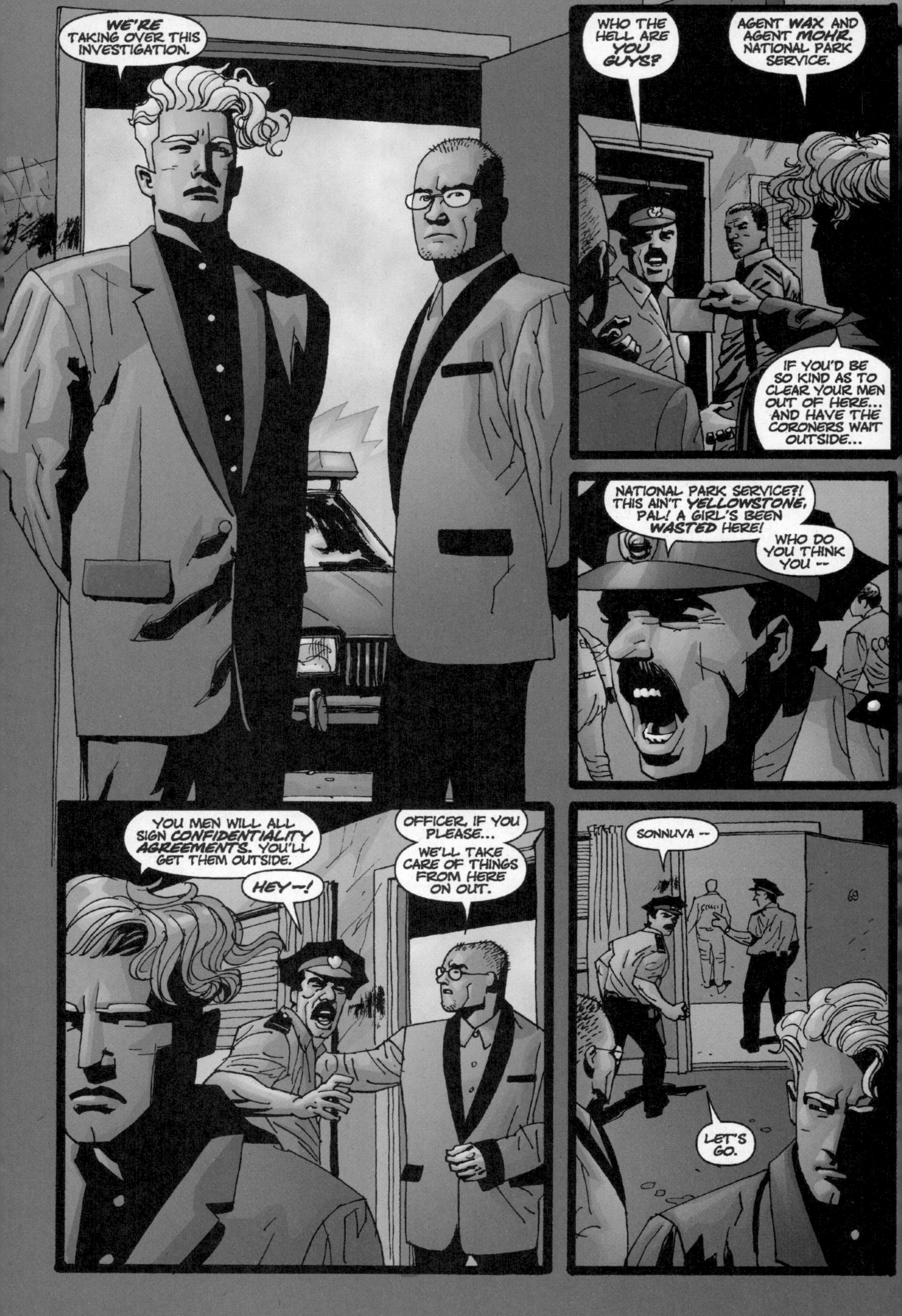
WE'RE TAKING OVER THIS INVESTIGATION.
WHO THE HELL ARE YOU GUYS?
AGENT WAX AND AGENT MOHR. NATIONAL PARK SERVICE.
IF YOU'D BE SO KIND AS TO CLEAR YOUR MEN OUT OF HERE... AND HAVE THE CORONERS WAIT OUTSIDE...
NATIONAL PARK SERVICE?! THIS AIN'T YELLOWSTONE, PAL! A GIRL'S BEEN WASTED HERE!
WHO DO YOU THINK YOU --
YOU MEN WILL ALL SIGN CONFIDENTIALITY AGREEMENTS. YOU'LL GET THEM OUTSIDE.
HEY--!
OFFICER, IF YOU PLEASE...
WE'LL TAKE CARE OF THINGS FROM HERE ON OUT.
SONNUVA --
LET'S GO.

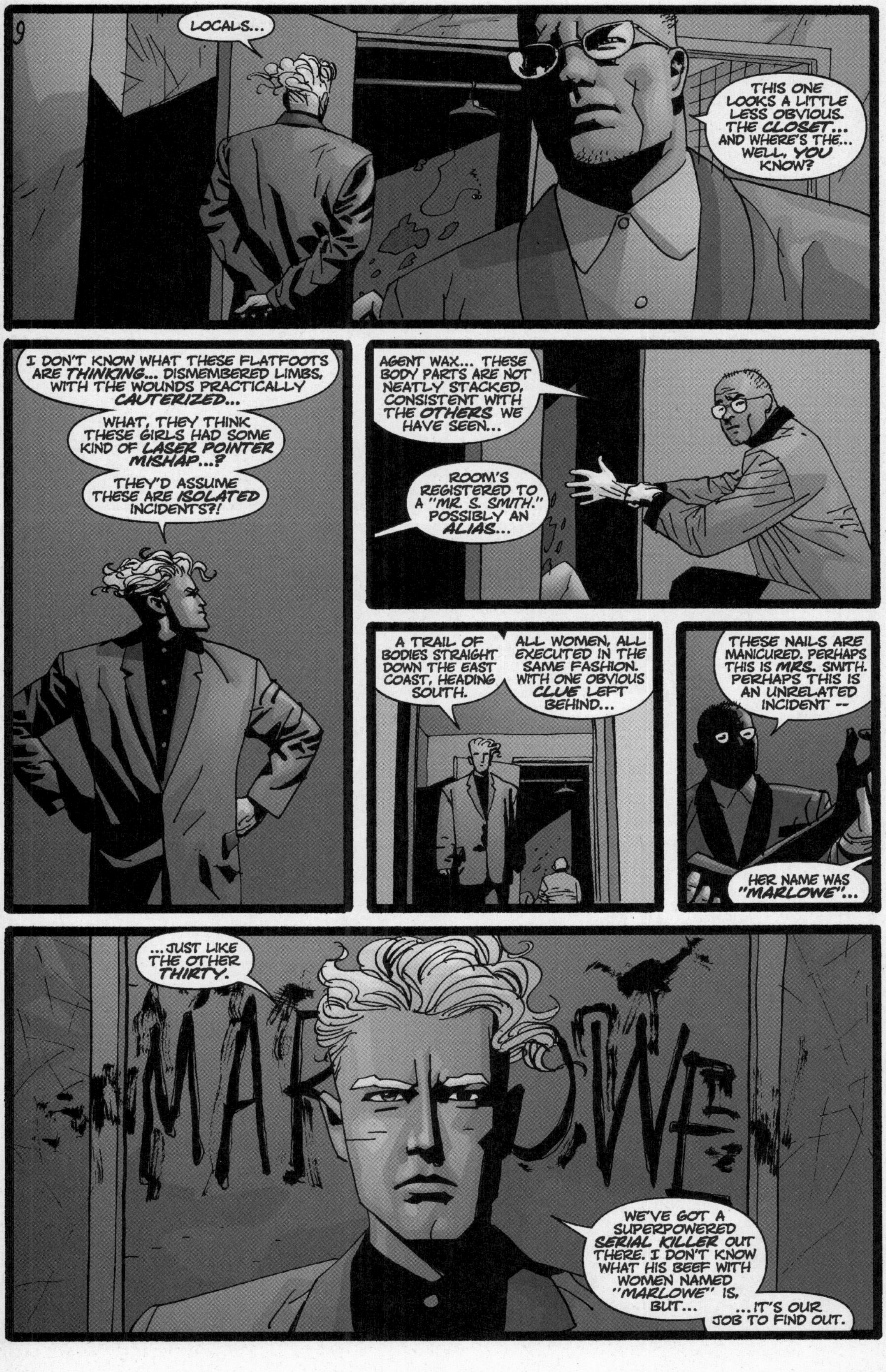
9
LOCALS...
THIS ONE LOOKS A LITTLE LESS OBVIOUS. THE CLOSET... AND WHERE'S THE... WELL, YOU KNOW?
I DON'T KNOW WHAT THESE FLATFOOTS ARE THINKING... DISMEMBERED LIMBS, WITH THE WOUNDS PRACTICALLY CAUTERIZED...
WHAT, THEY THINK THESE GIRLS HAD SOME KIND OF LASER POINTER MISHAP...?
THEY'D ASSUME THESE ARE ISOLATED INCIDENTS?!
AGENT WAX... THESE BODY PARTS ARE NOT NEATLY STACKED, CONSISTENT WITH THE OTHERS WE HAVE SEEN...
ROOM'S REGISTERED TO A "MR. S. SMITH." POSSIBLY AN ALIAS...
A TRAIL OF BODIES STRAIGHT DOWN THE EAST COAST, HEADING SOUTH.
ALL WOMEN, ALL EXECUTED IN THE SAME FASHION. WITH ONE OBVIOUS CLUE LEFT BEHIND...
THESE NAILS ARE MANICURED. PERHAPS THIS IS MRS. SMITH. PERHAPS THIS IS AN UNRELATED INCIDENT --
HER NAME WAS "MARLOWE"...
...JUST LIKE THE OTHER THIRTY.
WE'VE GOT A SUPERPOWERED SERIAL KILLER OUT THERE. I DON'T KNOW WHAT HIS BEEF WITH WOMEN NAMED "MARLOWE" IS, BUT...
...IT'S OUR JOB TO FIND OUT.

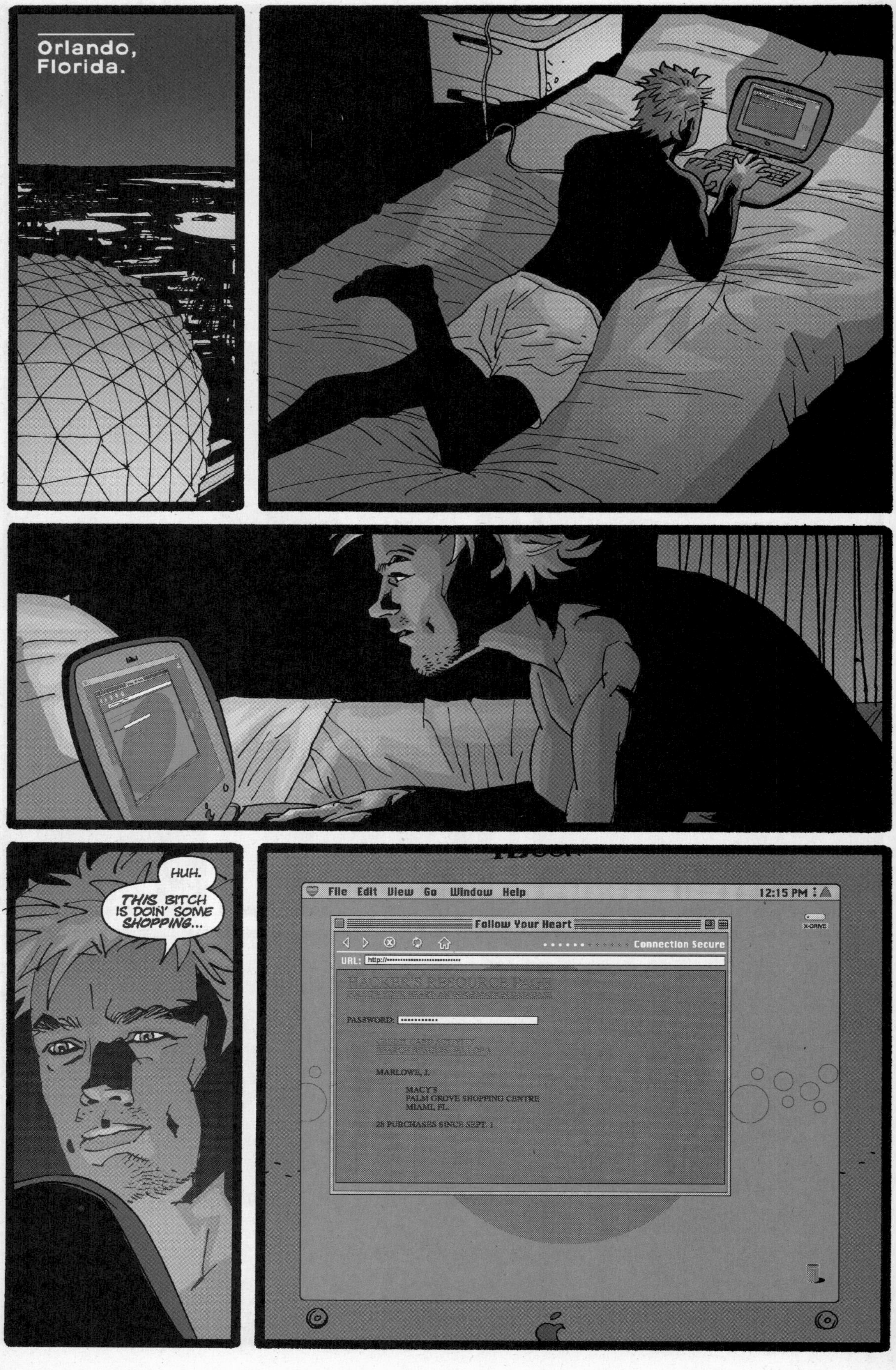
Orlando, Florida.
HUH.
THIS BITCH IS DOIN' SOME SHOPPING...
File Edit View Go Window Help
12:15 PM
X-DRIVE
Follow Your Heart
Connection Secure
URL: http://
HACKER'S RESOURCE PAGE
PASSWORD:
MARLOWE, J.
MACY'S
PALM GROVE SHOPPING CENTRE
MIAMI, FL.
28 PURCHASES SINCE SEPT. 1

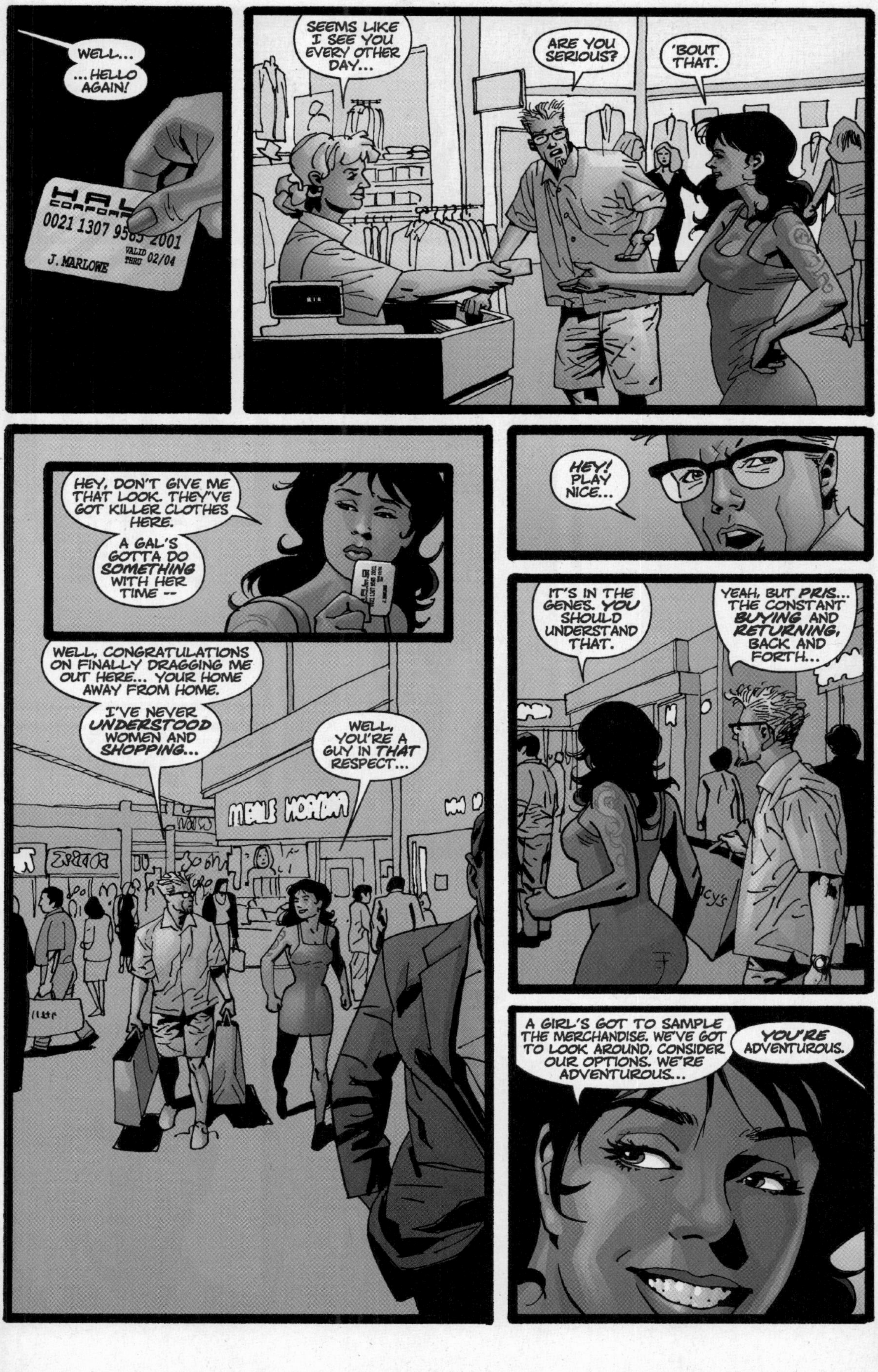
WELL...
...HELLO AGAIN!
HALO CORPORATION
0021 1307 9565 2001
VALID THRU 02/04
J. MARLOWE
SEEMS LIKE I SEE YOU EVERY OTHER DAY...
ARE YOU SERIOUS?
'BOUT THAT.
HEY, DON'T GIVE ME THAT LOOK. THEY'VE GOT KILLER CLOTHES HERE.
A GAL'S GOTTA DO *SOMETHING* WITH HER TIME --
HEY! PLAY NICE...
WELL, CONGRATULATIONS ON FINALLY DRAGGING ME OUT HERE... YOUR HOME AWAY FROM HOME.
I'VE NEVER *UNDERSTOOD* WOMEN AND *SHOPPING*...
WELL, YOU'RE A GUY IN *THAT* RESPECT...
IT'S IN THE GENES. *YOU* SHOULD UNDERSTAND THAT.
YEAH, BUT *PRIS*... THE CONSTANT *BUYING* AND *RETURNING*, BACK AND FORTH...
A GIRL'S GOT TO SAMPLE THE MERCHANDISE. WE'VE GOT TO LOOK AROUND, CONSIDER OUR OPTIONS. WE'RE ADVENTUROUS...
YOU'RE ADVENTUROUS.

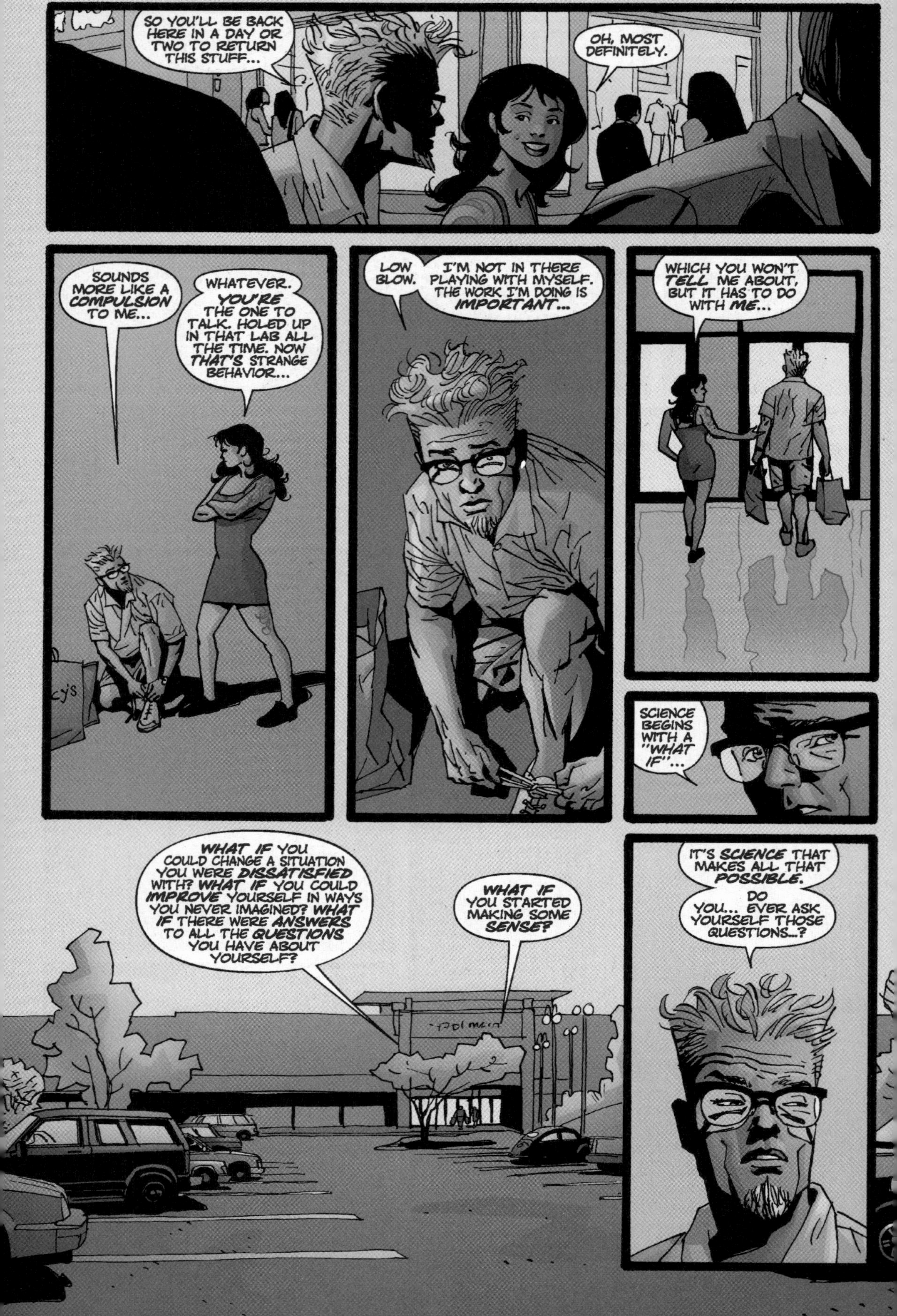
SO YOU'LL BE BACK HERE IN A DAY OR TWO TO RETURN THIS STUFF...
OH, MOST DEFINITELY.
SOUNDS MORE LIKE A COMPULSION TO ME...
WHATEVER. YOU'RE THE ONE TO TALK. HOLED UP IN THAT LAB ALL THE TIME. NOW THAT'S STRANGE BEHAVIOR...
LOW BLOW.
I'M NOT IN THERE PLAYING WITH MYSELF. THE WORK I'M DOING IS IMPORTANT...
WHICH YOU WON'T TELL ME ABOUT, BUT IT HAS TO DO WITH ME...
SCIENCE BEGINS WITH A "WHAT IF"...
WHAT IF YOU COULD CHANGE A SITUATION YOU WERE DISSATISFIED WITH? WHAT IF YOU COULD IMPROVE YOURSELF IN WAYS YOU NEVER IMAGINED? WHAT IF THERE WERE ANSWERS TO ALL THE QUESTIONS YOU HAVE ABOUT YOURSELF?
WHAT IF YOU STARTED MAKING SOME SENSE?
IT'S SCIENCE THAT MAKES ALL THAT POSSIBLE.
DO YOU... EVER ASK YOURSELF THOSE QUESTIONS...?

ARE WE REALLY TALKING ABOUT *ME* NOW...?

WELL, WE BOTH KNOW... WHAT YOUR *SITUATION* IS...

-:SIGH:- IS THIS WHERE I'M SUPPOSED TO SAY, "YOU MEAN THE FACT THAT I HAVE *DAEMONITE* GENES, DR. STONE?"

I KNOW WHAT I AM.

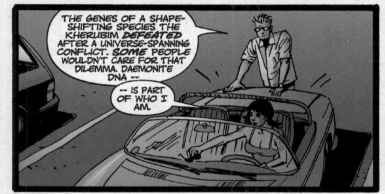

THE GENES OF A SHAPE-SHIFTING SPECIES THE KHERUBIM *DEFEATED* AFTER A UNIVERSE-SPANNING CONFLICT. *SOME* PEOPLE WOULDN'T CARE FOR THAT DILEMMA. DAEMONITE DNA --

-- IS PART OF WHO I AM.

NOT MUCH I CAN DO ABOUT IT, IS THERE?

SO YOU JUST *IGNORE* IT?

YOU'RE HALF-KHERUBIM. HOW DO YOU FEEL ABOUT IT?

WE'RE NOT TALKING ABOUT *ME*...

WHY? 'CAUSE THE KHERUBIM WERE THE *GOOD GUYS*?! WHAT DIFFERENCE DOES *THAT* MAKE NOW?

THE WAR'S OVER. HOW MANY TIMES DO WE HAVE TO DREDGE UP THE WHOLE KHERUBIM-DAEMONITE THING?

I'M *SICK* OF IT.

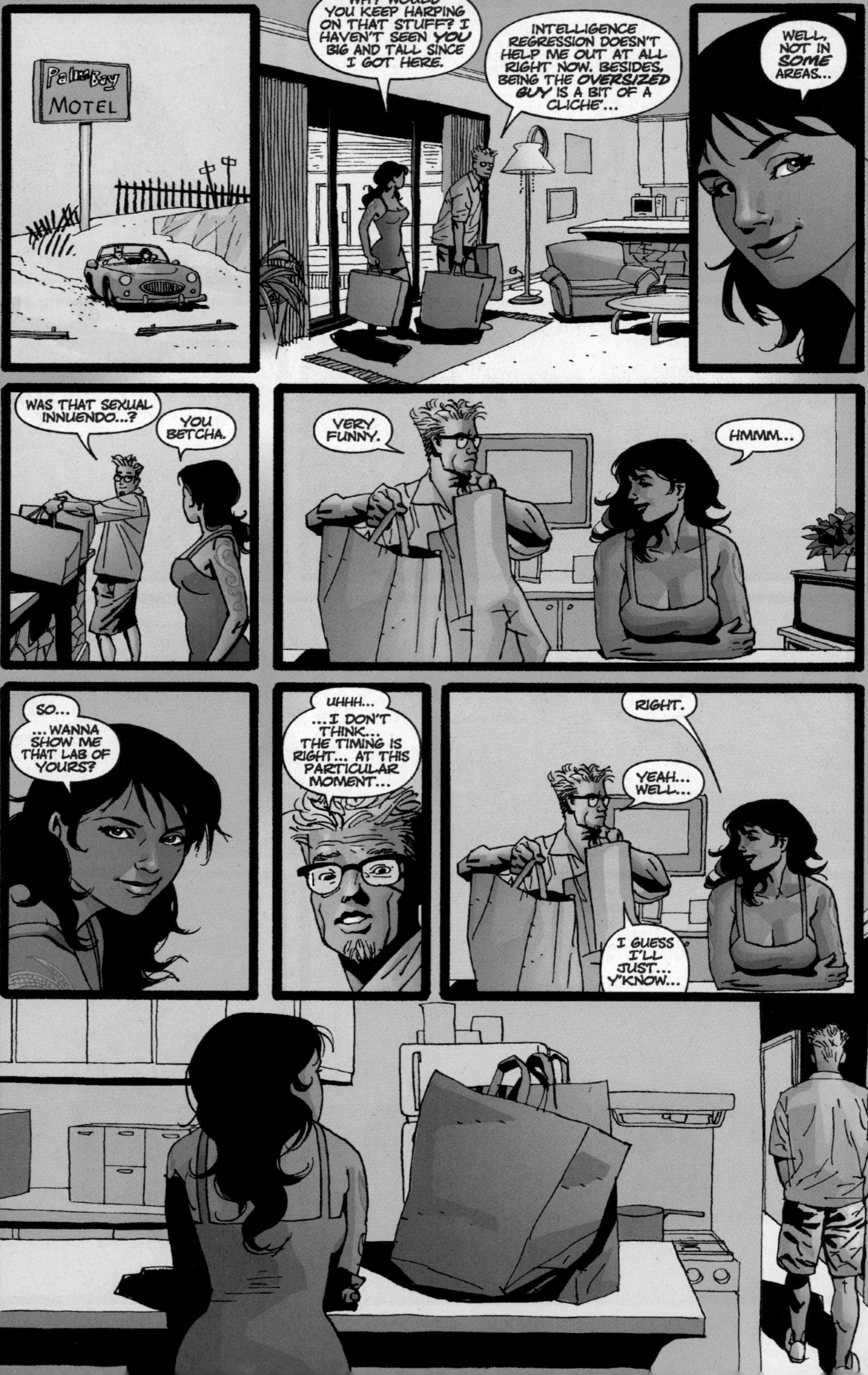
Palm Bay
MOTEL
WHY WOULD YOU KEEP HARPING ON THAT STUFF? I HAVEN'T SEEN YOU BIG AND TALL SINCE I GOT HERE.
INTELLIGENCE REGRESSION DOESN'T HELP ME OUT AT ALL RIGHT NOW. BESIDES, BEING THE OVERSIZED GUY IS A BIT OF A CLICHE'...
WELL, NOT IN SOME AREAS...
WAS THAT SEXUAL INNUENDO...?
YOU BETCHA.
VERY FUNNY.
HMMM...
SO...
...WANNA SHOW ME THAT LAB OF YOURS?
UHHH...
...I DON'T THINK... THE TIMING IS RIGHT... AT THIS PARTICULAR MOMENT...
RIGHT.
YEAH... WELL...
I GUESS I'LL JUST... Y'KNOW...

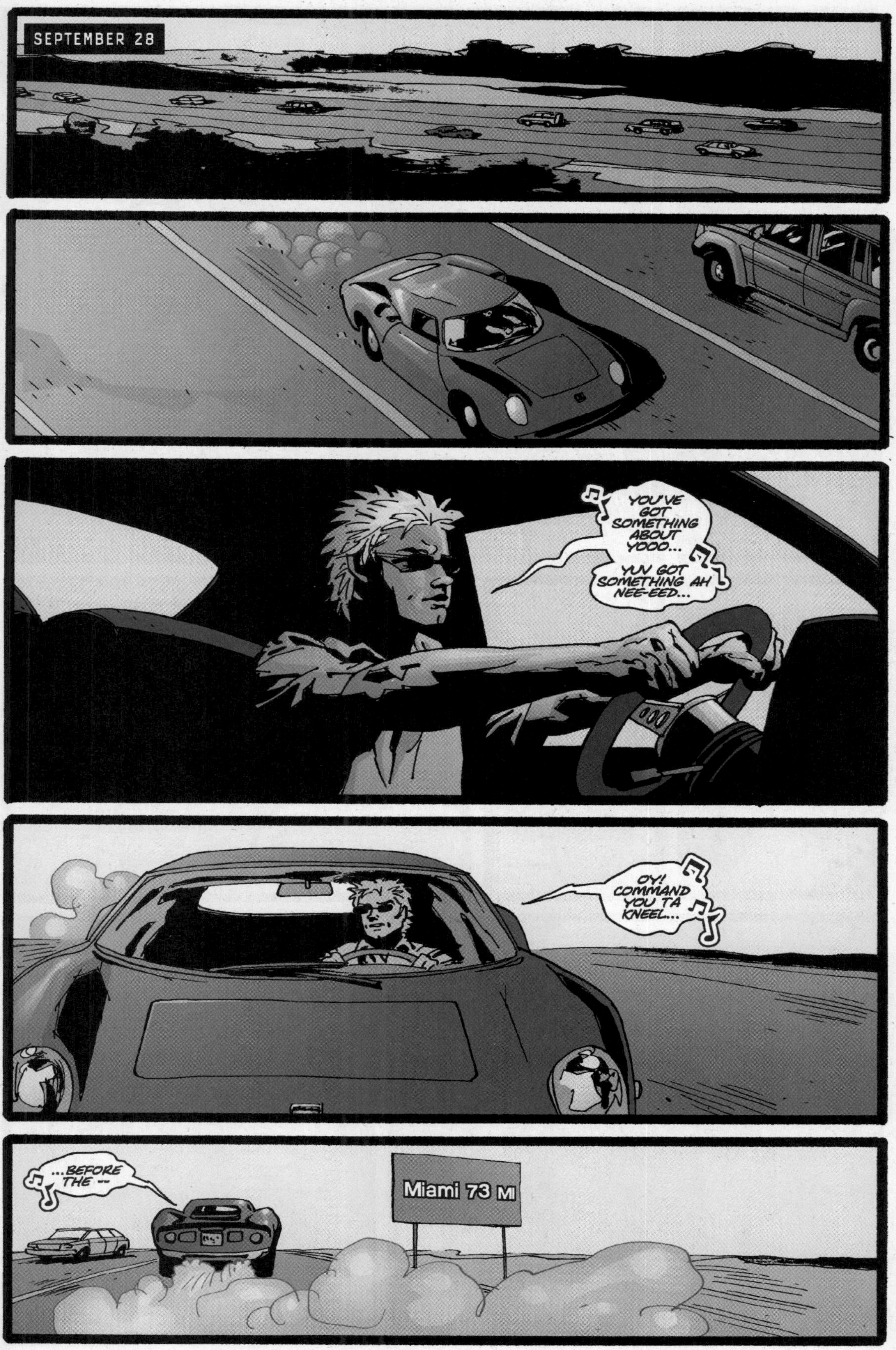
SEPTEMBER 28
YOU'VE GOT SOMETHING ABOUT YOOO... YUV GOT SOMETHING AH NEE-EED...
OY! COMMAND YOU TA KNEEL...
...BEFORE THE --
Miami 73 MI

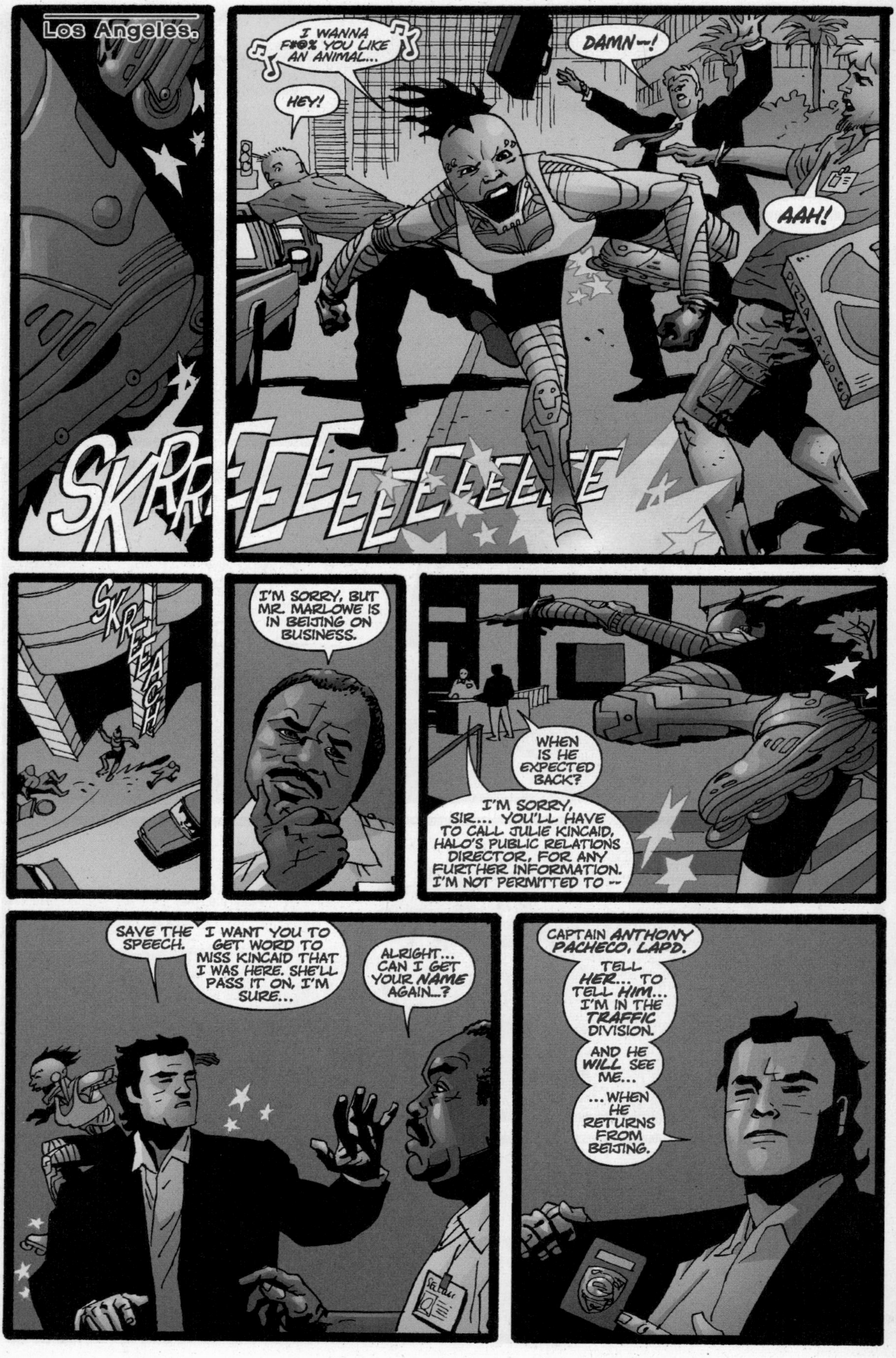
Los Angeles.
I WANNA F#@% YOU LIKE AN ANIMAL...
HEY!
DAMN--!
AAH!
PIZZA-A-GO-GO
SKRREEEEEEEEEEEE
SKREEACH
I'M SORRY, BUT MR. MARLOWE IS IN BEIJING ON BUSINESS.
WHEN IS HE EXPECTED BACK?
I'M SORRY, SIR... YOU'LL HAVE TO CALL JULIE KINCAID, HALO'S PUBLIC RELATIONS DIRECTOR, FOR ANY FURTHER INFORMATION. I'M NOT PERMITTED TO --
SAVE THE SPEECH.
I WANT YOU TO GET WORD TO MISS KINCAID THAT I WAS HERE. SHE'LL PASS IT ON, I'M SURE...
ALRIGHT... CAN I GET YOUR NAME AGAIN...?
CAPTAIN ANTHONY PACHECO, LAPD.
TELL HER... TO TELL HIM... I'M IN THE TRAFFIC DIVISION.
AND HE WILL SEE ME...
...WHEN HE RETURNS FROM BEIJING.

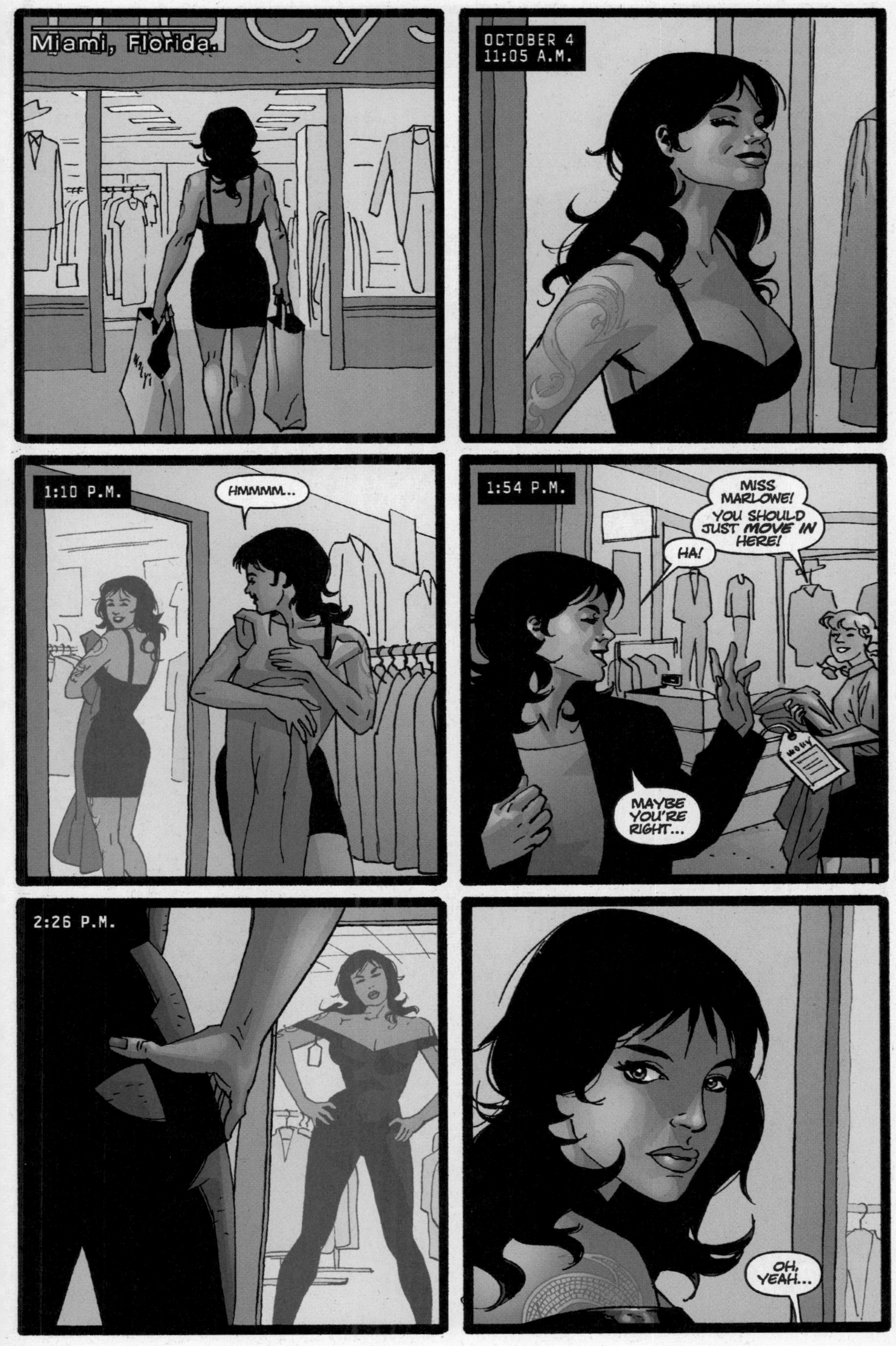
Miami, Florida.
OCTOBER 4
11:05 A.M.
1:10 P.M.
HMMMM..
1:54 P.M.
MISS MARLOWE! YOU SHOULD JUST MOVE IN HERE!
HA!
MAYBE YOU'RE RIGHT...
2:26 P.M.
OH, YEAH...

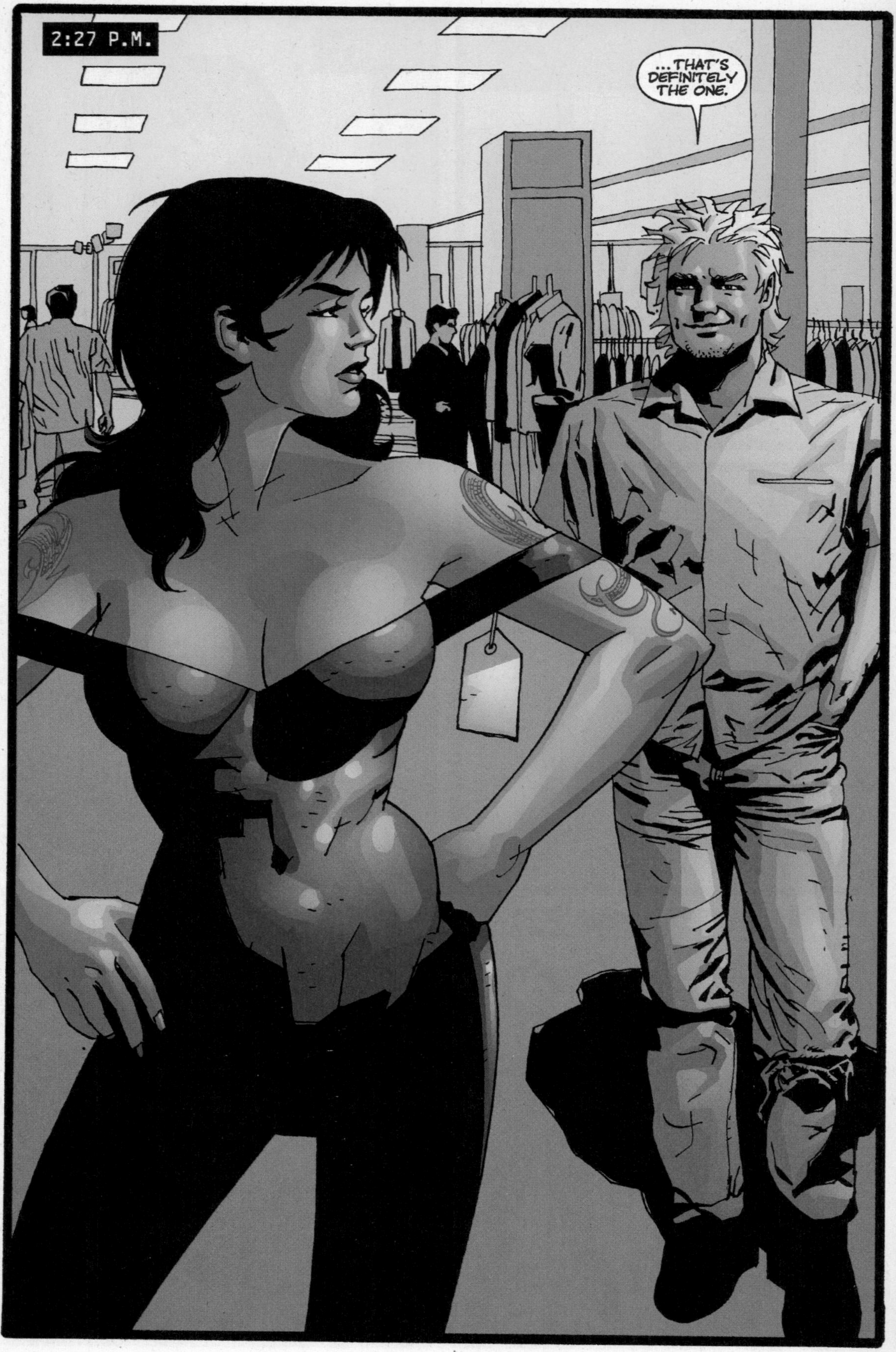
2:27 P.M.
...THAT'S DEFINITELY THE ONE.

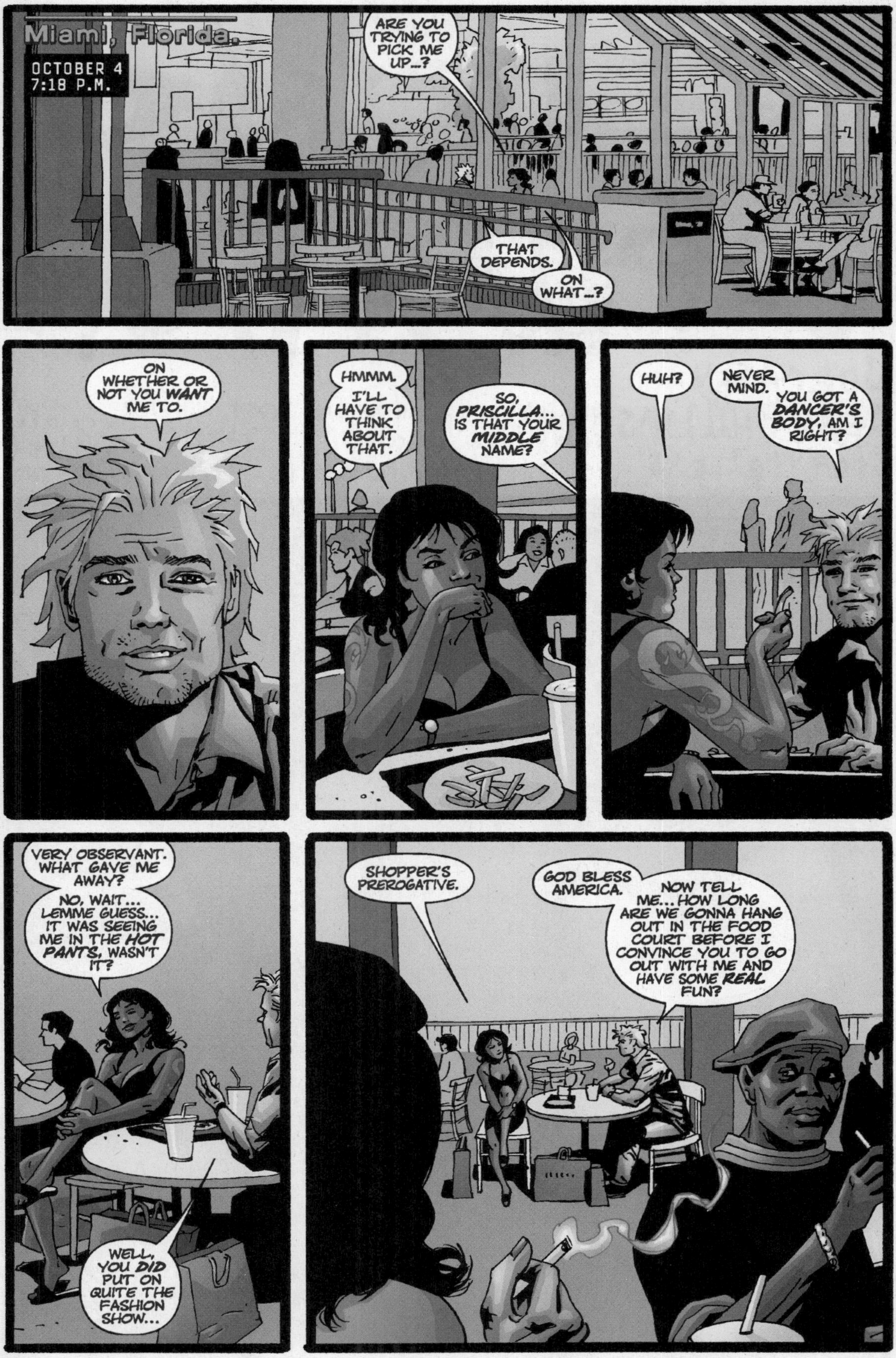
Miami, Florida.
OCTOBER 4
7:18 P.M.
ARE YOU TRYING TO PICK ME UP...?
THAT DEPENDS.
ON WHAT...?
ON WHETHER OR NOT YOU WANT ME TO.
HMMM.
I'LL HAVE TO THINK ABOUT THAT.
SO, PRISCILLA... IS THAT YOUR MIDDLE NAME?
HUH?
NEVER MIND.
YOU GOT A DANCER'S BODY, AM I RIGHT?
VERY OBSERVANT. WHAT GAVE ME AWAY?
NO, WAIT... LEMME GUESS... IT WAS SEEING ME IN THE HOT PANTS, WASN'T IT?
WELL, YOU DID PUT ON QUITE THE FASHION SHOW...
SHOPPER'S PREROGATIVE.
GOD BLESS AMERICA.
NOW TELL ME... HOW LONG ARE WE GONNA HANG OUT IN THE FOOD COURT BEFORE I CONVINCE YOU TO GO OUT WITH ME AND HAVE SOME REAL FUN?

SEARING COPULATION

JOE CASEY
SEAN PHILLIPS
STORYTELLERS

RICHARD STARKINGS & COMICRAFT'S SAIDA TEMOFONTE LETTERS

DAN BROWN COLORS

SCOTT DUNBIER EDITOR

WILDCATS CREATED BY JIM LEE & BRANDON CHOI

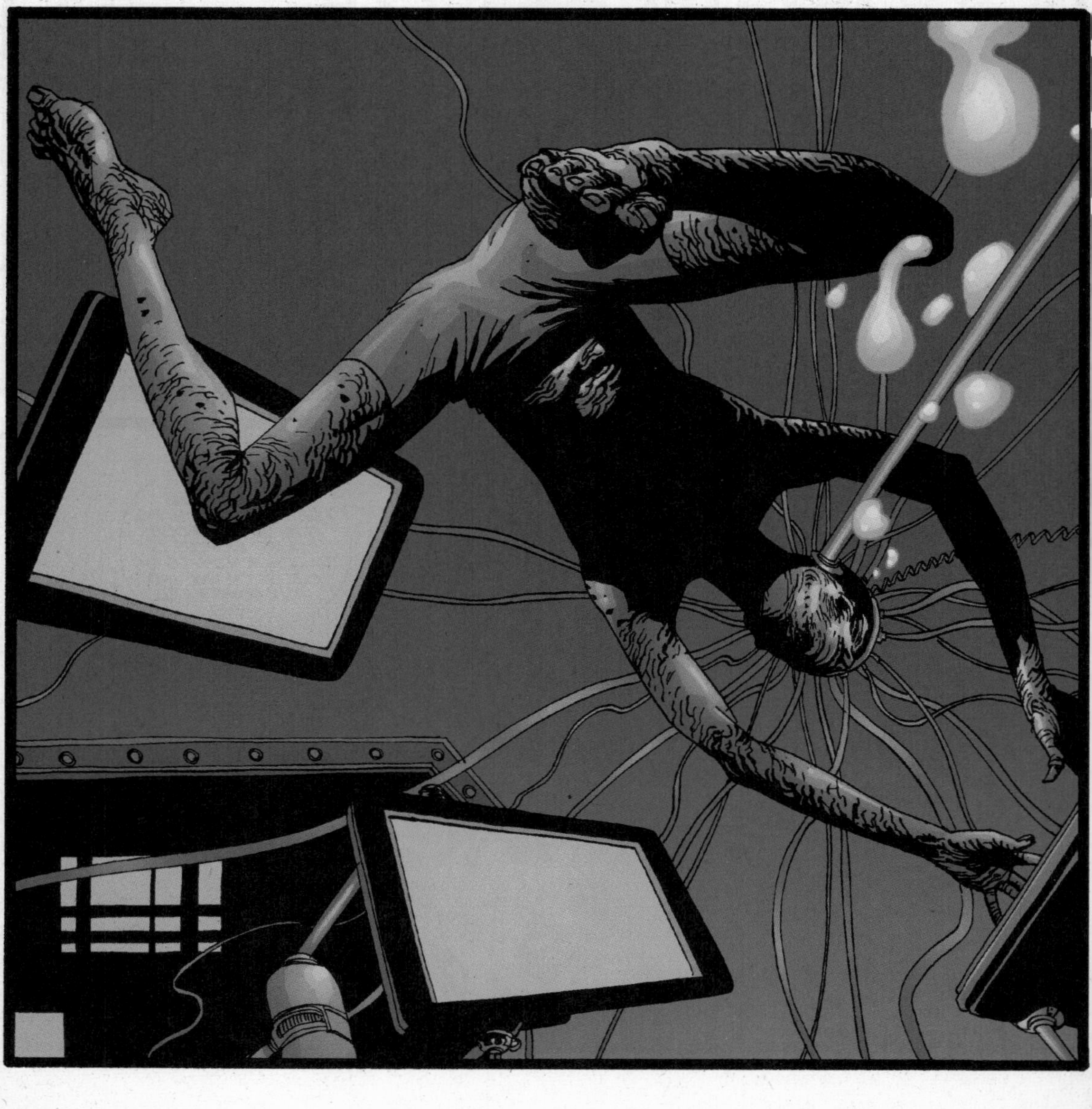

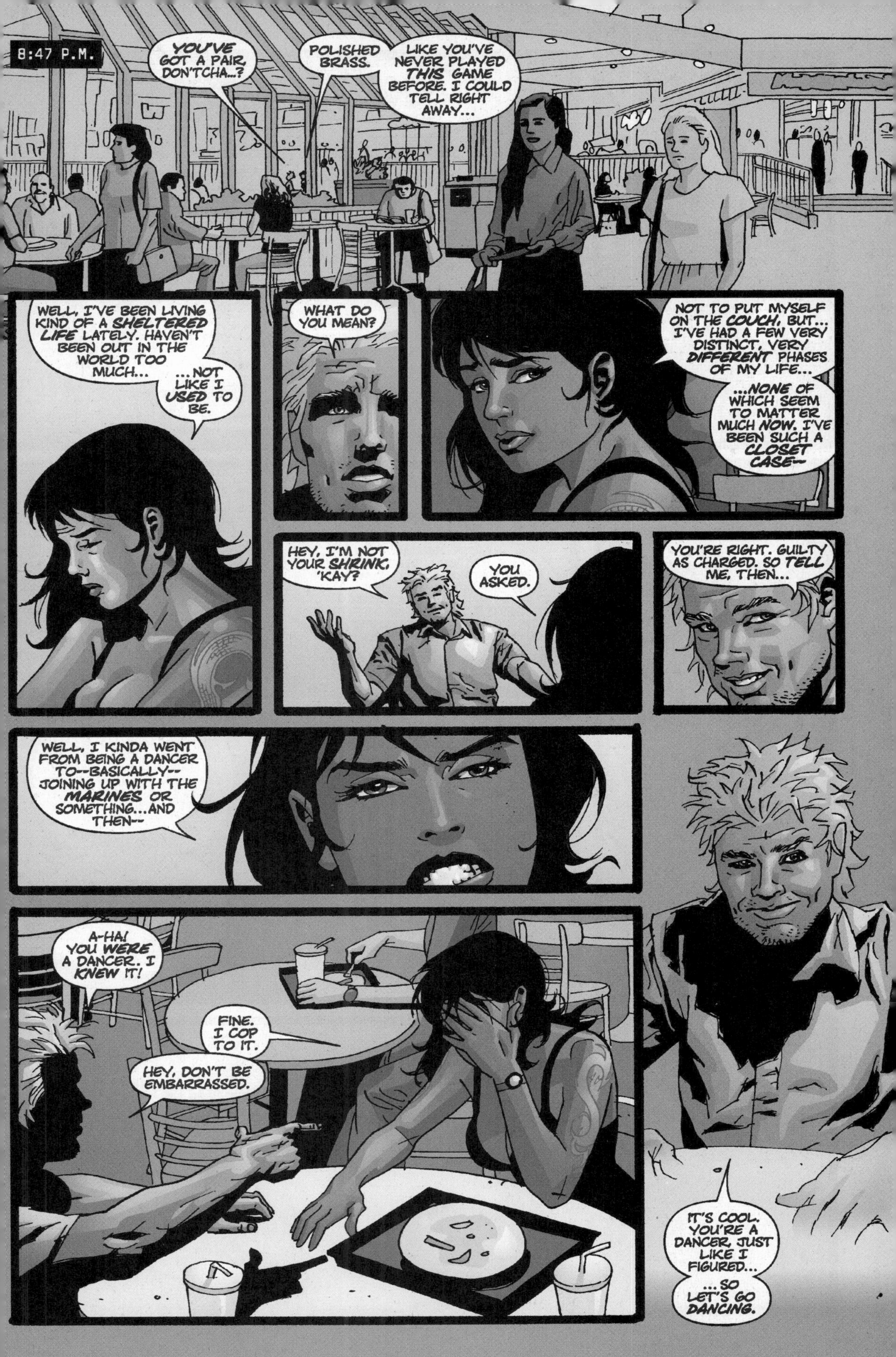
8:47 P.M.
YOU'VE GOT A PAIR, DON'TCHA...?
POLISHED BRASS.
LIKE YOU'VE NEVER PLAYED THIS GAME BEFORE. I COULD TELL RIGHT AWAY...
WELL, I'VE BEEN LIVING KIND OF A SHELTERED LIFE LATELY. HAVEN'T BEEN OUT IN THE WORLD TOO MUCH...
...NOT LIKE I USED TO BE.
WHAT DO YOU MEAN?
NOT TO PUT MYSELF ON THE COUCH, BUT... I'VE HAD A FEW VERY DISTINCT, VERY DIFFERENT PHASES OF MY LIFE...
...NONE OF WHICH SEEM TO MATTER MUCH NOW. I'VE BEEN SUCH A CLOSET CASE--
HEY, I'M NOT YOUR SHRINK, 'KAY?
YOU ASKED.
YOU'RE RIGHT. GUILTY AS CHARGED. SO TELL ME, THEN...
WELL, I KINDA WENT FROM BEING A DANCER TO--BASICALLY--JOINING UP WITH THE MARINES OR SOMETHING...AND THEN--
A-HA! YOU WERE A DANCER. I KNEW IT!
FINE. I COP TO IT.
HEY, DON'T BE EMBARRASSED.
IT'S COOL. YOU'RE A DANCER, JUST LIKE I FIGURED...
...SO LET'S GO DANCING.

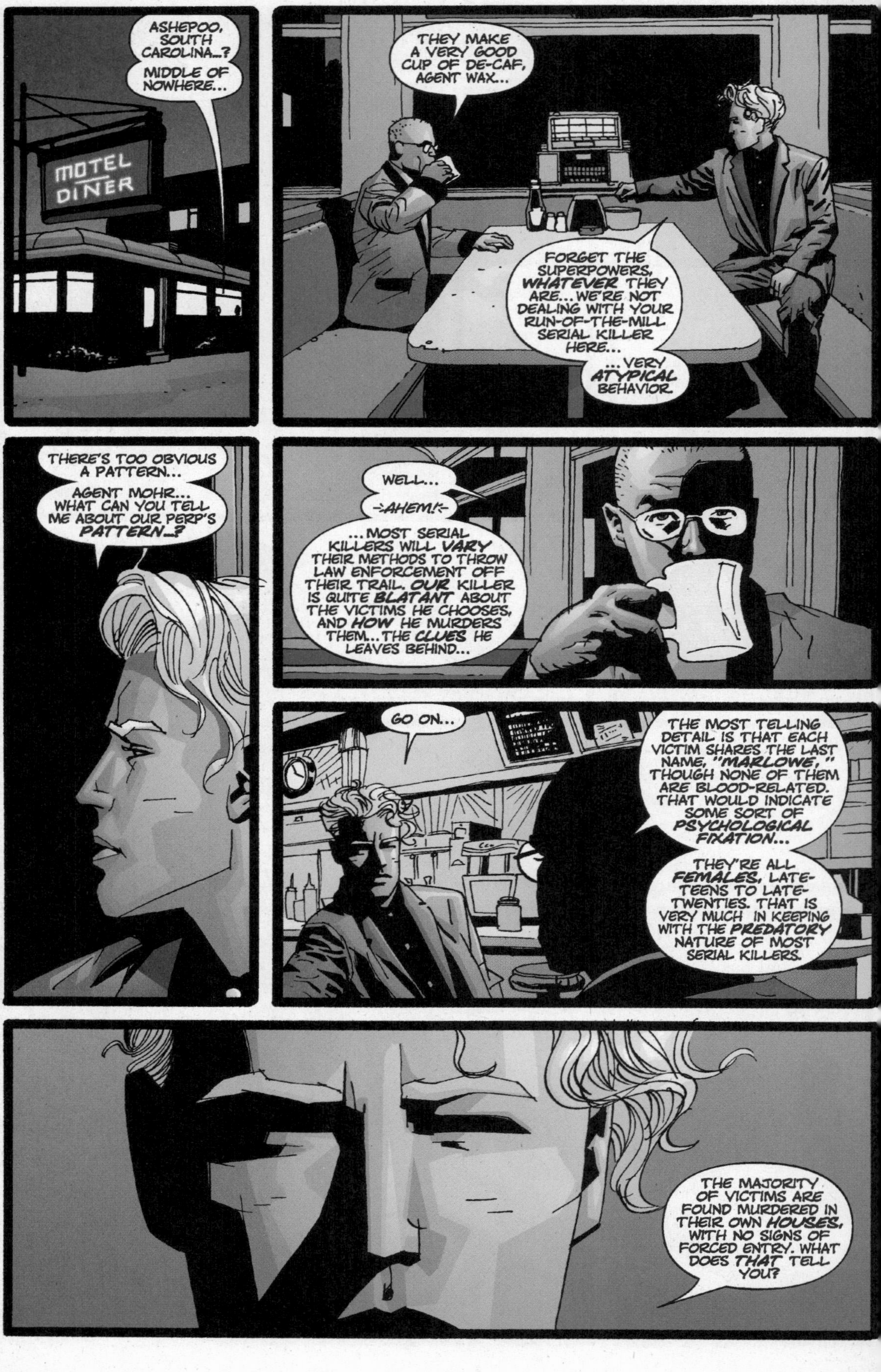
ASHEPOO, SOUTH CAROLINA...?
MIDDLE OF NOWHERE...
MOTEL DINER
THEY MAKE A VERY GOOD CUP OF DE-CAF, AGENT WAX...
FORGET THE SUPERPOWERS, WHATEVER THEY ARE... WE'RE NOT DEALING WITH YOUR RUN-OF-THE-MILL SERIAL KILLER HERE...
...VERY ATYPICAL BEHAVIOR.
THERE'S TOO OBVIOUS A PATTERN...
AGENT MOHR... WHAT CAN YOU TELL ME ABOUT OUR PERP'S PATTERN...?
WELL...
-AHEM!-
...MOST SERIAL KILLERS WILL VARY THEIR METHODS TO THROW LAW ENFORCEMENT OFF THEIR TRAIL. OUR KILLER IS QUITE BLATANT ABOUT THE VICTIMS HE CHOOSES, AND HOW HE MURDERS THEM... THE CLUES HE LEAVES BEHIND...
GO ON...
THE MOST TELLING DETAIL IS THAT EACH VICTIM SHARES THE LAST NAME, "MARLOWE," THOUGH NONE OF THEM ARE BLOOD-RELATED. THAT WOULD INDICATE SOME SORT OF PSYCHOLOGICAL FIXATION...
THEY'RE ALL FEMALES, LATE-TEENS TO LATE-TWENTIES. THAT IS VERY MUCH IN KEEPING WITH THE PREDATORY NATURE OF MOST SERIAL KILLERS.
THE MAJORITY OF VICTIMS ARE FOUND MURDERED IN THEIR OWN HOUSES, WITH NO SIGNS OF FORCED ENTRY. WHAT DOES THAT TELL YOU?

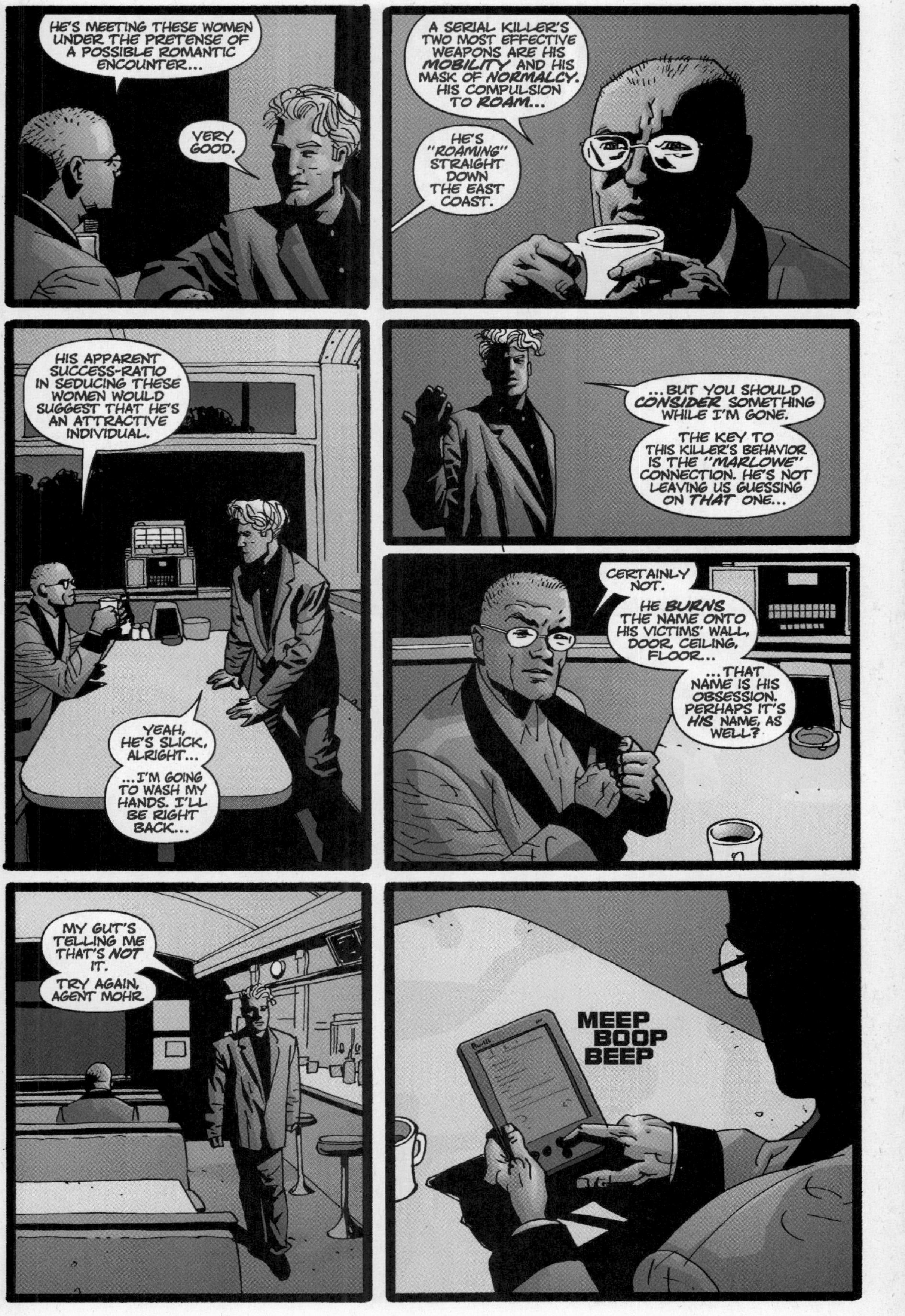
HE'S MEETING THESE WOMEN UNDER THE PRETENSE OF A POSSIBLE ROMANTIC ENCOUNTER...
VERY GOOD.
A SERIAL KILLER'S TWO MOST EFFECTIVE WEAPONS ARE HIS MOBILITY AND HIS MASK OF NORMALCY. HIS COMPULSION TO ROAM...
HE'S "ROAMING" STRAIGHT DOWN THE EAST COAST.
HIS APPARENT SUCCESS-RATIO IN SEDUCING THESE WOMEN WOULD SUGGEST THAT HE'S AN ATTRACTIVE INDIVIDUAL.
YEAH, HE'S SLICK, ALRIGHT...
...I'M GOING TO WASH MY HANDS. I'LL BE RIGHT BACK...
...BUT YOU SHOULD CONSIDER SOMETHING WHILE I'M GONE.
THE KEY TO THIS KILLER'S BEHAVIOR IS THE "MARLOWE" CONNECTION. HE'S NOT LEAVING US GUESSING ON THAT ONE...
CERTAINLY NOT.
HE BURNS THE NAME ONTO HIS VICTIMS' WALL, DOOR CEILING, FLOOR...
...THAT NAME IS HIS OBSESSION. PERHAPS IT'S HIS NAME, AS WELL?
MY GUT'S TELLING ME THAT'S NOT IT.
TRY AGAIN, AGENT MOHR
MEEP
BOOP
BEEP

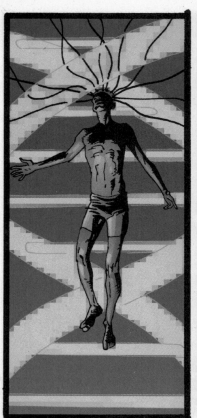

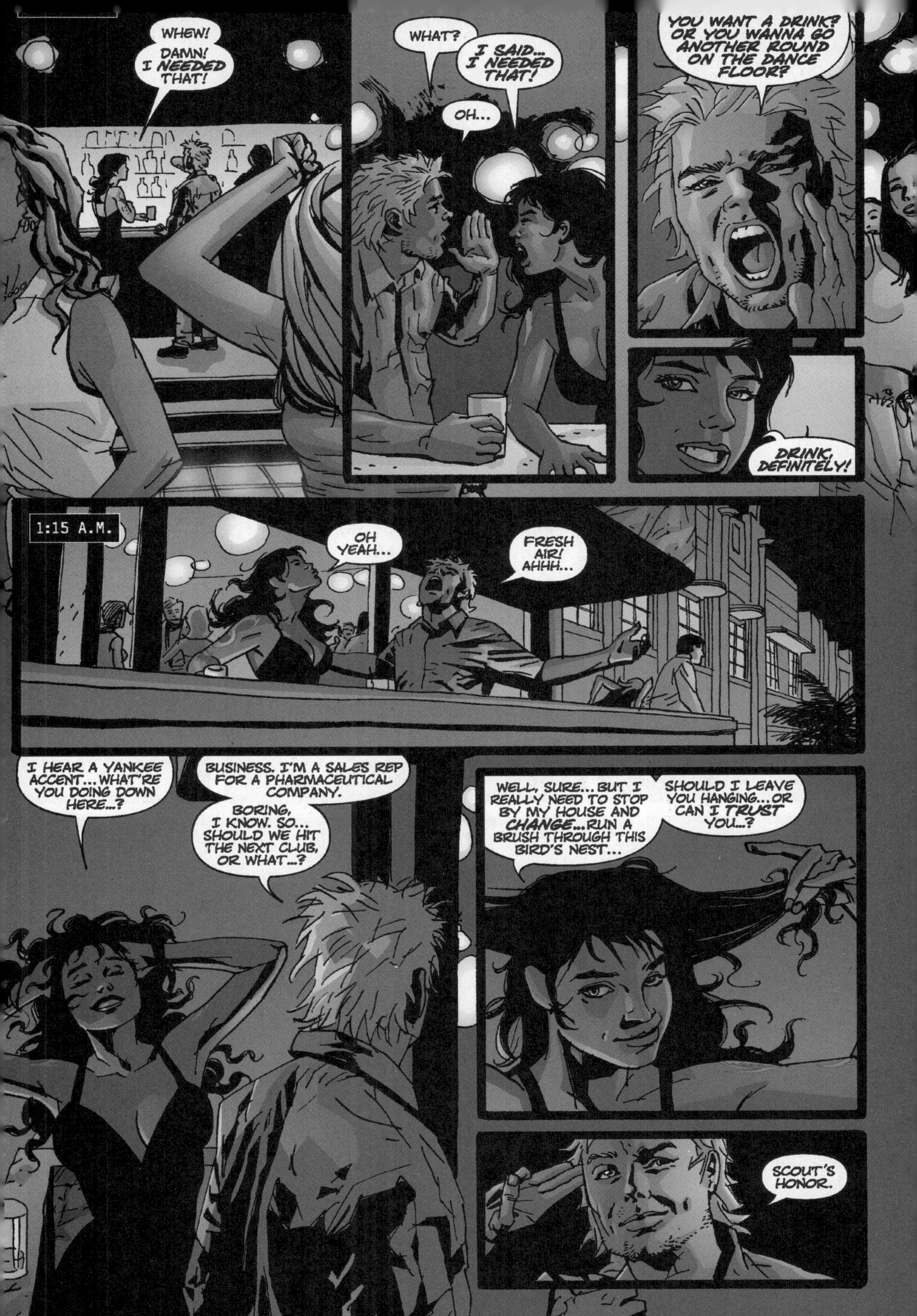
WHEW! DAMN! I NEEDED THAT!
WHAT?
I SAID... I NEEDED THAT!
OH...
YOU WANT A DRINK? OR YOU WANNA GO ANOTHER ROUND ON THE DANCE FLOOR?
DRINK, DEFINITELY!
1:15 A.M.
OH YEAH...
FRESH AIR! AHHH...
I HEAR A YANKEE ACCENT...WHAT'RE YOU DOING DOWN HERE...?
BUSINESS. I'M A SALES REP FOR A PHARMACEUTICAL COMPANY.
BORING, I KNOW. SO... SHOULD WE HIT THE NEXT CLUB, OR WHAT...?
WELL, SURE... BUT I REALLY NEED TO STOP BY MY HOUSE AND CHANGE...RUN A BRUSH THROUGH THIS BIRD'S NEST...
SHOULD I LEAVE YOU HANGING...OR CAN I TRUST YOU...?
SCOUT'S HONOR.

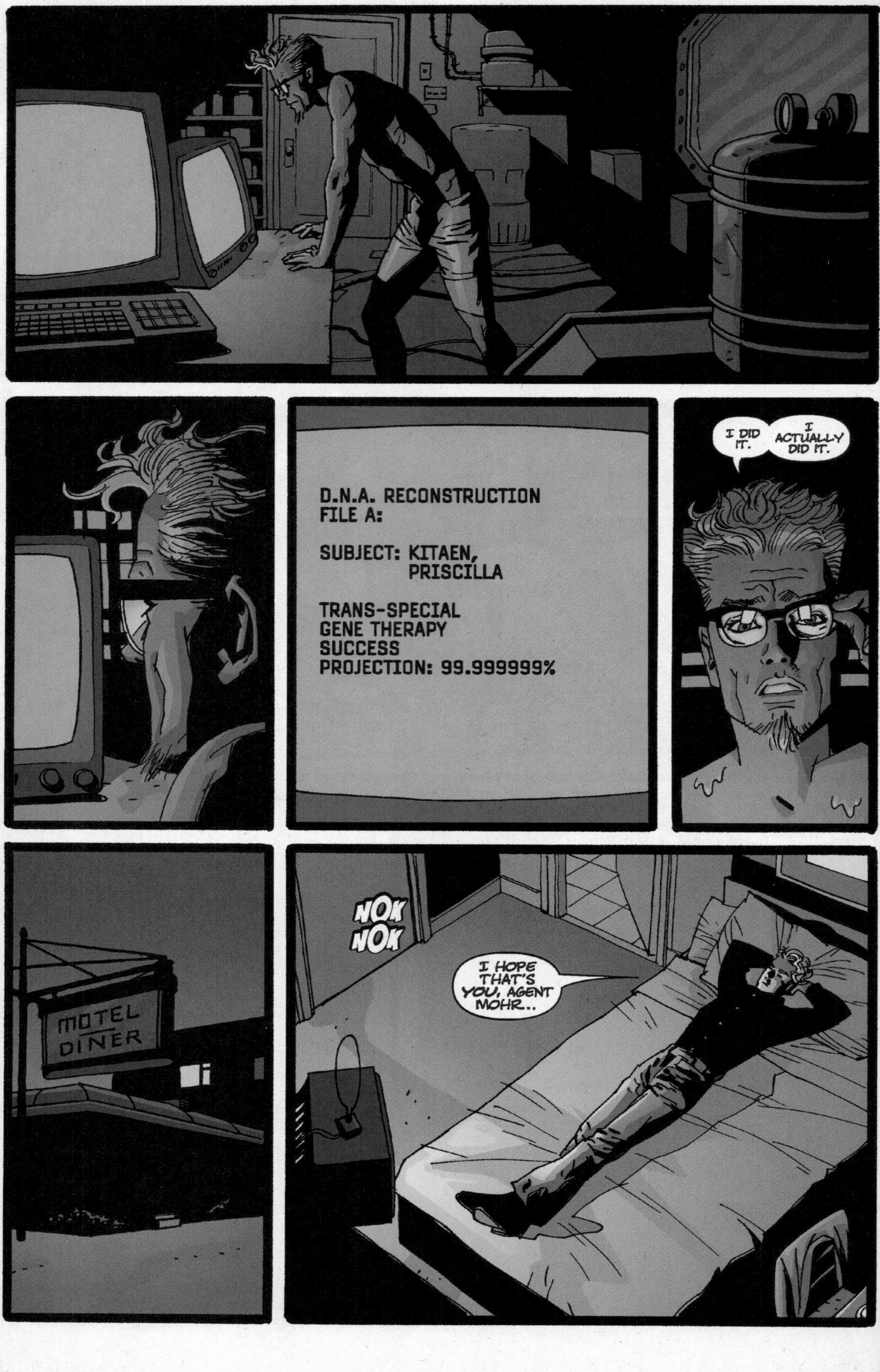
D.N.A. RECONSTRUCTION
FILE A:
SUBJECT: KITAEN, PRISCILLA
TRANS-SPECIAL GENE THERAPY SUCCESS PROJECTION: 99.999999%
I DID IT.
I ACTUALLY DID IT.
MOTEL DINER
NOK NOK
I HOPE THAT'S YOU, AGENT MOHR..

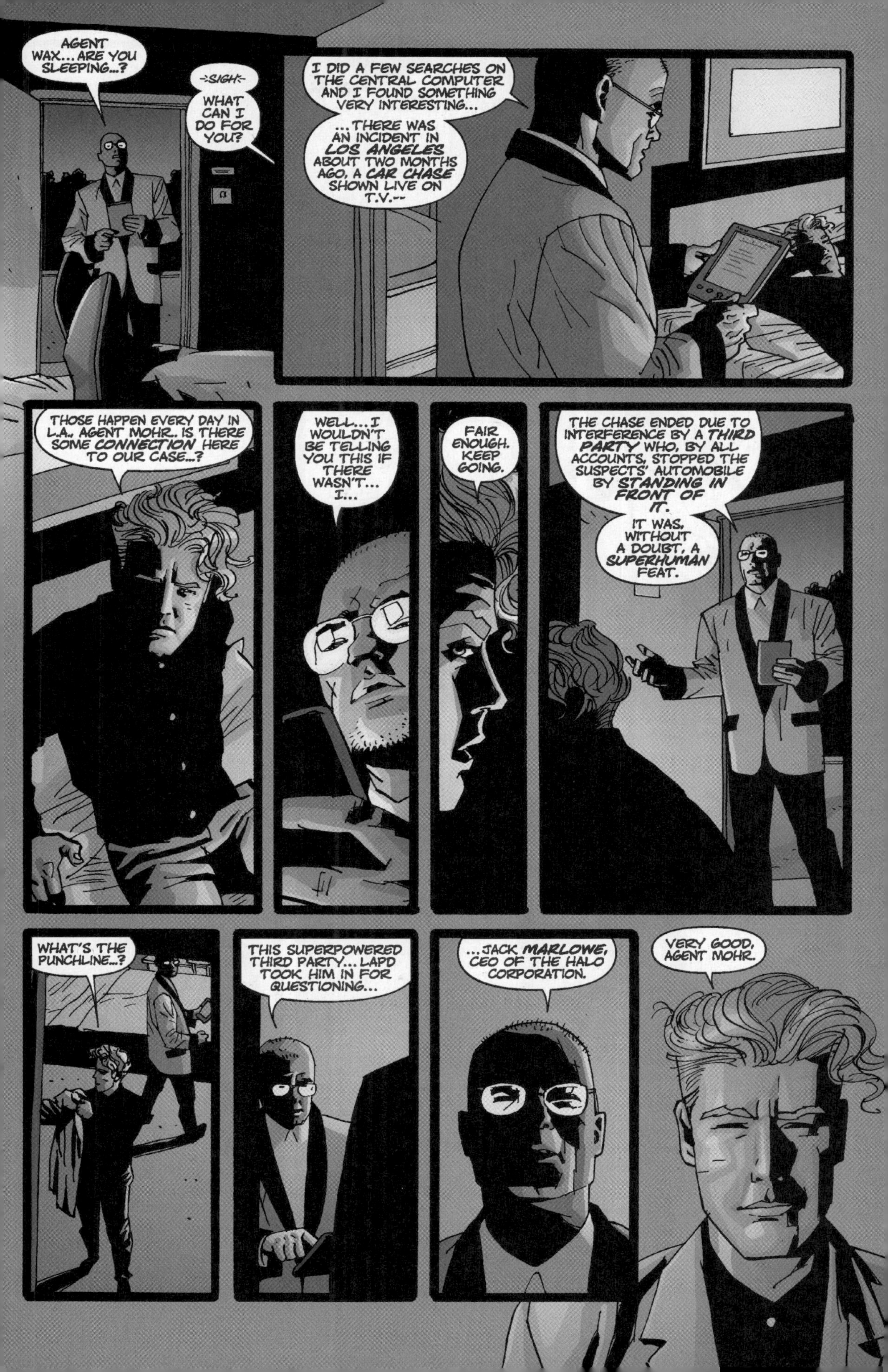
AGENT WAX... ARE YOU SLEEPING...?
-SIGH-
WHAT CAN I DO FOR YOU?
I DID A FEW SEARCHES ON THE CENTRAL COMPUTER AND I FOUND SOMETHING VERY INTERESTING...
...THERE WAS AN INCIDENT IN LOS ANGELES ABOUT TWO MONTHS AGO, A CAR CHASE SHOWN LIVE ON T.V.--
THOSE HAPPEN EVERY DAY IN L.A., AGENT MOHR.. IS THERE SOME CONNECTION HERE TO OUR CASE...?
WELL... I WOULDN'T BE TELLING YOU THIS IF THERE WASN'T... I...
FAIR ENOUGH. KEEP GOING.
THE CHASE ENDED DUE TO INTERFERENCE BY A THIRD PARTY WHO, BY ALL ACCOUNTS, STOPPED THE SUSPECTS' AUTOMOBILE BY STANDING IN FRONT OF IT.
IT WAS, WITHOUT A DOUBT, A SUPERHUMAN FEAT.
WHAT'S THE PUNCHLINE...?
THIS SUPERPOWERED THIRD PARTY... LAPD TOOK HIM IN FOR QUESTIONING...
...JACK MARLOWE, CEO OF THE HALO CORPORATION.
VERY GOOD, AGENT MOHR.

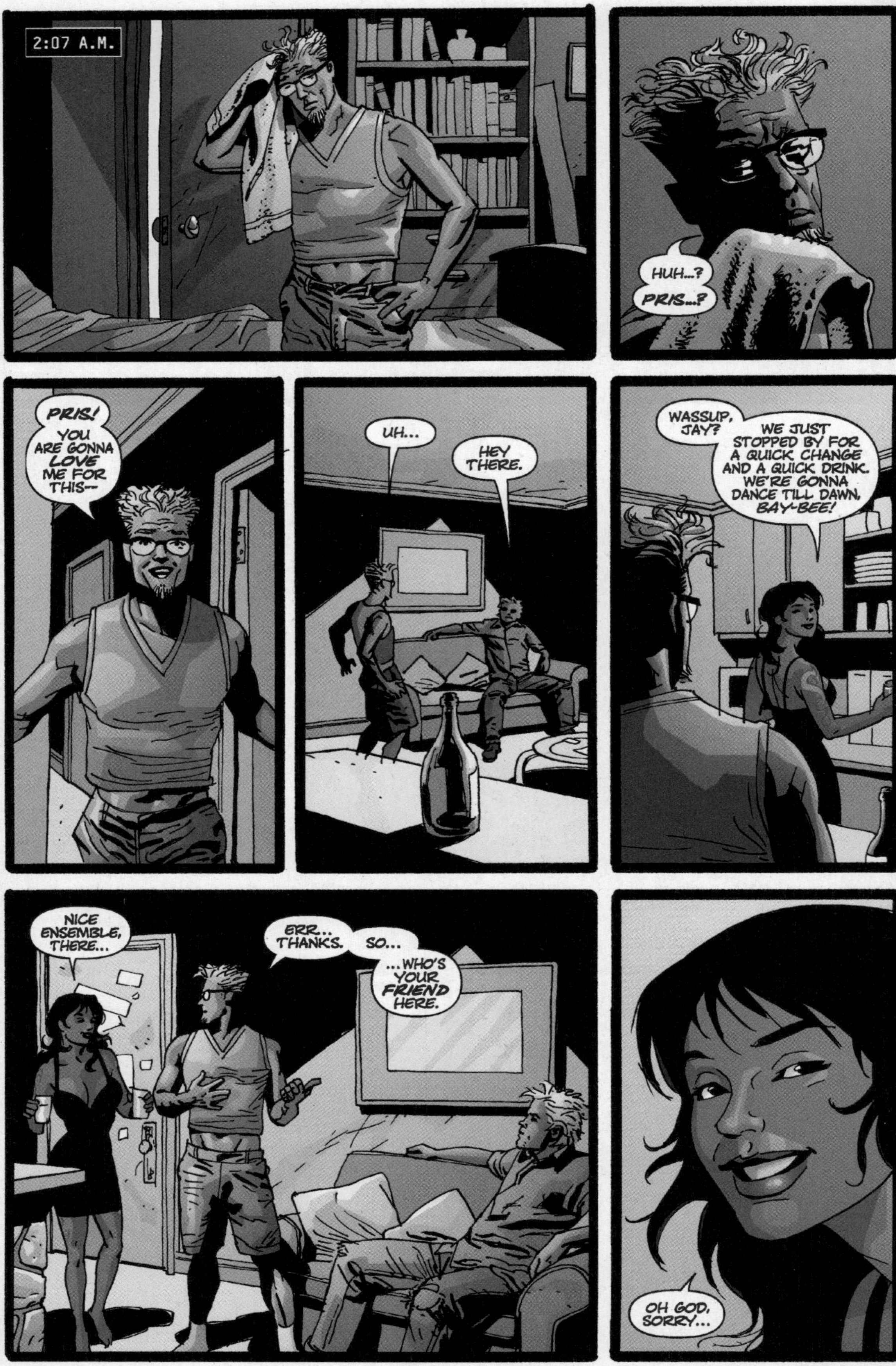
2:07 A.M.
HUH...? PRIS...?
PRIS! YOU ARE GONNA LOVE ME FOR THIS--
UH...
HEY THERE.
WASSUP, JAY?
WE JUST STOPPED BY FOR A QUICK CHANGE AND A QUICK DRINK. WE'RE GONNA DANCE TILL DAWN, BAY-BEE!
NICE ENSEMBLE, THERE...
ERR... THANKS.
SO... ...WHO'S YOUR FRIEND HERE.
OH GOD, SORRY...

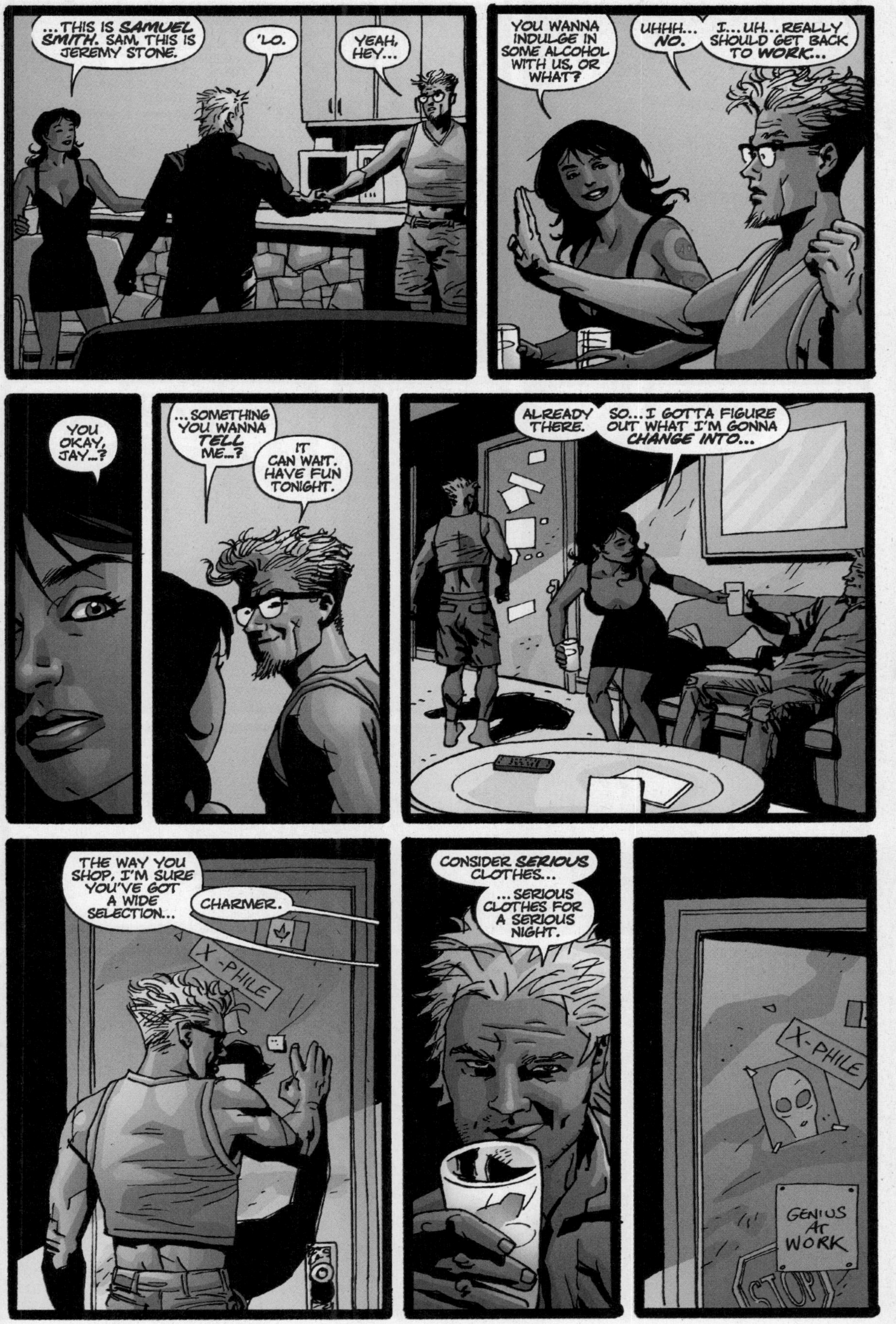

...THIS IS SAMUEL SMITH. SAM, THIS IS JEREMY STONE.
'LO.
YEAH, HEY...
YOU WANNA INDULGE IN SOME ALCOHOL WITH US, OR WHAT?
UHHH... NO.
I... UH... REALLY SHOULD GET BACK TO WORK...
YOU OKAY, JAY...?
...SOMETHING YOU WANNA TELL ME...?
IT CAN WAIT. HAVE FUN TONIGHT.
ALREADY THERE.
SO... I GOTTA FIGURE OUT WHAT I'M GONNA CHANGE INTO...
THE WAY YOU SHOP, I'M SURE YOU'VE GOT A WIDE SELECTION...
CHARMER.
X-PHILE
CONSIDER SERIOUS CLOTHES...
...SERIOUS CLOTHES FOR A SERIOUS NIGHT.
X-PHILE
GENIUS AT WORK
STOP

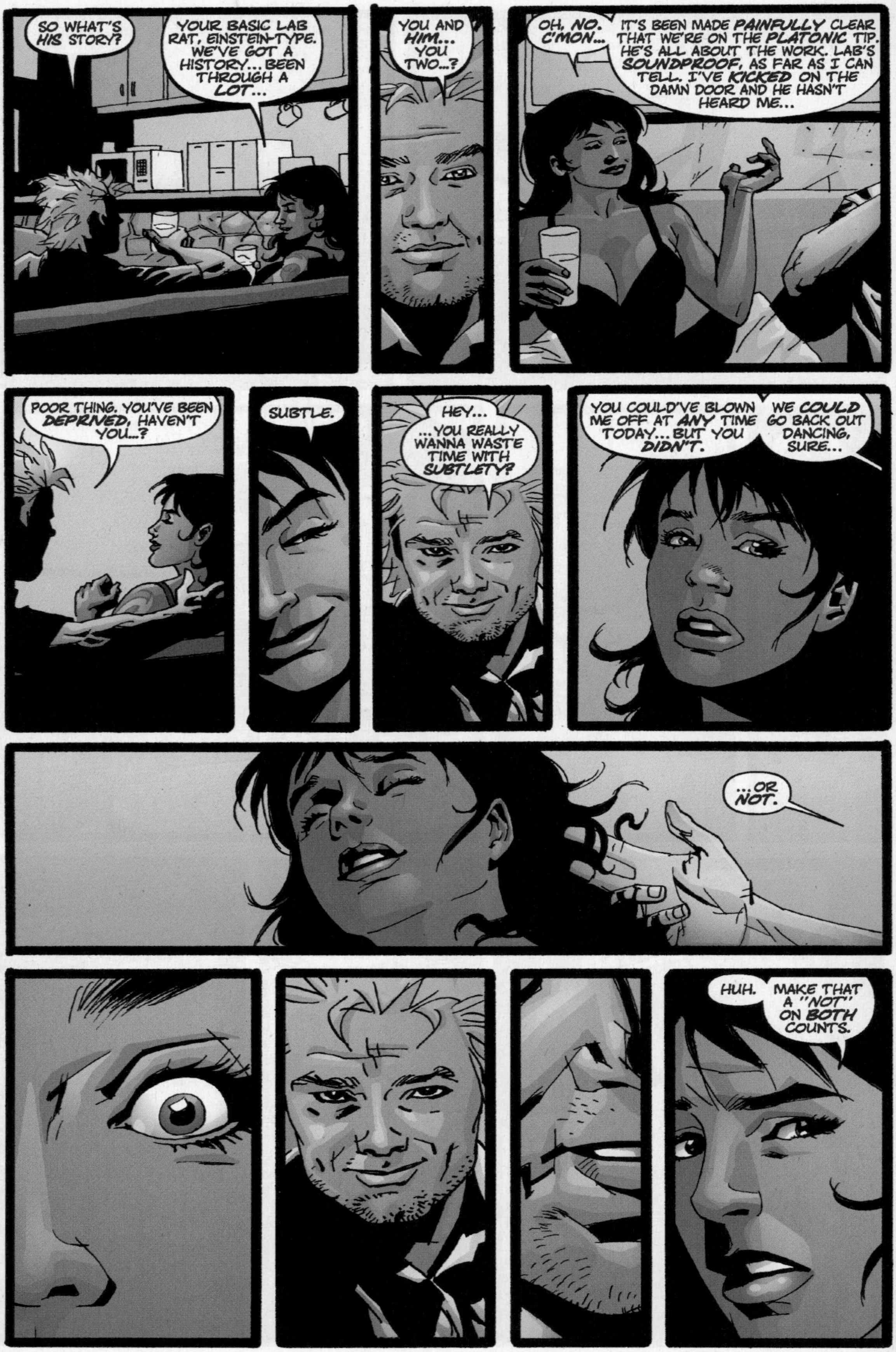
SO WHAT'S HIS STORY?
YOUR BASIC LAB RAT, EINSTEIN-TYPE. WE'VE GOT A HISTORY... BEEN THROUGH A LOT...
YOU AND HIM... YOU TWO...?
OH, NO. C'MON...
IT'S BEEN MADE PAINFULLY CLEAR THAT WE'RE ON THE PLATONIC TIP. HE'S ALL ABOUT THE WORK. LAB'S SOUNDPROOF, AS FAR AS I CAN TELL. I'VE KICKED ON THE DAMN DOOR AND HE HASN'T HEARD ME...
POOR THING. YOU'VE BEEN DEPRIVED, HAVEN'T YOU...?
SUBTLE.
HEY...
...YOU REALLY WANNA WASTE TIME WITH SUBTLETY?
YOU COULD'VE BLOWN ME OFF AT ANY TIME TODAY... BUT YOU DIDN'T.
WE COULD GO BACK OUT DANCING, SURE...
...OR NOT.
HUH.
MAKE THAT A "NOT" ON BOTH COUNTS.

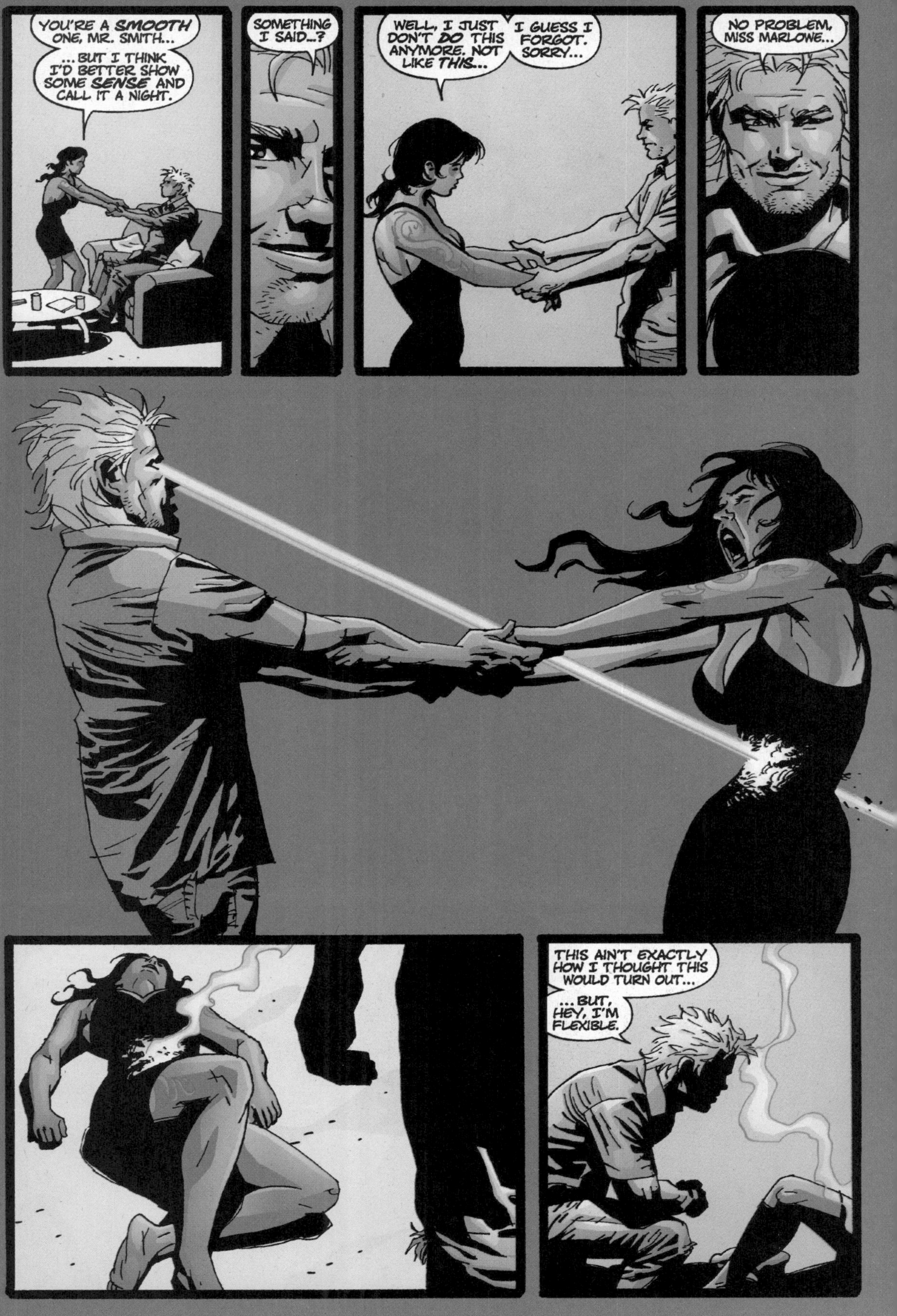

YOU'RE A SMOOTH ONE, MR. SMITH...
... BUT I THINK I'D BETTER SHOW SOME SENSE AND CALL IT A NIGHT.
SOMETHING I SAID...?
WELL, I JUST DON'T DO THIS ANYMORE. NOT LIKE THIS...
I GUESS I FORGOT. SORRY...
NO PROBLEM, MISS MARLOWE...
THIS AIN'T EXACTLY HOW I THOUGHT THIS WOULD TURN OUT...
... BUT, HEY, I'M FLEXIBLE.

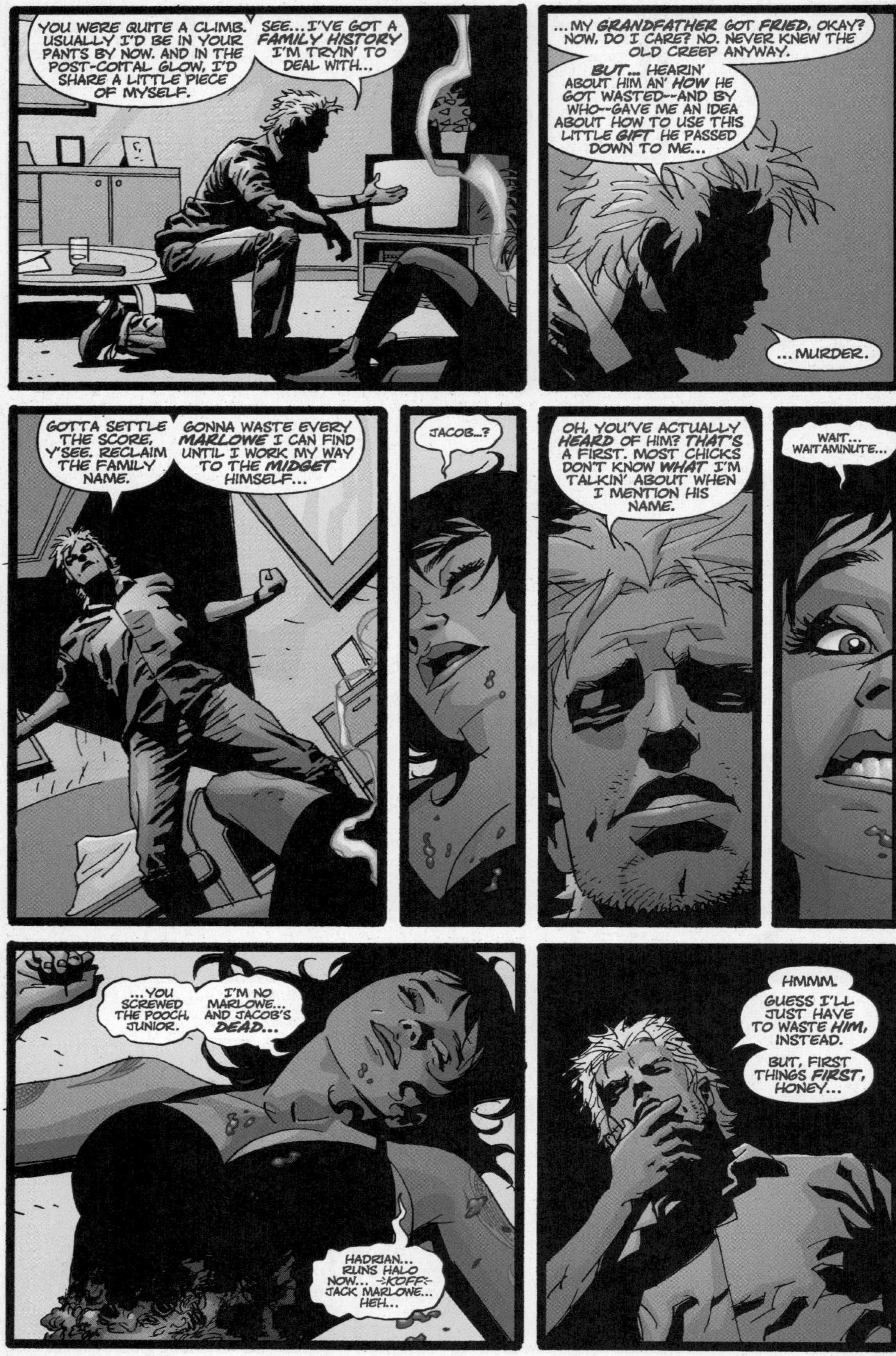
YOU WERE QUITE A CLIMB. USUALLY I'D BE IN YOUR PANTS BY NOW. AND IN THE POST-COITAL GLOW, I'D SHARE A LITTLE PIECE OF MYSELF.
SEE... I'VE GOT A FAMILY HISTORY I'M TRYIN' TO DEAL WITH...
...MY GRANDFATHER GOT FRIED, OKAY? NOW, DO I CARE? NO. NEVER KNEW THE OLD CREEP ANYWAY.
BUT... HEARIN' ABOUT HIM AN' HOW HE GOT WASTED--AND BY WHO--GAVE ME AN IDEA ABOUT HOW TO USE THIS LITTLE GIFT HE PASSED DOWN TO ME...
...MURDER.
GOTTA SETTLE THE SCORE, Y'SEE. RECLAIM THE FAMILY NAME.
GONNA WASTE EVERY MARLOWE I CAN FIND UNTIL I WORK MY WAY TO THE MIDGET HIMSELF...
JACOB...?
OH, YOU'VE ACTUALLY HEARD OF HIM? THAT'S A FIRST. MOST CHICKS DON'T KNOW WHAT I'M TALKIN' ABOUT WHEN I MENTION HIS NAME.
WAIT... WAITAMINUTE...
...YOU SCREWED THE POOCH, JUNIOR.
I'M NO MARLOWE... AND JACOB'S DEAD...
HADRIAN... RUNS HALO NOW... -KOFF- JACK MARLOWE... HEH...
HMMM.
GUESS I'LL JUST HAVE TO WASTE HIM, INSTEAD.
BUT, FIRST THINGS FIRST, HONEY...

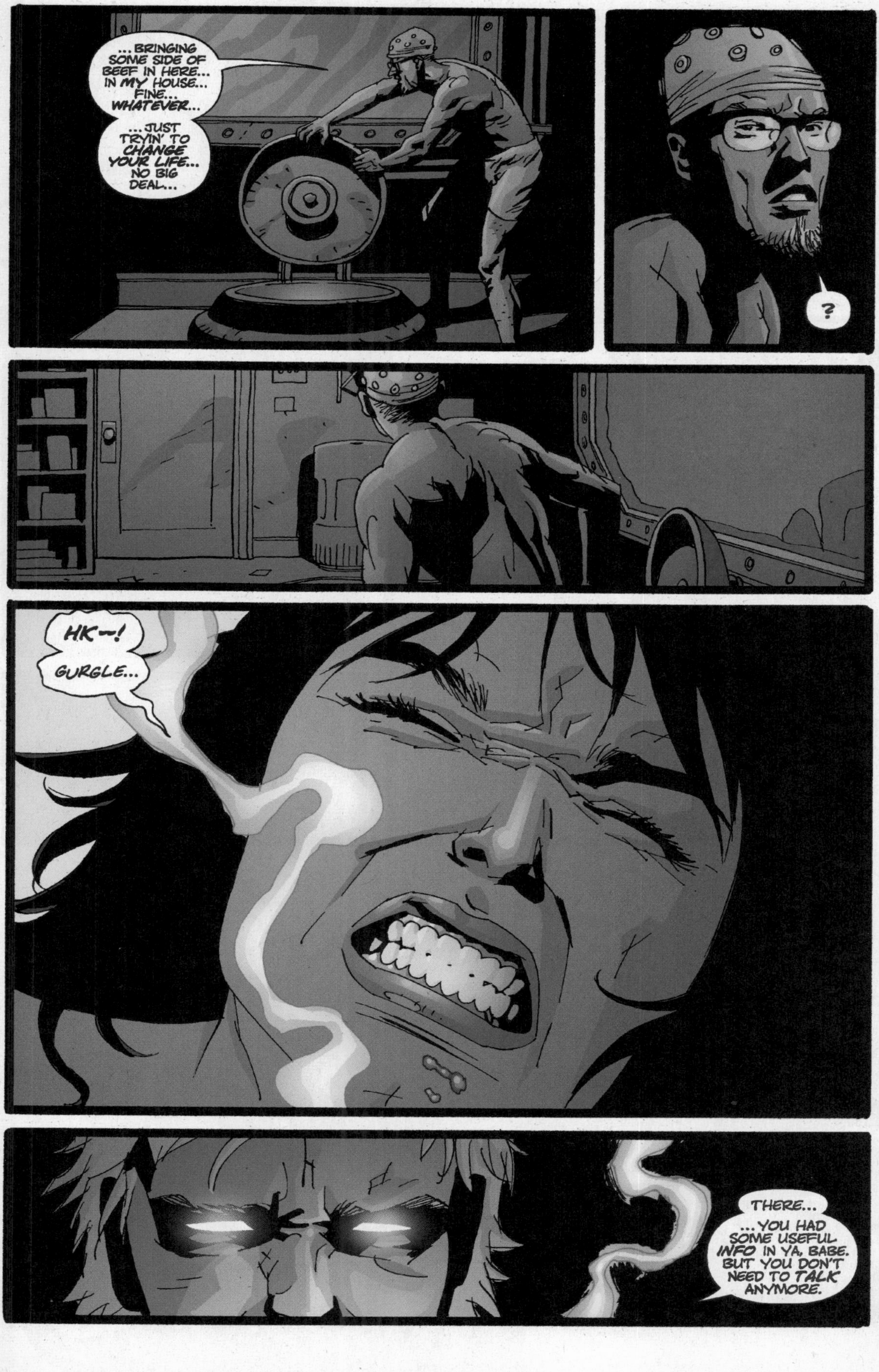
... BRINGING SOME SIDE OF BEEF IN HERE... IN MY HOUSE... FINE... WHATEVER...
... JUST TRYIN' TO CHANGE YOUR LIFE... NO BIG DEAL...
?
HK--!
GURGLE...
THERE...
... YOU HAD SOME USEFUL INFO IN YA, BABE. BUT YOU DON'T NEED TO TALK ANYMORE.

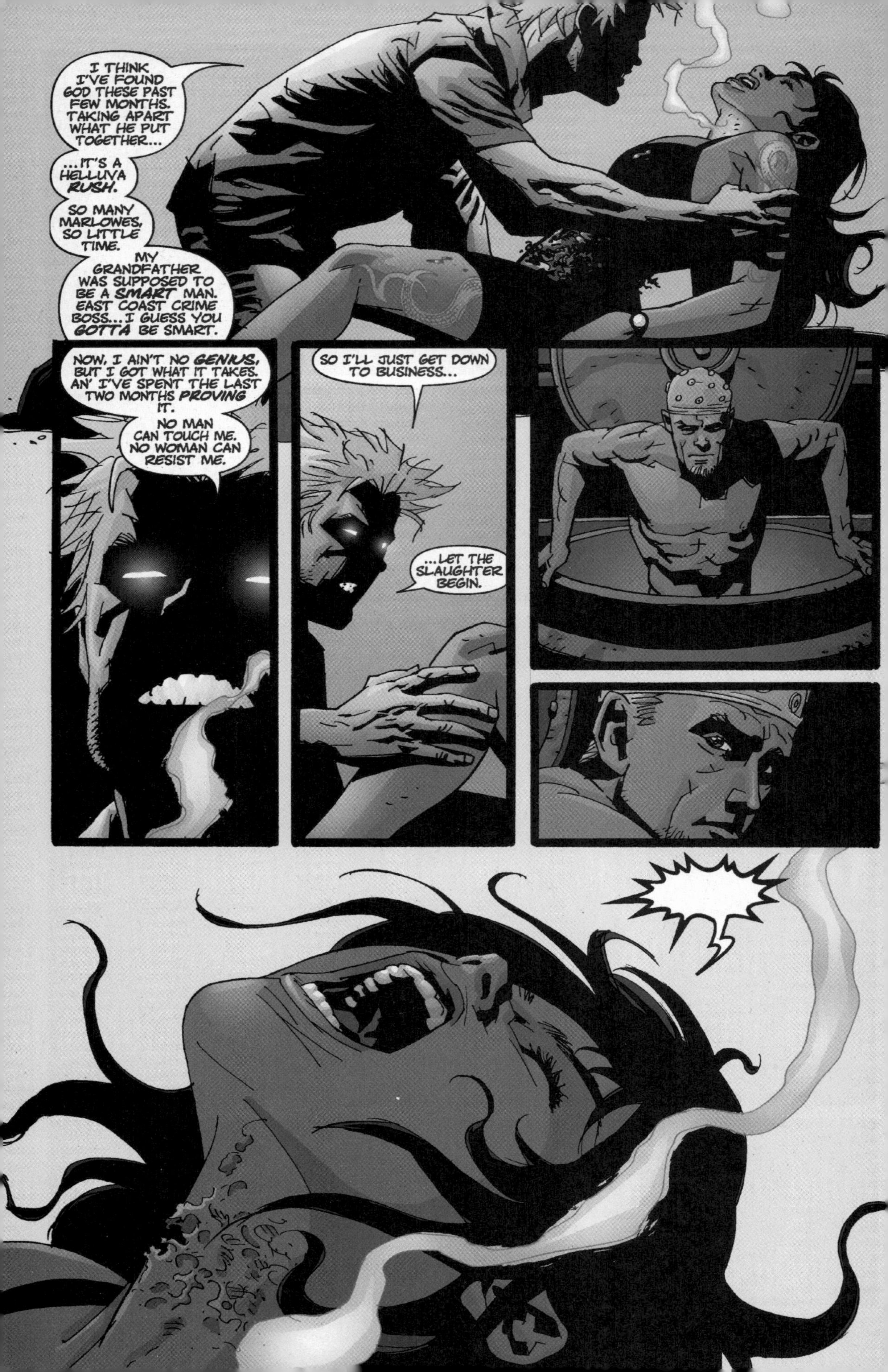
I THINK I'VE FOUND GOD THESE PAST FEW MONTHS. TAKING APART WHAT HE PUT TOGETHER...
...IT'S A HELLUVA RUSH.
SO MANY MARLOWES, SO LITTLE TIME.
MY GRANDFATHER WAS SUPPOSED TO BE A SMART MAN. EAST COAST CRIME BOSS...I GUESS YOU GOTTA BE SMART.
NOW, I AIN'T NO GENIUS, BUT I GOT WHAT IT TAKES. AN' I'VE SPENT THE LAST TWO MONTHS PROVING IT.
NO MAN CAN TOUCH ME. NO WOMAN CAN RESIST ME.
SO I'LL JUST GET DOWN TO BUSINESS...
...LET THE SLAUGHTER BEGIN.

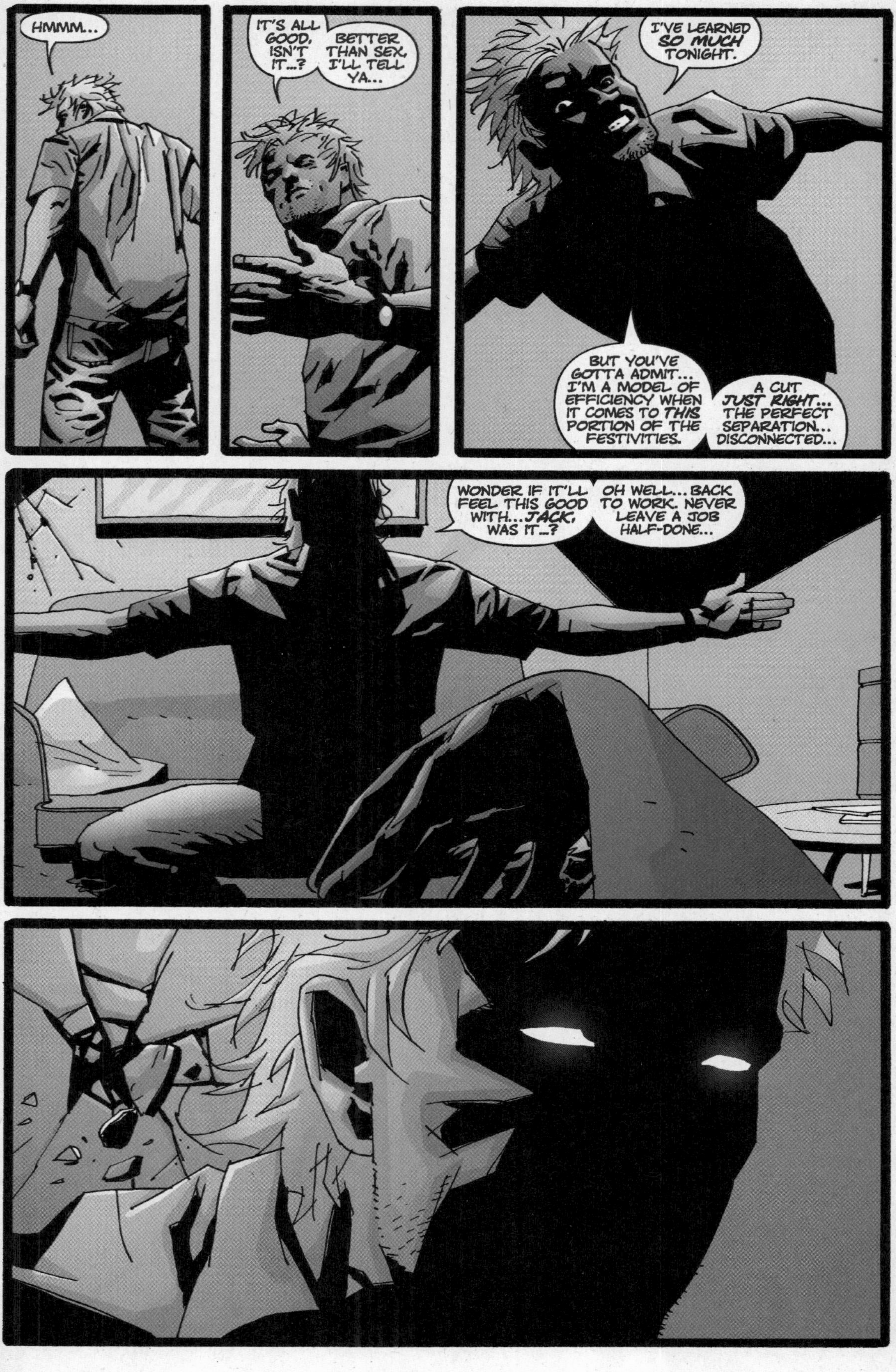
HMMM...
IT'S ALL GOOD, ISN'T IT...?
BETTER THAN SEX, I'LL TELL YA...
I'VE LEARNED SO MUCH TONIGHT.
BUT YOU'VE GOTTA ADMIT... I'M A MODEL OF EFFICIENCY WHEN IT COMES TO THIS PORTION OF THE FESTIVITIES.
A CUT JUST RIGHT... THE PERFECT SEPARATION... DISCONNECTED...
WONDER IF IT'LL FEEL THIS GOOD WITH... JACK, WAS IT...?
OH WELL... BACK TO WORK. NEVER LEAVE A JOB HALF-DONE...

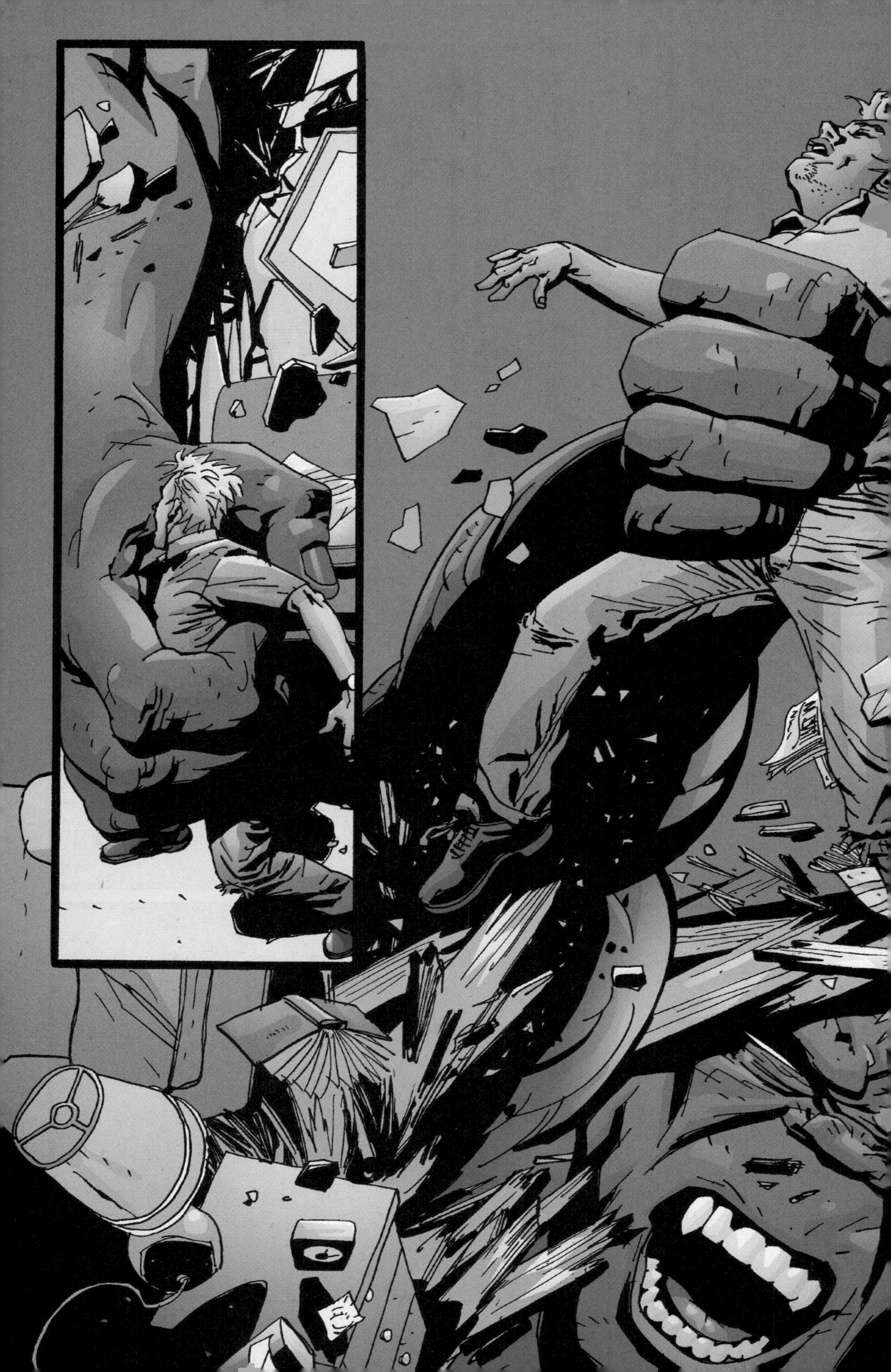

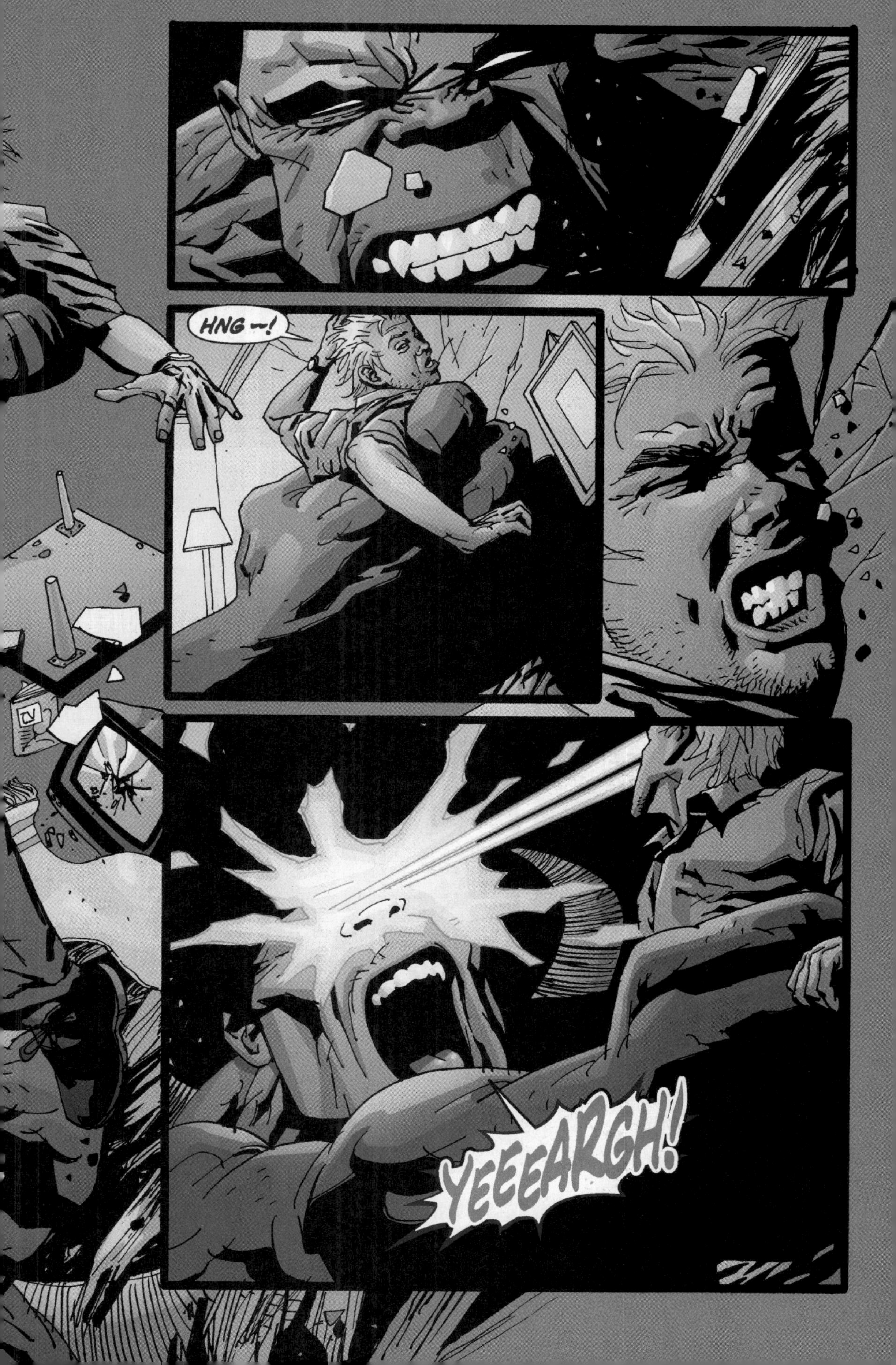
HNG --!
YEEEARGH!

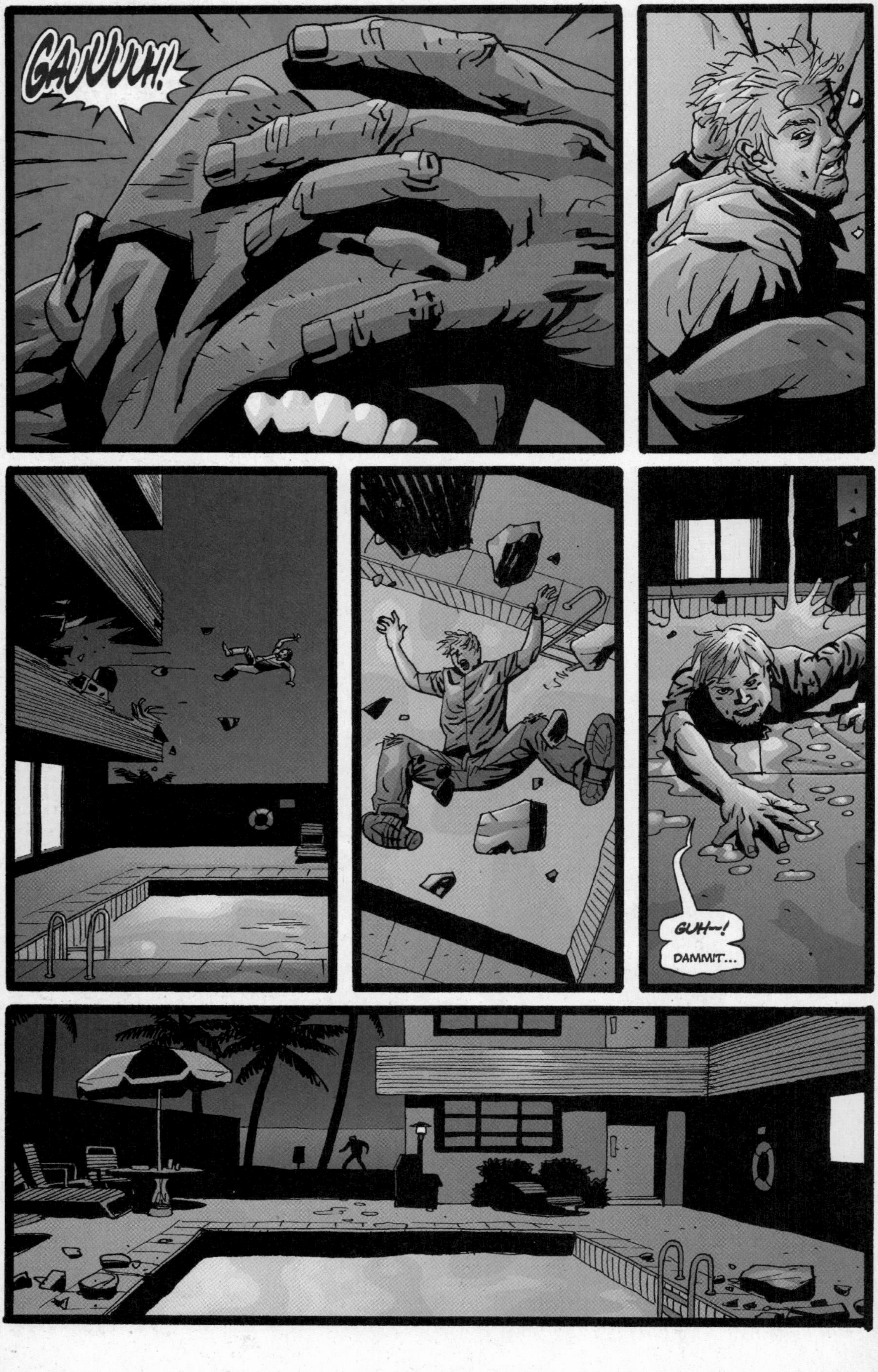
GAUUUUH!
GUH--!
DAMMIT...

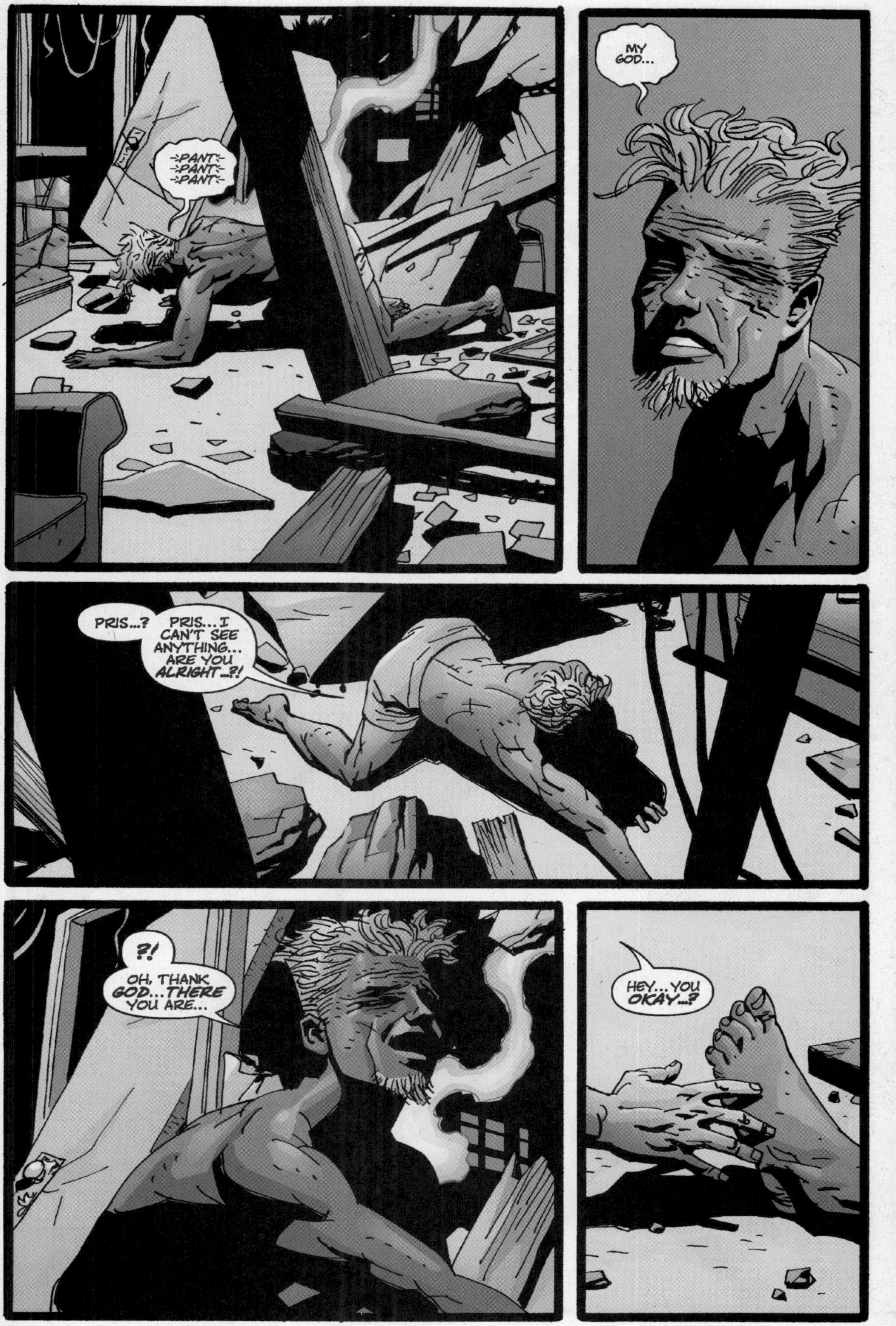
-PANT-
-PANT-
-PANT
MY GOD...
PRIS...?
PRIS... I CAN'T SEE ANYTHING... ARE YOU *ALRIGHT*...?!
?!
OH, THANK *GOD*... *THERE* YOU ARE...
HEY... YOU *OKAY*...?

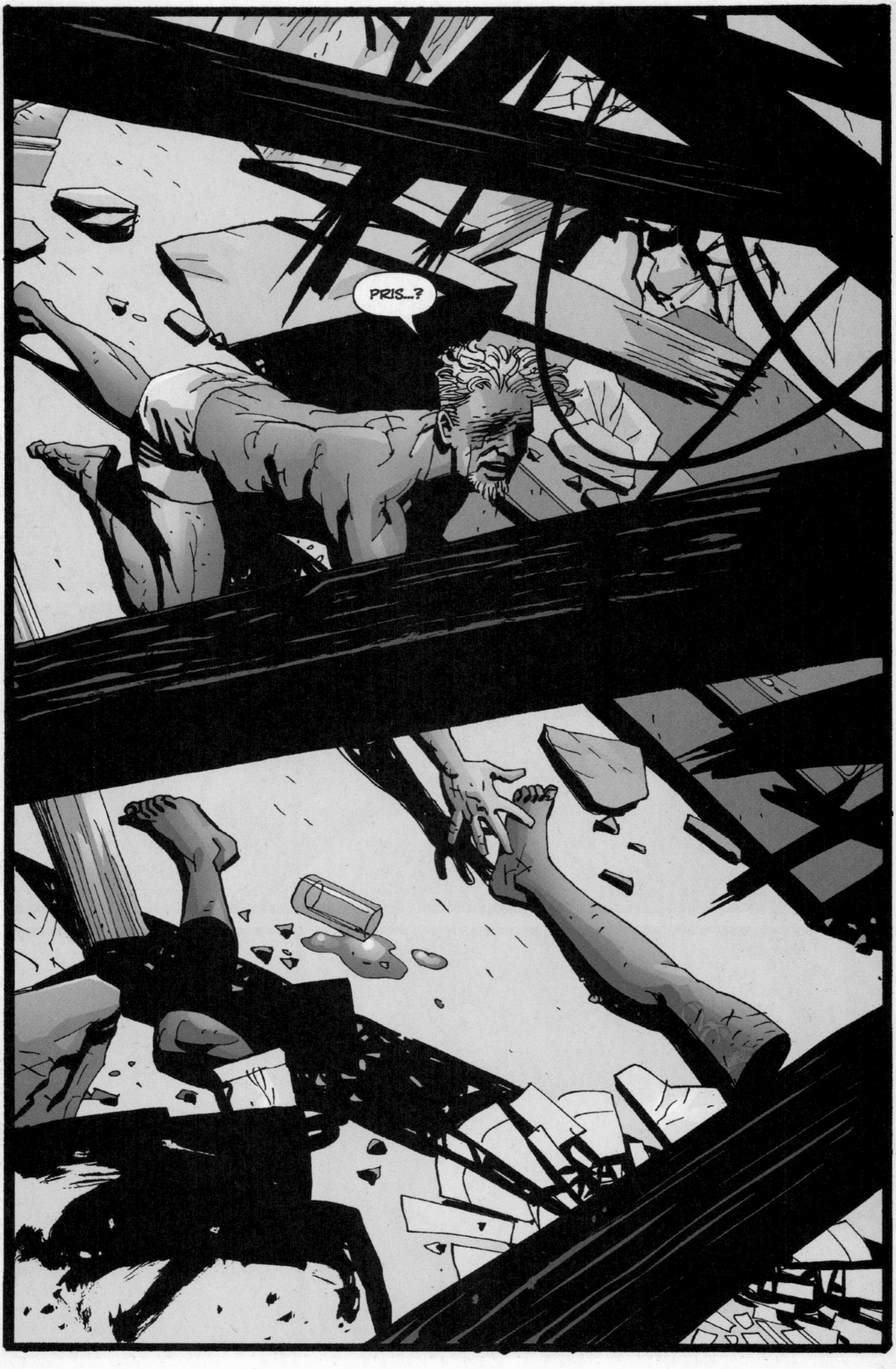
PRIS...?

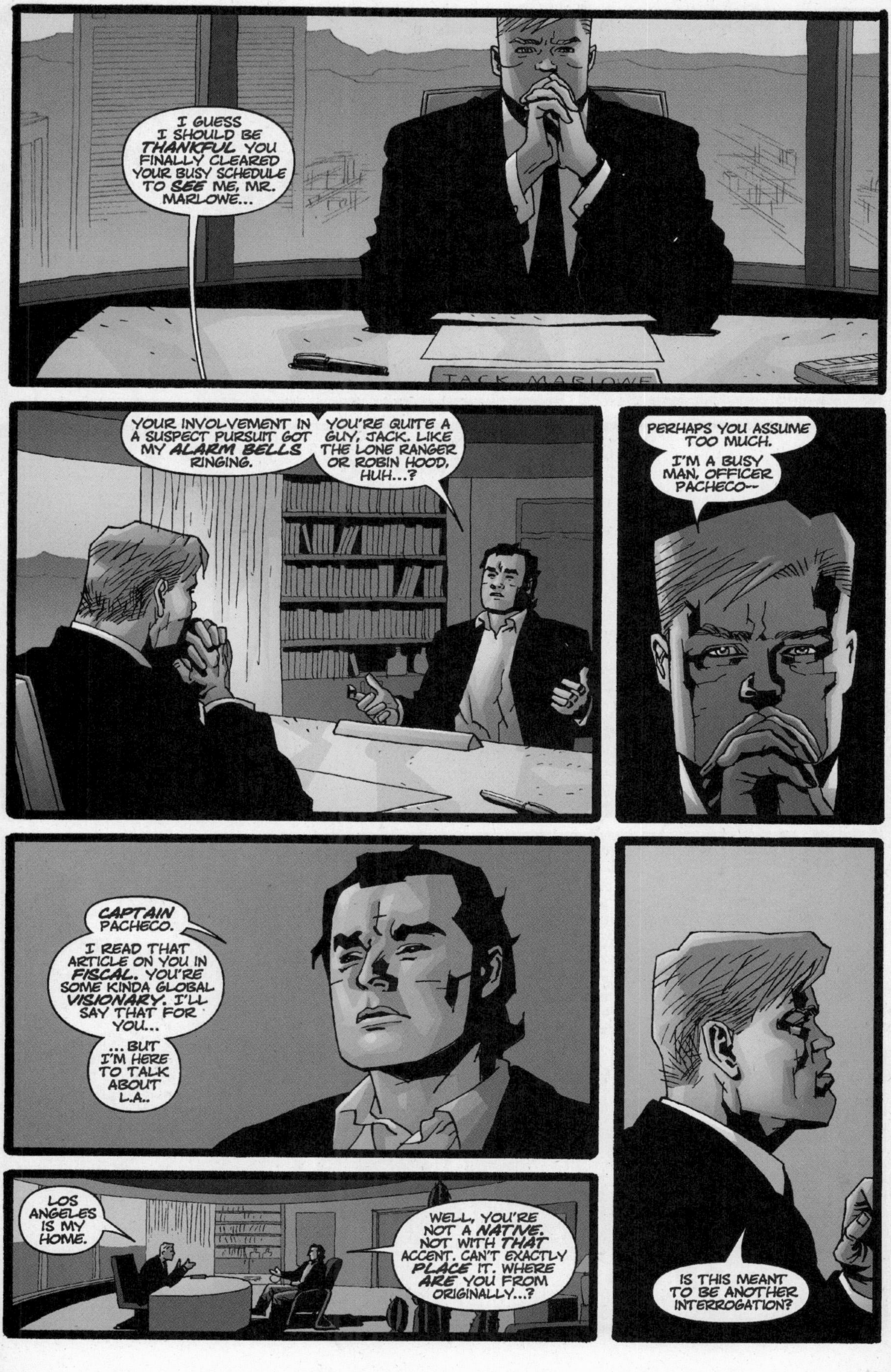
I GUESS I SHOULD BE THANKFUL YOU FINALLY CLEARED YOUR BUSY SCHEDULE TO SEE ME, MR. MARLOWE...
JACK MARLOWE
YOUR INVOLVEMENT IN A SUSPECT PURSUIT GOT MY ALARM BELLS RINGING.
YOU'RE QUITE A GUY, JACK. LIKE THE LONE RANGER OR ROBIN HOOD, HUH...?
PERHAPS YOU ASSUME TOO MUCH.
I'M A BUSY MAN, OFFICER PACHECO--
CAPTAIN PACHECO.
I READ THAT ARTICLE ON YOU IN FISCAL. YOU'RE SOME KINDA GLOBAL VISIONARY. I'LL SAY THAT FOR YOU...
...BUT I'M HERE TO TALK ABOUT L.A..
LOS ANGELES IS MY HOME.
WELL, YOU'RE NOT A NATIVE. NOT WITH THAT ACCENT. CAN'T EXACTLY PLACE IT. WHERE ARE YOU FROM ORIGINALLY...?
IS THIS MEANT TO BE ANOTHER INTERROGATION?

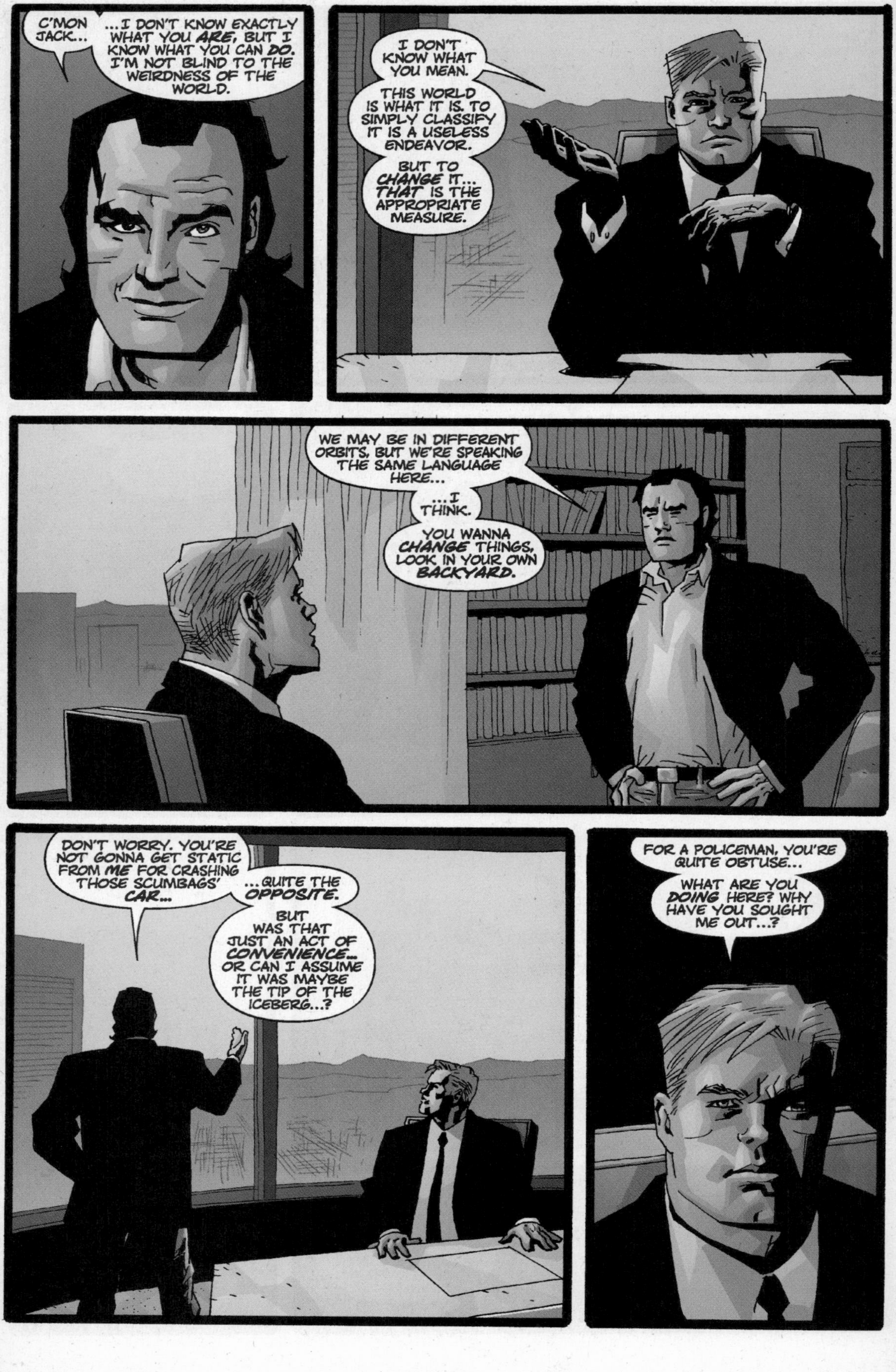
C'MON JACK...
...I DON'T KNOW EXACTLY WHAT YOU ARE, BUT I KNOW WHAT YOU CAN DO. I'M NOT BLIND TO THE WEIRDNESS OF THE WORLD.
I DON'T KNOW WHAT YOU MEAN.
THIS WORLD IS WHAT IT IS. TO SIMPLY CLASSIFY IT IS A USELESS ENDEAVOR.
BUT TO CHANGE IT... THAT IS THE APPROPRIATE MEASURE.
WE MAY BE IN DIFFERENT ORBITS, BUT WE'RE SPEAKING THE SAME LANGUAGE HERE...
...I THINK.
YOU WANNA CHANGE THINGS, LOOK IN YOUR OWN BACKYARD.
DON'T WORRY. YOU'RE NOT GONNA GET STATIC FROM ME FOR CRASHING THOSE SCUMBAGS' CAR...
...QUITE THE OPPOSITE.
BUT WAS THAT JUST AN ACT OF CONVENIENCE... OR CAN I ASSUME IT WAS MAYBE THE TIP OF THE ICEBERG...?
FOR A POLICEMAN, YOU'RE QUITE OBTUSE...
WHAT ARE YOU DOING HERE? WHY HAVE YOU SOUGHT ME OUT...?

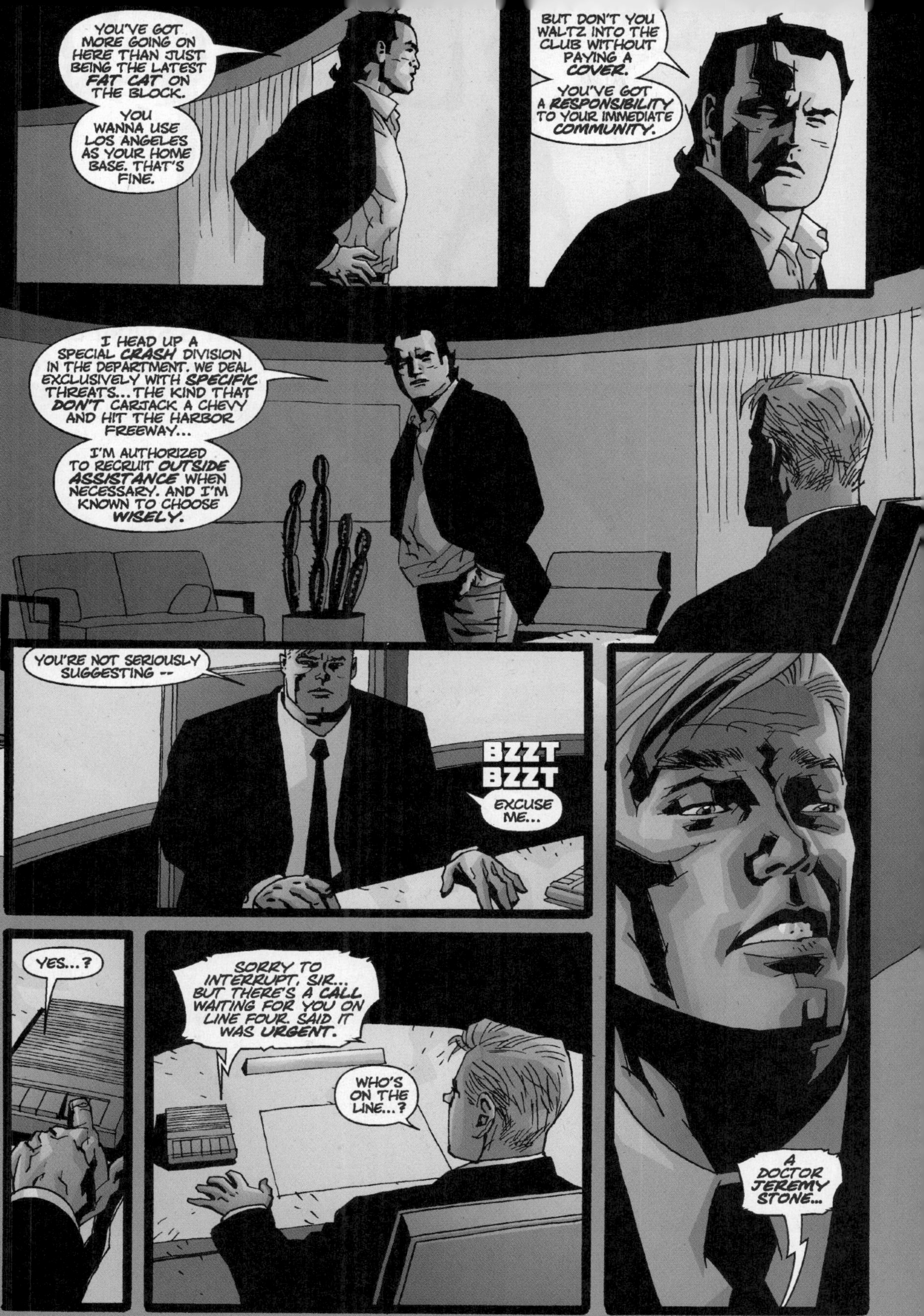

YOU'VE GOT MORE GOING ON HERE THAN JUST BEING THE LATEST FAT CAT ON THE BLOCK.
YOU WANNA USE LOS ANGELES AS YOUR HOME BASE. THAT'S FINE.
BUT DON'T YOU WALTZ INTO THE CLUB WITHOUT PAYING A COVER.
YOU'VE GOT A RESPONSIBILITY TO YOUR IMMEDIATE COMMUNITY.
I HEAD UP A SPECIAL CRASH DIVISION IN THE DEPARTMENT. WE DEAL EXCLUSIVELY WITH SPECIFIC THREATS... THE KIND THAT DON'T CARJACK A CHEVY AND HIT THE HARBOR FREEWAY...
I'M AUTHORIZED TO RECRUIT OUTSIDE ASSISTANCE WHEN NECESSARY. AND I'M KNOWN TO CHOOSE WISELY.
YOU'RE NOT SERIOUSLY SUGGESTING --
BZZT BZZT
EXCUSE ME...
YES...?
SORRY TO INTERRUPT, SIR... BUT THERE'S A CALL WAITING FOR YOU ON LINE FOUR. SAID IT WAS URGENT.
WHO'S ON THE LINE...?
A DOCTOR JEREMY STONE...

DESOLATION WARD

JOE CASEY AND SEAN PHILLIPS STORYTELLERS
DAN BROWN COLORS RICHARD STARKINGS AND COMICRAFT'S SAIDA! LETTERS
SCOTT DUNBIER EDITOR JIM LEE AND BRANDON CHOI WILDCATS CREATORS

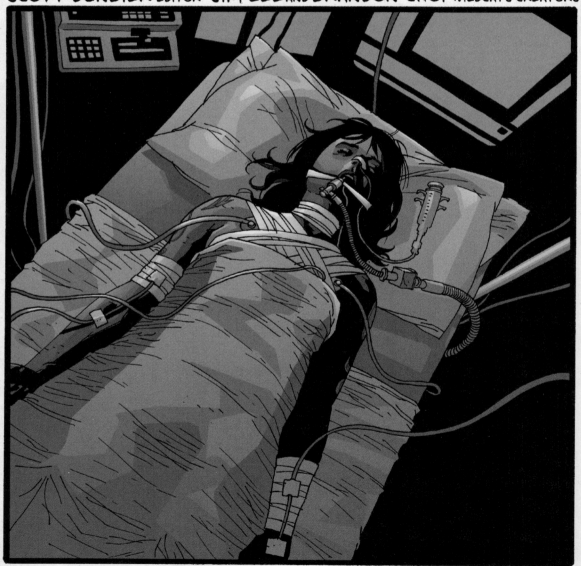

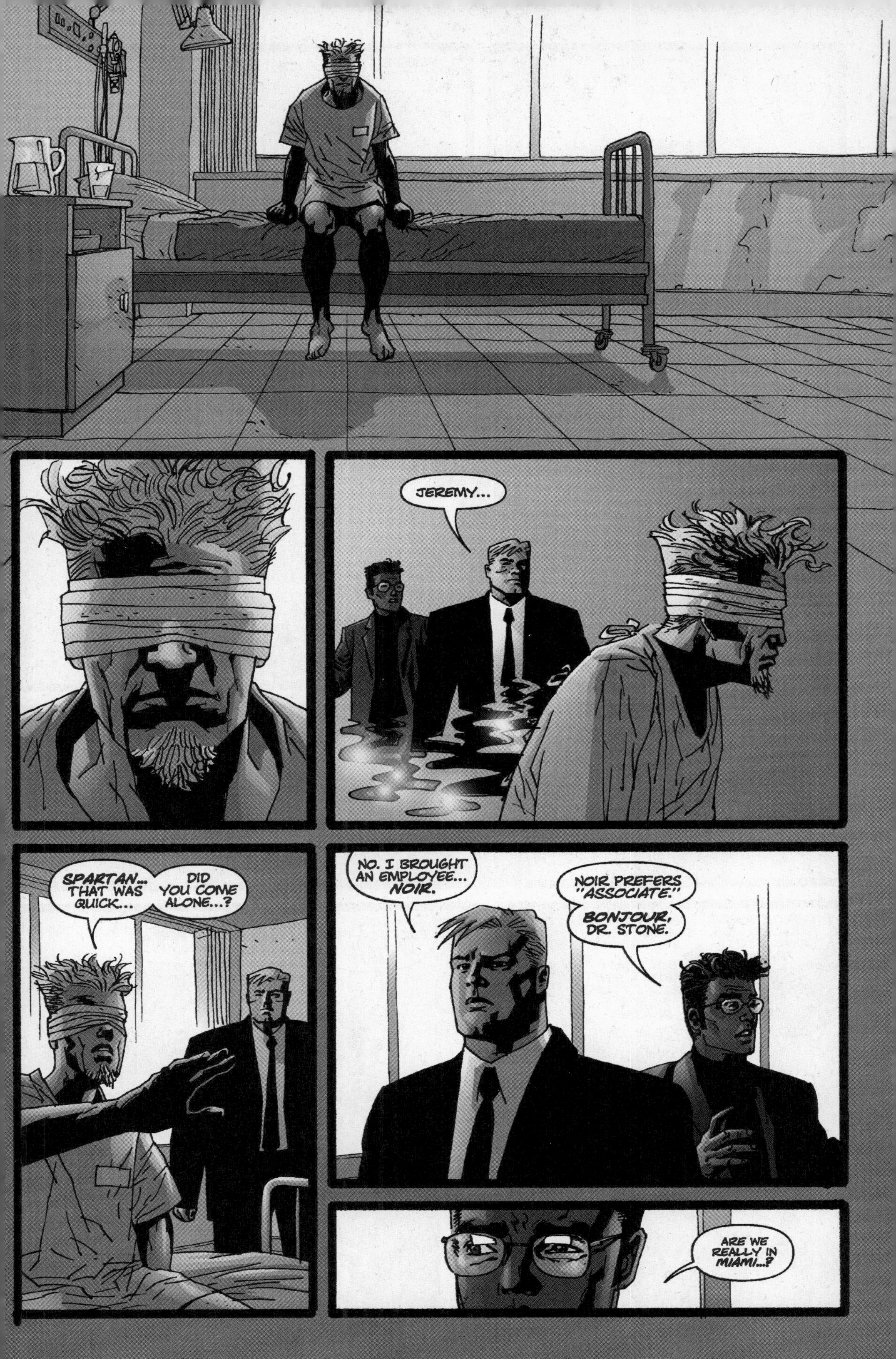
JEREMY...
SPARTAN... THAT WAS QUICK...
DID YOU COME ALONE...?
NO. I BROUGHT AN EMPLOYEE... NOIR.
NOIR PREFERS "ASSOCIATE."
BONJOUR, DR. STONE.
ARE WE REALLY IN MIAMI...?

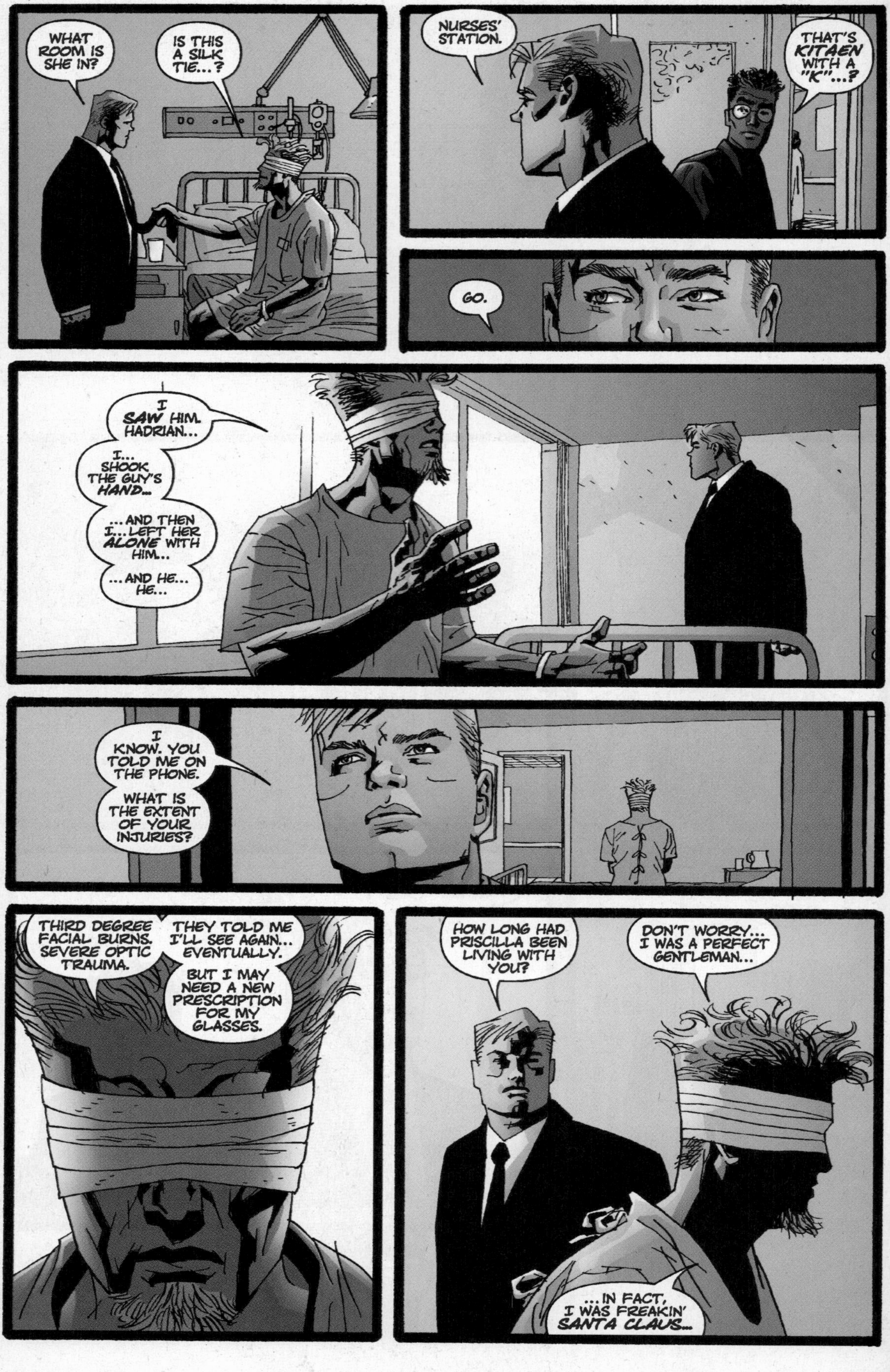
WHAT ROOM IS SHE IN?
IS THIS A SILK TIE...?
NURSES' STATION.
THAT'S KITAEN WITH A "K"...?
GO.
I SAW HIM. HADRIAN...
I... SHOOK THE GUY'S HAND...
...AND THEN I...LEFT HER ALONE WITH HIM...
...AND HE... HE...
I KNOW. YOU TOLD ME ON THE PHONE.
WHAT IS THE EXTENT OF YOUR INJURIES?
THIRD DEGREE FACIAL BURNS. SEVERE OPTIC TRAUMA.
THEY TOLD ME I'LL SEE AGAIN... EVENTUALLY.
BUT I MAY NEED A NEW PRESCRIPTION FOR MY GLASSES.
HOW LONG HAD PRISCILLA BEEN LIVING WITH YOU?
DON'T WORRY... I WAS A PERFECT GENTLEMAN...
...IN FACT, I WAS FREAKIN' SANTA CLAUS...

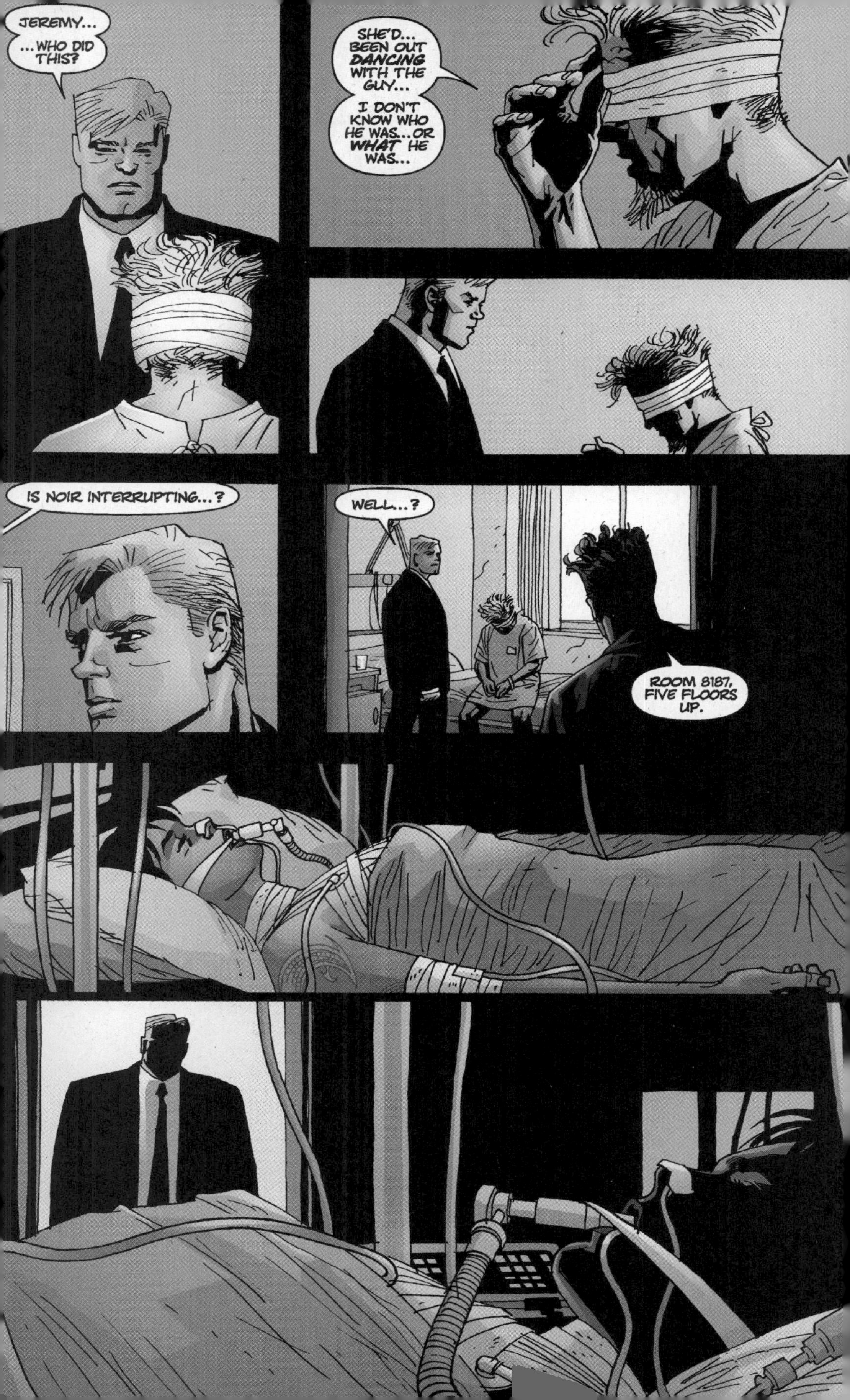
JEREMY...
...WHO DID THIS?
SHE'D... BEEN OUT DANCING WITH THE GUY...
I DON'T KNOW WHO HE WAS...OR WHAT HE WAS...
IS NOIR INTERRUPTING...?
WELL...?
ROOM 8187, FIVE FLOORS UP.

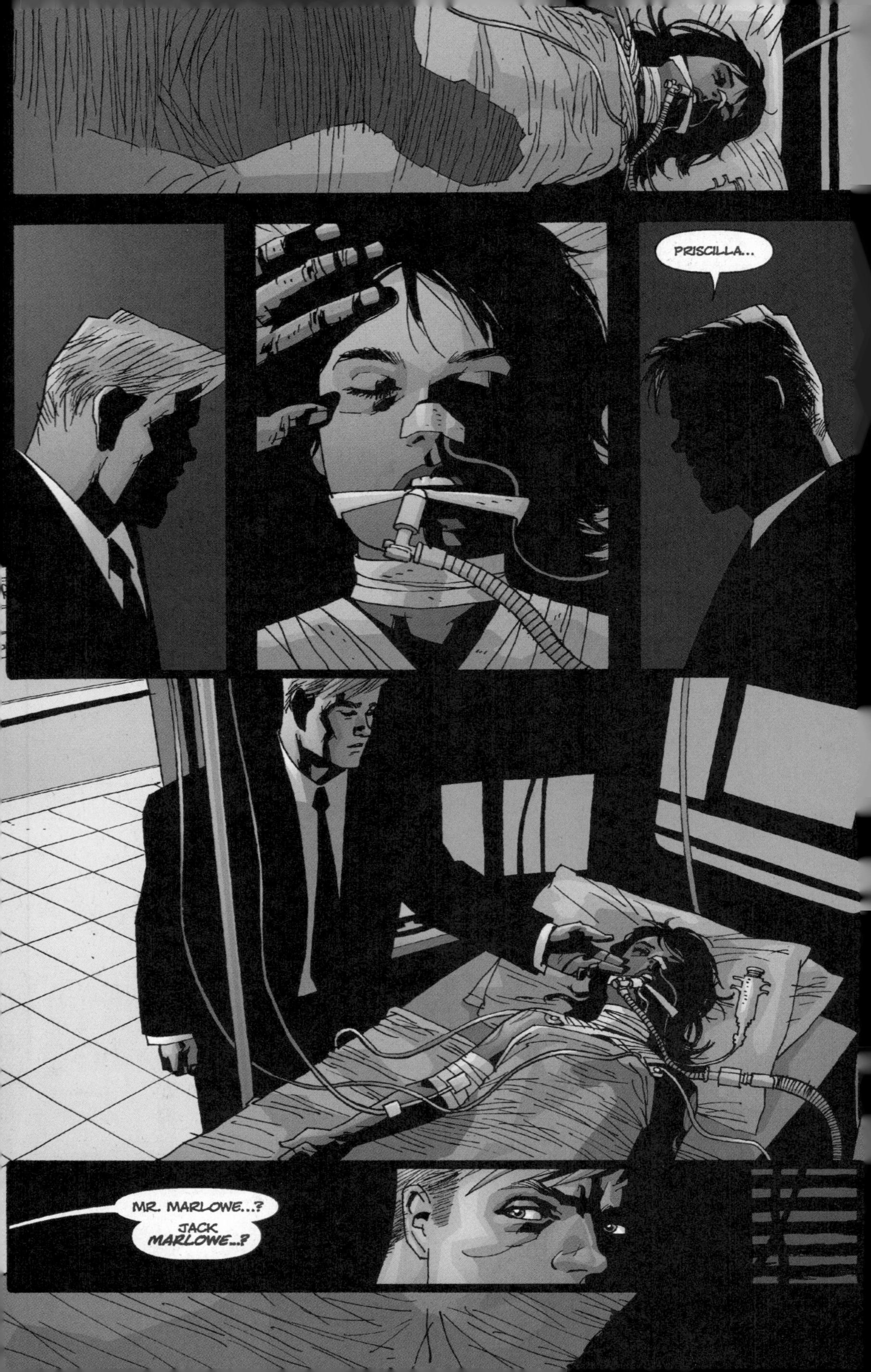
PRISCILLA...
MR. MARLOWE...?
JACK MARLOWE...?

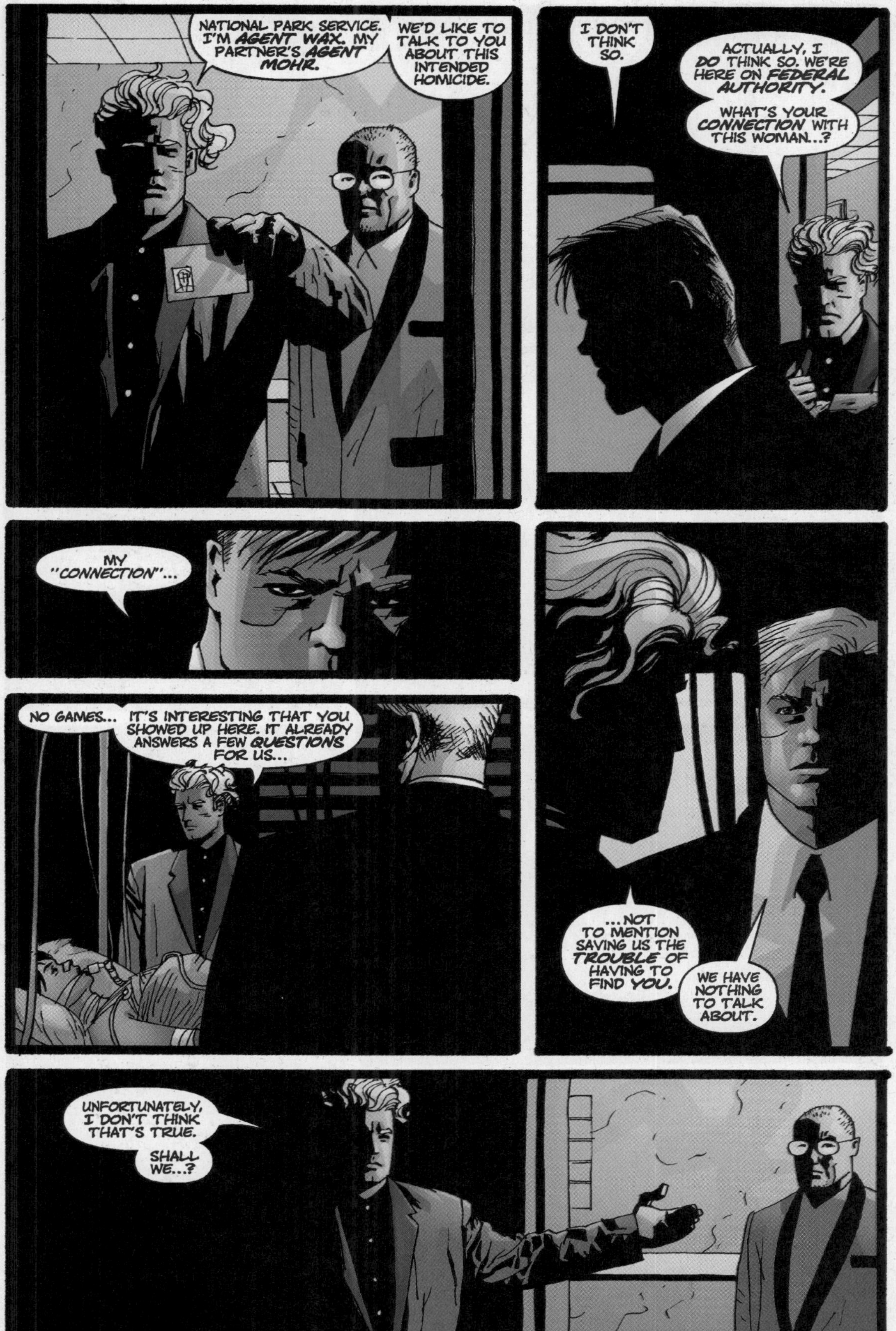
NATIONAL PARK SERVICE. I'M AGENT WAX. MY PARTNER'S AGENT MOHR.
WE'D LIKE TO TALK TO YOU ABOUT THIS INTENDED HOMICIDE.
I DON'T THINK SO.
ACTUALLY, I DO THINK SO. WE'RE HERE ON FEDERAL AUTHORITY.
WHAT'S YOUR CONNECTION WITH THIS WOMAN...?
MY "CONNECTION"...
NO GAMES...
IT'S INTERESTING THAT YOU SHOWED UP HERE. IT ALREADY ANSWERS A FEW QUESTIONS FOR US...
...NOT TO MENTION SAVING US THE TROUBLE OF HAVING TO FIND YOU.
WE HAVE NOTHING TO TALK ABOUT.
UNFORTUNATELY, I DON'T THINK THAT'S TRUE.
SHALL WE...?

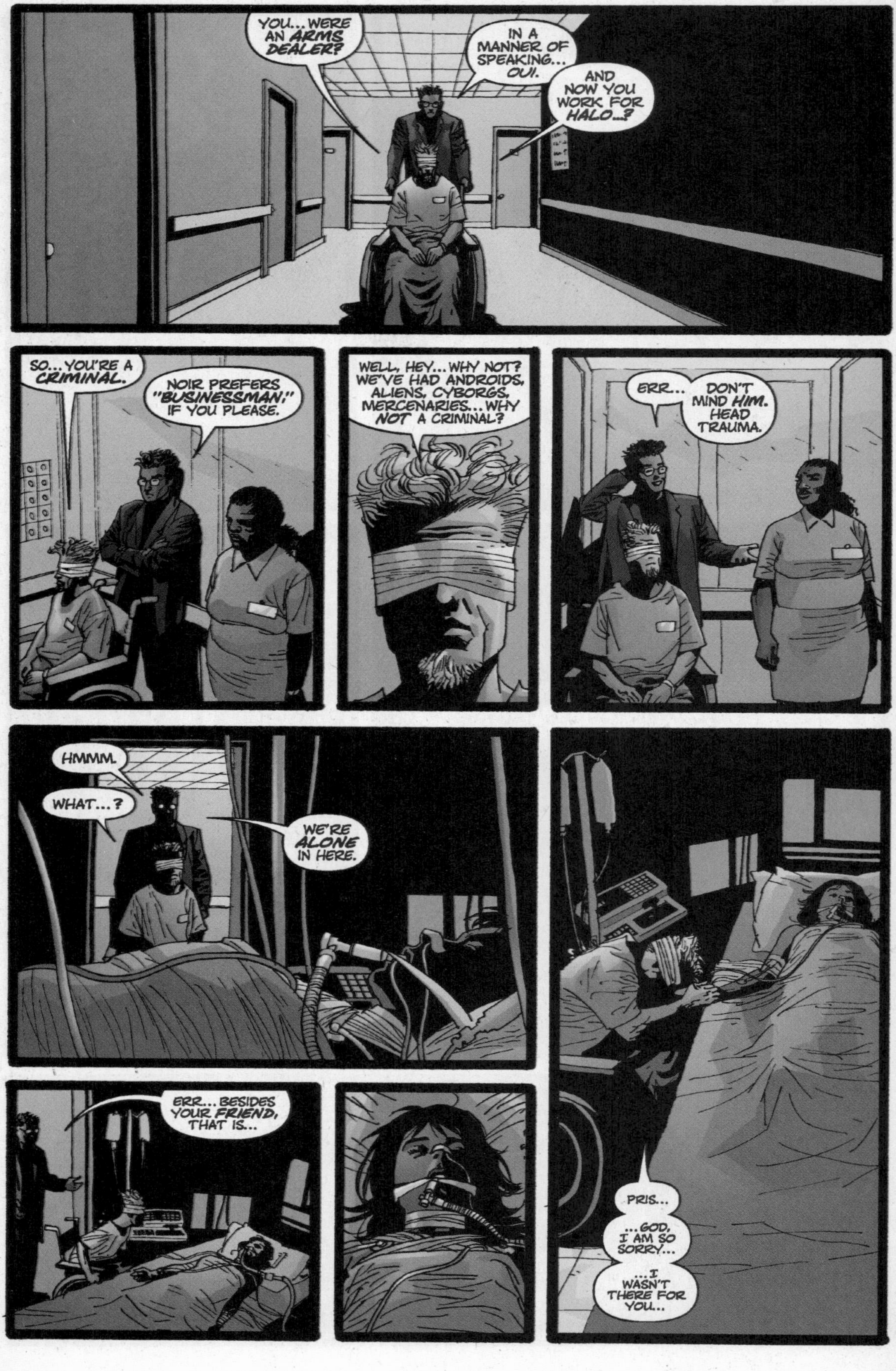
YOU... WERE AN ARMS DEALER?
IN A MANNER OF SPEAKING... OUI.
AND NOW YOU WORK FOR HALO...?
SO... YOU'RE A CRIMINAL.
NOIR PREFERS "BUSINESSMAN," IF YOU PLEASE.
WELL, HEY... WHY NOT? WE'VE HAD ANDROIDS, ALIENS, CYBORGS, MERCENARIES... WHY NOT A CRIMINAL?
ERR...
DON'T MIND HIM. HEAD TRAUMA.
HMMM.
WHAT...?
WE'RE ALONE IN HERE.
ERR... BESIDES YOUR FRIEND, THAT IS...
PRIS...
...GOD, I AM SO SORRY...
...I WASN'T THERE FOR YOU...

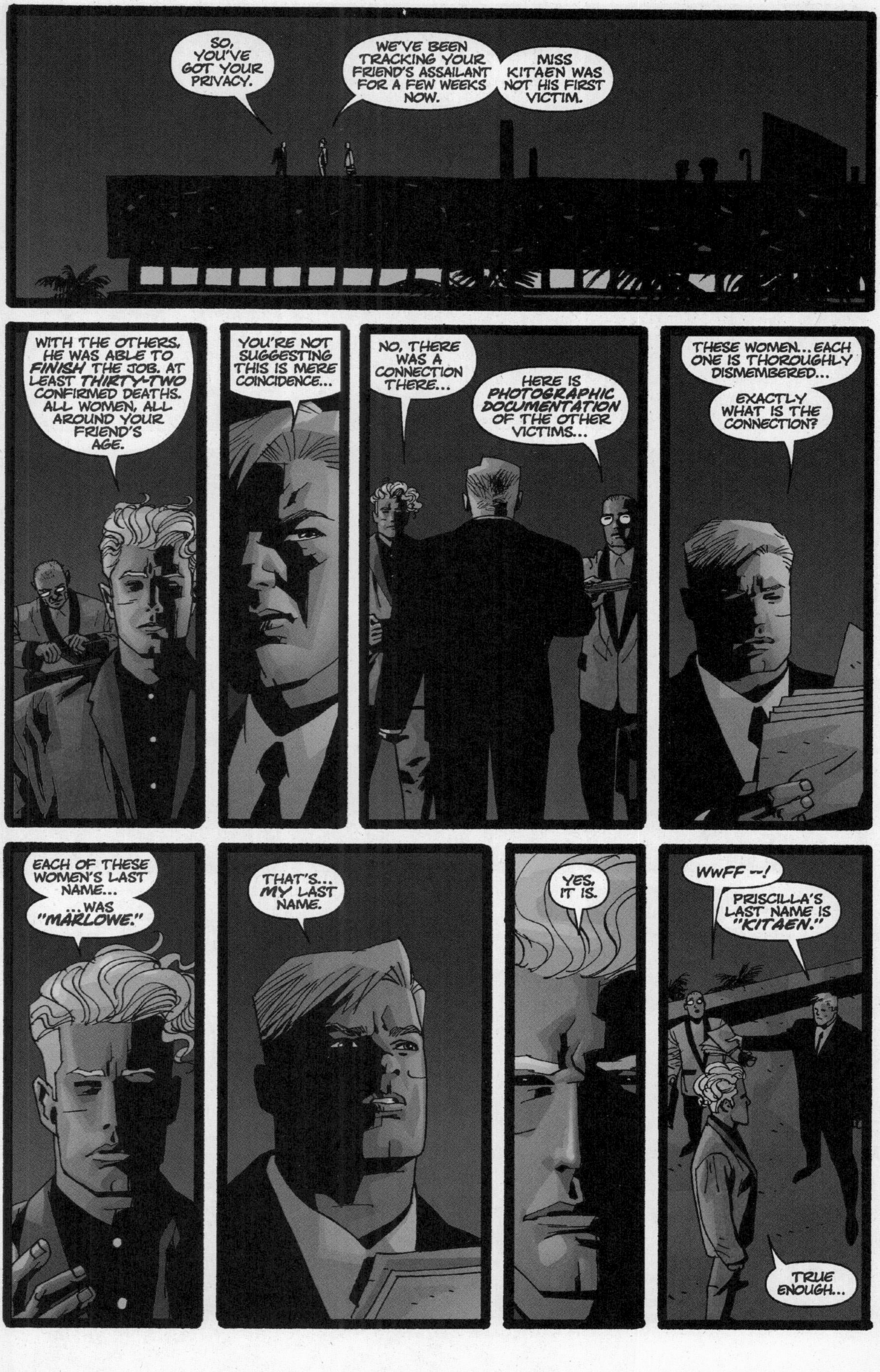

SO, YOU'VE GOT YOUR PRIVACY.
WE'VE BEEN TRACKING YOUR FRIEND'S ASSAILANT FOR A FEW WEEKS NOW.
MISS KITAEN WAS NOT HIS FIRST VICTIM.
WITH THE OTHERS, HE WAS ABLE TO FINISH THE JOB. AT LEAST THIRTY-TWO CONFIRMED DEATHS. ALL WOMEN, ALL AROUND YOUR FRIEND'S AGE.
YOU'RE NOT SUGGESTING THIS IS MERE COINCIDENCE...
NO, THERE WAS A CONNECTION THERE...
HERE IS PHOTOGRAPHIC DOCUMENTATION OF THE OTHER VICTIMS...
THESE WOMEN... EACH ONE IS THOROUGHLY DISMEMBERED...
EXACTLY WHAT IS THE CONNECTION?
EACH OF THESE WOMEN'S LAST NAME...
...WAS "MARLOWE."
THAT'S... MY LAST NAME.
YES, IT IS.
WWFF --!
PRISCILLA'S LAST NAME IS "KITAEN."
TRUE ENOUGH...

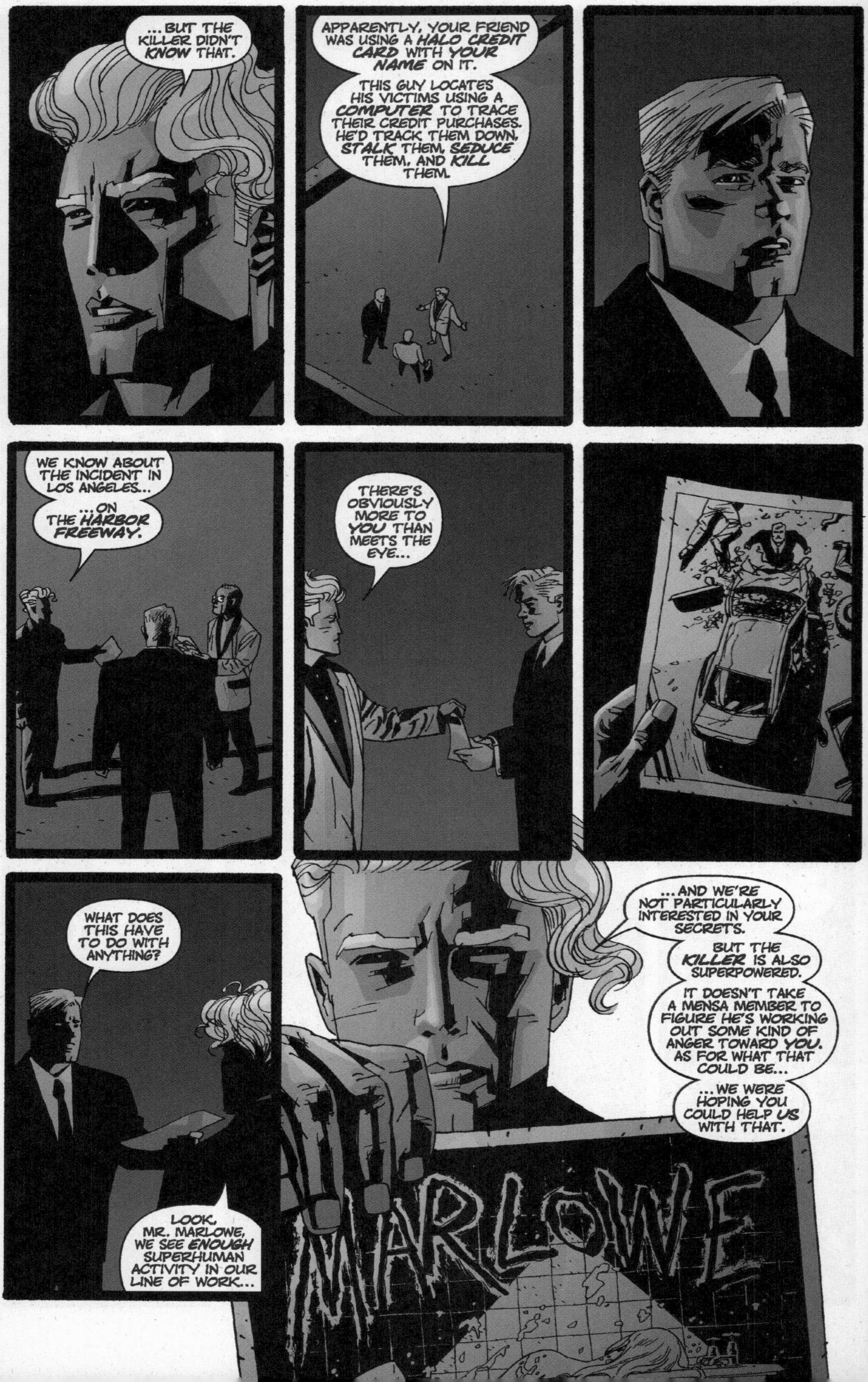
...BUT THE KILLER DIDN'T KNOW THAT.
APPARENTLY, YOUR FRIEND WAS USING A HALO CREDIT CARD WITH YOUR NAME ON IT.
THIS GUY LOCATES HIS VICTIMS USING A COMPUTER TO TRACE THEIR CREDIT PURCHASES. HE'D TRACK THEM DOWN, STALK THEM, SEDUCE THEM, AND KILL THEM.
WE KNOW ABOUT THE INCIDENT IN LOS ANGELES...
...ON THE HARBOR FREEWAY.
THERE'S OBVIOUSLY MORE TO YOU THAN MEETS THE EYE...
WHAT DOES THIS HAVE TO DO WITH ANYTHING?
LOOK, MR. MARLOWE, WE SEE ENOUGH SUPERHUMAN ACTIVITY IN OUR LINE OF WORK...
...AND WE'RE NOT PARTICULARLY INTERESTED IN YOUR SECRETS.
BUT THE KILLER IS ALSO SUPERPOWERED.
IT DOESN'T TAKE A MENSA MEMBER TO FIGURE HE'S WORKING OUT SOME KIND OF ANGER TOWARD YOU. AS FOR WHAT THAT COULD BE...
...WE WERE HOPING YOU COULD HELP US WITH THAT.
MARLOWE

-- LADIES AND GENTLEMEN, THIS IS YOUR CAPTAIN... WE'VE REACHED AN ALTITUDE OF THIRTY-THREE THOUSAND FEET.

SHOULD BE A SMOOTH FLIGHT ALL THE WAY INTO LOS ANGELES. THE WEATHER THERE IS PRESENTLY PARTLY CLOUDY AND SEVENTY-ONE DEGREES --

BROWN NOW. BROWN DOWN

FISCAL

PRICE $ 4.99 US

DISPLAY UNTIL NOV 3, 2000

MARLOWE ON THE MOVE

REBUILDING HALO:

WILL JACK MARLOWE HELP THE ANGEL OF CORPORATE AMERICA FLY HIGHER

Corporate Co
What's He
Acquisition

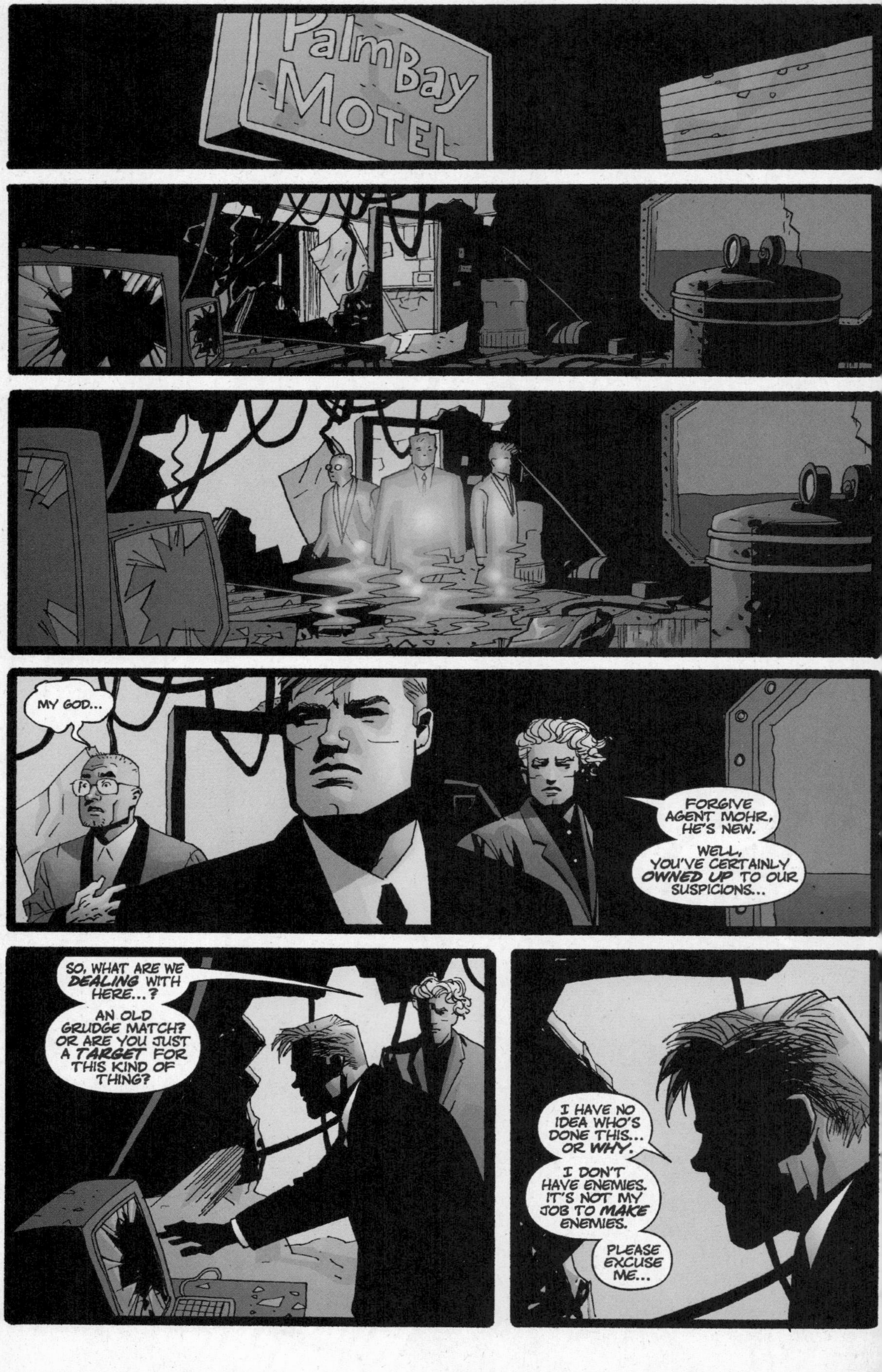

Palm Bay
MOTEL
MY GOD...
FORGIVE AGENT MOHR, HE'S NEW.
WELL, YOU'VE CERTAINLY OWNED UP TO OUR SUSPICIONS...
SO, WHAT ARE WE DEALING WITH HERE...?
AN OLD GRUDGE MATCH? OR ARE YOU JUST A TARGET FOR THIS KIND OF THING?
I HAVE NO IDEA WHO'S DONE THIS... OR WHY.
I DON'T HAVE ENEMIES. IT'S NOT MY JOB TO MAKE ENEMIES.
PLEASE EXCUSE ME...

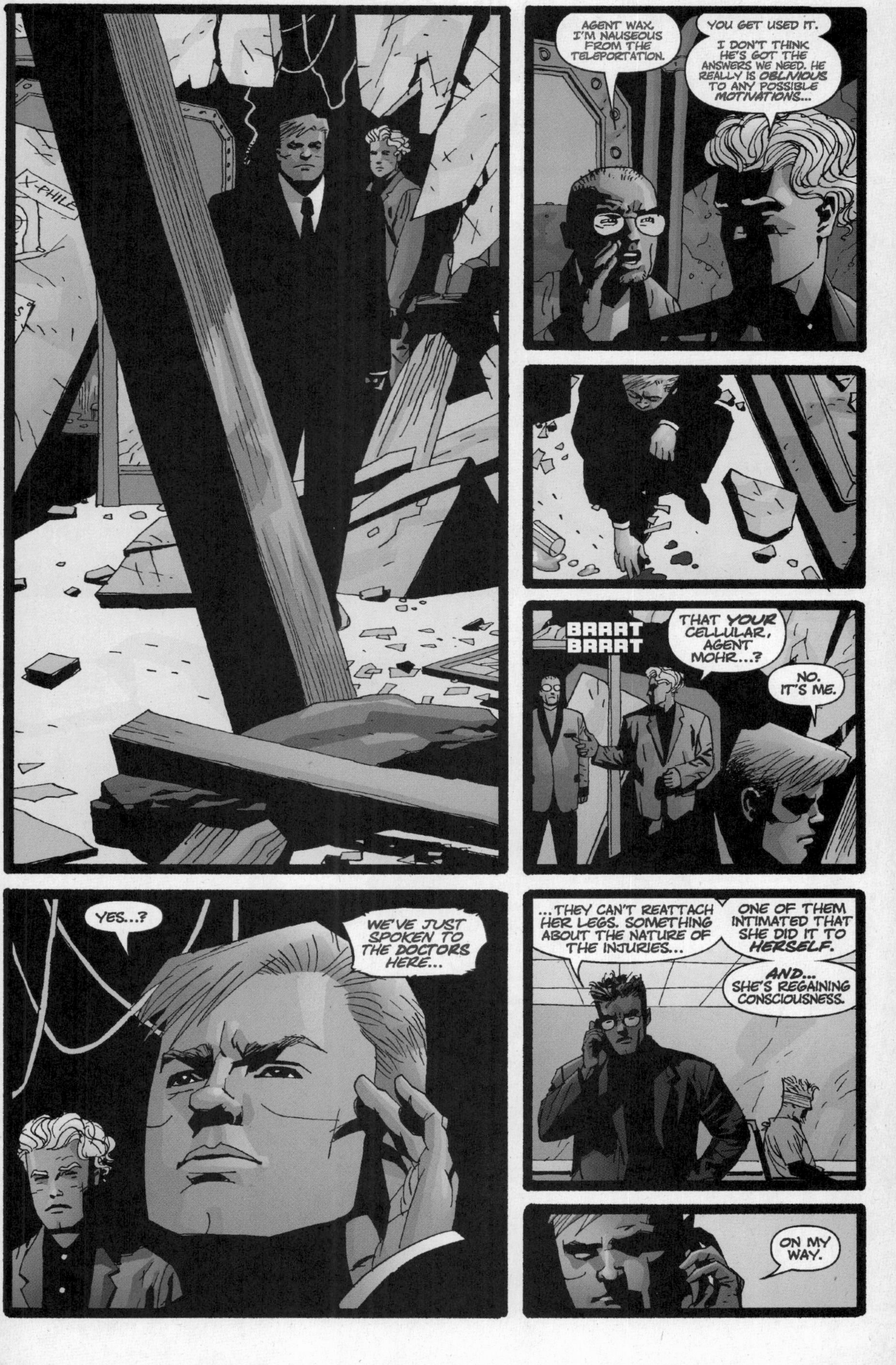
AGENT WAX, I'M NAUSEOUS FROM THE TELEPORTATION.
YOU GET USED IT.
I DON'T THINK HE'S GOT THE ANSWERS WE NEED. HE REALLY IS *OBLIVIOUS* TO ANY POSSIBLE *MOTIVATIONS*...
BRAAT BRAAT
THAT *YOUR* CELLULAR, AGENT MOHR...?
NO. IT'S ME.
YES...?
WE'VE JUST SPOKEN TO THE *DOCTORS* HERE...
...THEY CAN'T REATTACH HER LEGS. SOMETHING ABOUT THE NATURE OF THE INJURIES...
ONE OF THEM INTIMATED THAT SHE DID IT TO ***HERSELF.***
AND... SHE'S REGAINING CONSCIOUSNESS.
ON MY WAY.

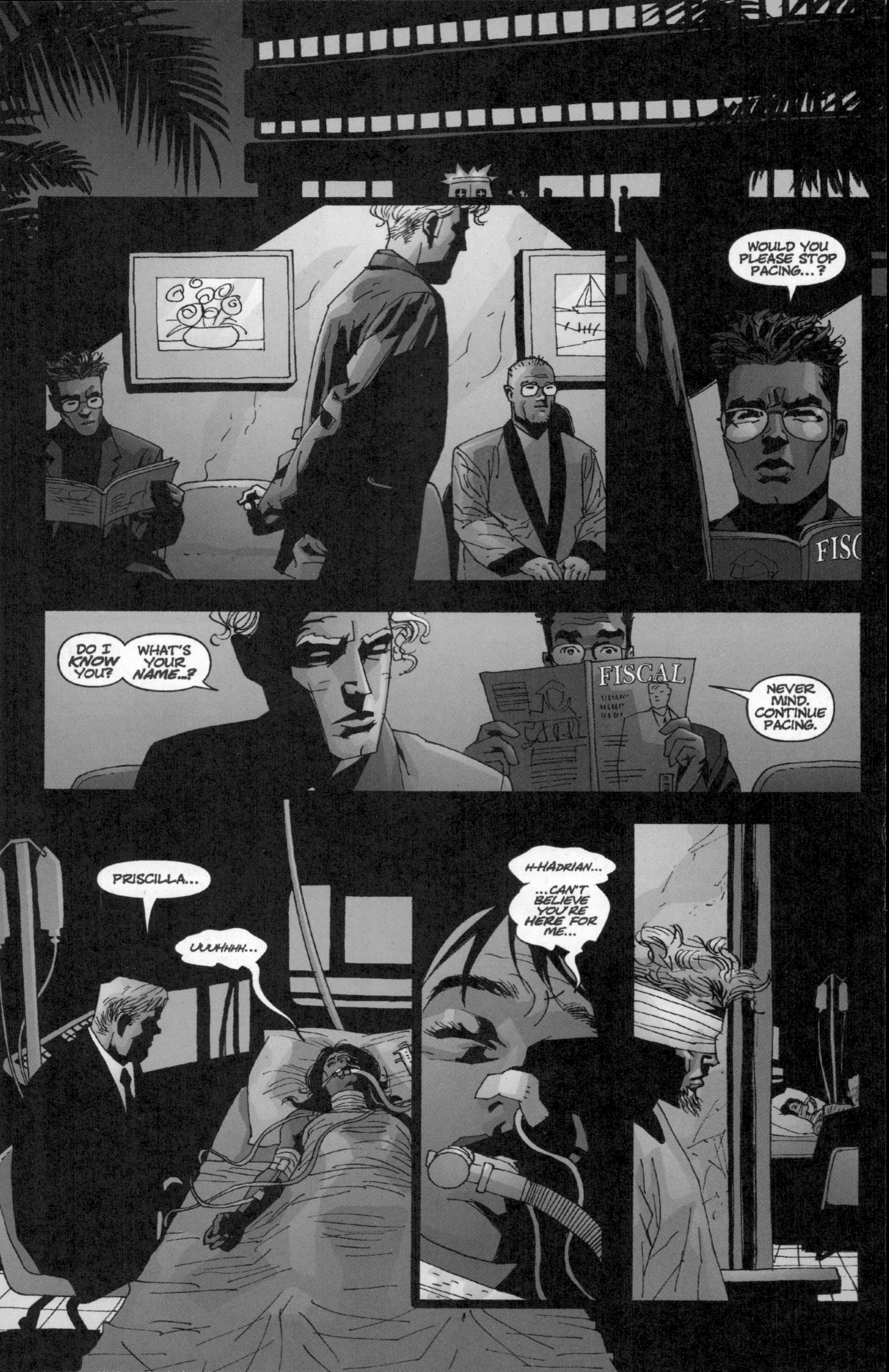
WOULD YOU PLEASE STOP PACING...?
FISC
DO I KNOW YOU?
WHAT'S YOUR NAME...?
FISCAL
NEVER MIND. CONTINUE PACING.
PRISCILLA...
UUUHHHH...
H-HADRIAN...
...CAN'T BELIEVE YOU'RE HERE FOR ME...

DO YOU REMEMBER ANYTHING?

I... MET THIS GUY... I WAS...AT THE MALL...

WE WENT... DANCING...

WHO...?

TOLD ME...HIS NAME WAS... SMITH...

...SAMUEL SMITH.

WHAT...DID HE DO TO ME...?

HADRIAN... I CAN'T FEEL...

WAIT... I... REMEMBER... HE SAID...SOME THINGS...

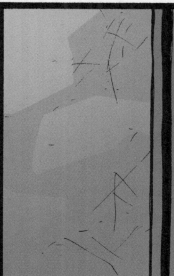

...ABOUT HIS FAMILY...

...AND YOURS.

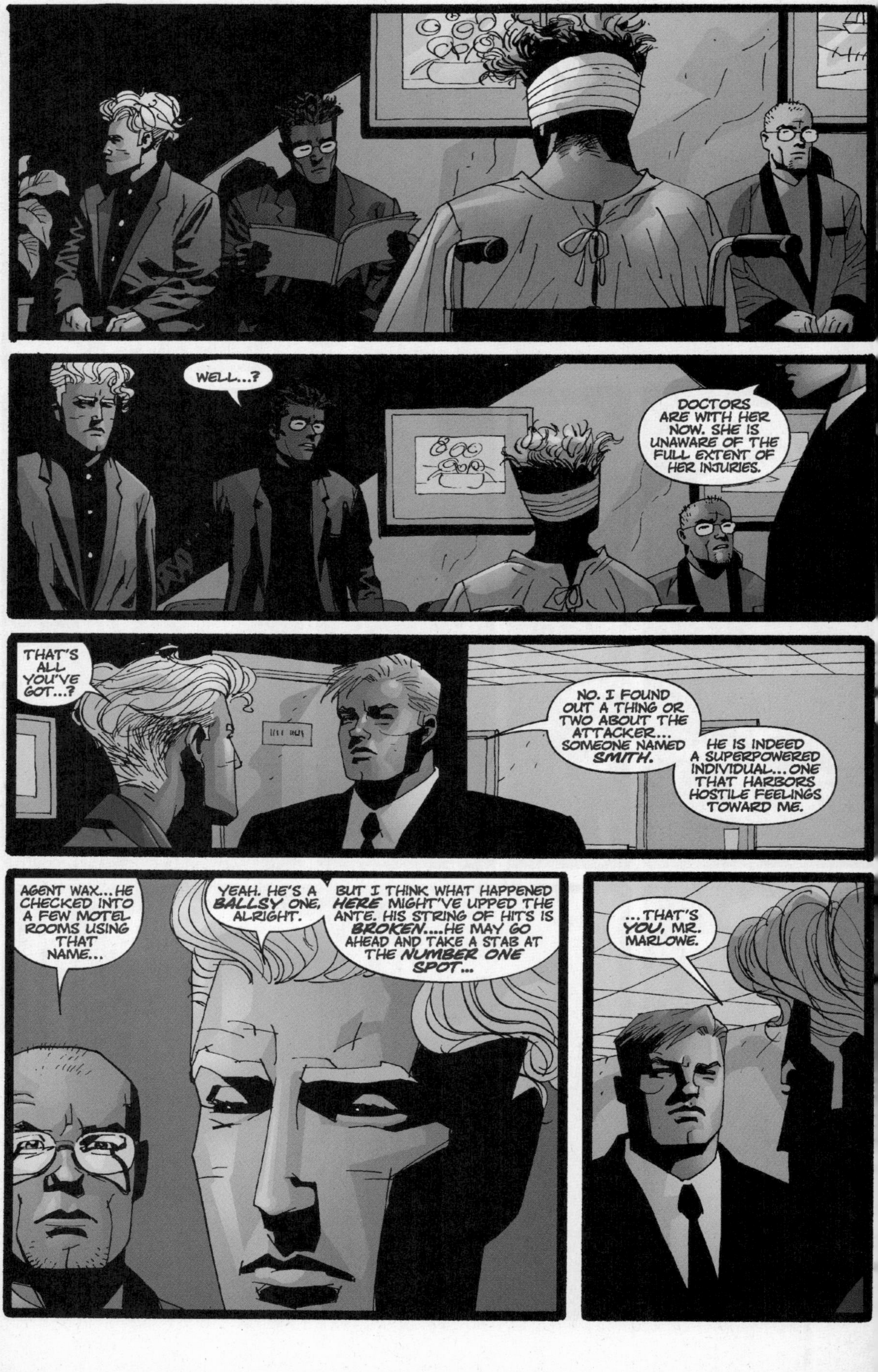
WELL...?
DOCTORS ARE WITH HER NOW. SHE IS UNAWARE OF THE FULL EXTENT OF HER INJURIES.
THAT'S ALL YOU'VE GOT...?
NO. I FOUND OUT A THING OR TWO ABOUT THE ATTACKER... SOMEONE NAMED SMITH.
HE IS INDEED A SUPERPOWERED INDIVIDUAL... ONE THAT HARBORS HOSTILE FEELINGS TOWARD ME.
AGENT WAX... HE CHECKED INTO A FEW MOTEL ROOMS USING THAT NAME...
YEAH. HE'S A BALLSY ONE, ALRIGHT.
BUT I THINK WHAT HAPPENED HERE MIGHT'VE UPPED THE ANTE. HIS STRING OF HITS IS BROKEN.... HE MAY GO AHEAD AND TAKE A STAB AT THE NUMBER ONE SPOT...
...THAT'S YOU, MR. MARLOWE.

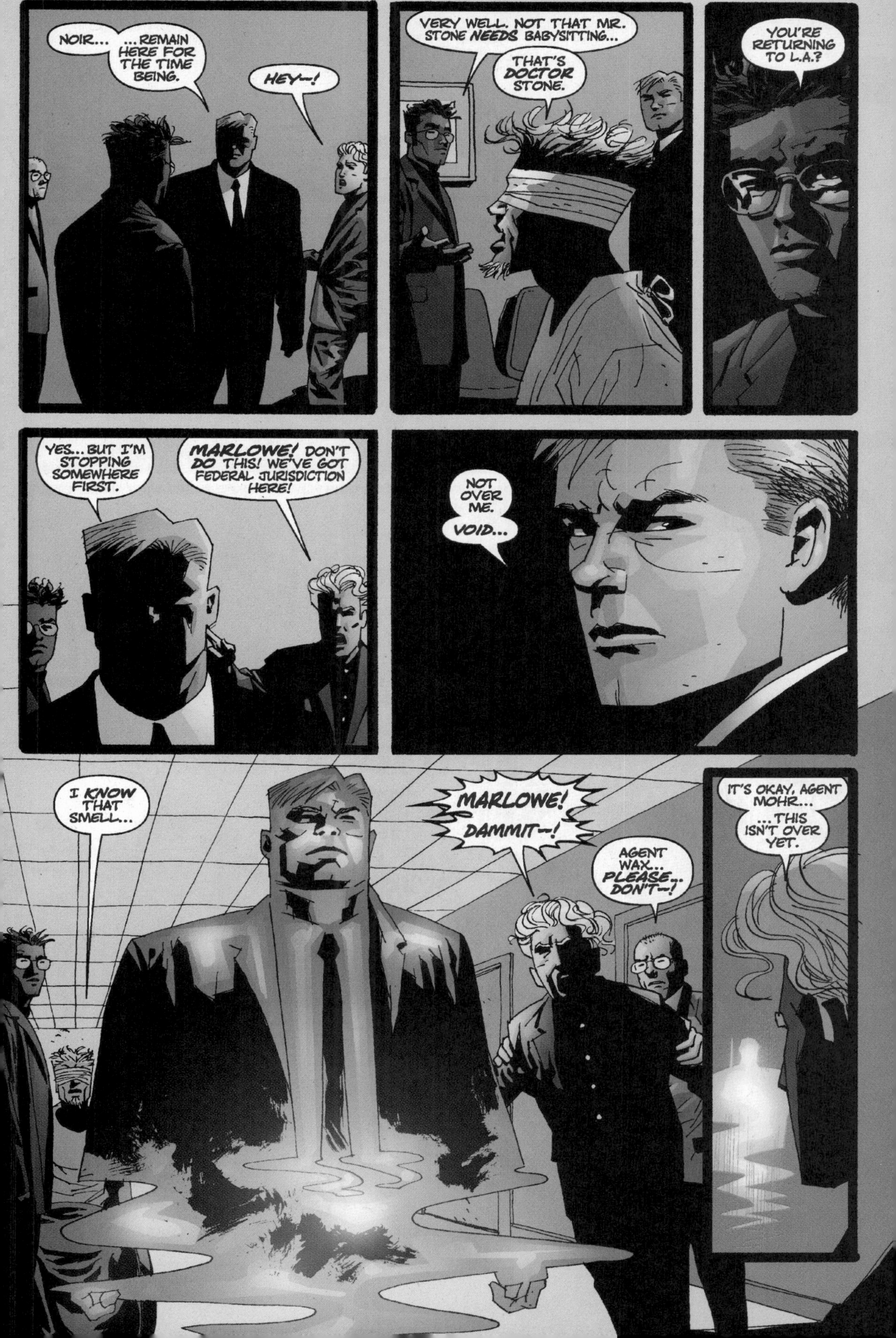

NOIR...
...REMAIN HERE FOR THE TIME BEING.
HEY--!
VERY WELL. NOT THAT MR. STONE NEEDS BABYSITTING...
THAT'S DOCTOR STONE.
YOU'RE RETURNING TO L.A.?
YES... BUT I'M STOPPING SOMEWHERE FIRST.
MARLOWE! DON'T DO THIS! WE'VE GOT FEDERAL JURISDICTION HERE!
NOT OVER ME.
VOID...
I KNOW THAT SMELL...
MARLOWE! DAMMIT--!
AGENT WAX... PLEASE... DON'T--!
IT'S OKAY, AGENT MOHR...
...THIS ISN'T OVER YET.

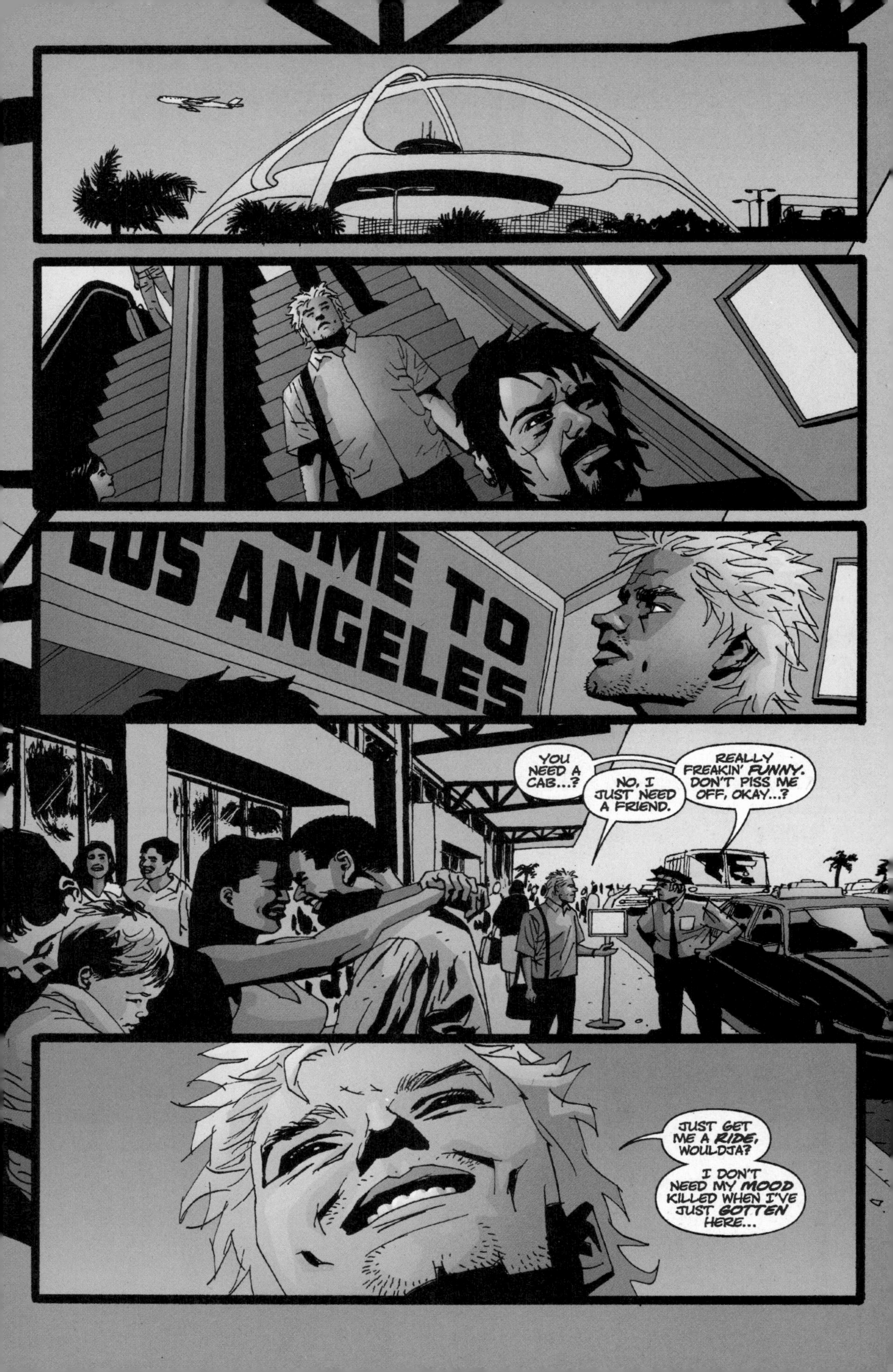

COME TO
LOS ANGELES
YOU NEED A CAB...?
NO, I JUST NEED A FRIEND.
REALLY FREAKIN' FUNNY. DON'T PISS ME OFF, OKAY...?
JUST GET ME A RIDE, WOULDJA?
I DON'T NEED MY MOOD KILLED WHEN I'VE JUST GOTTEN HERE...

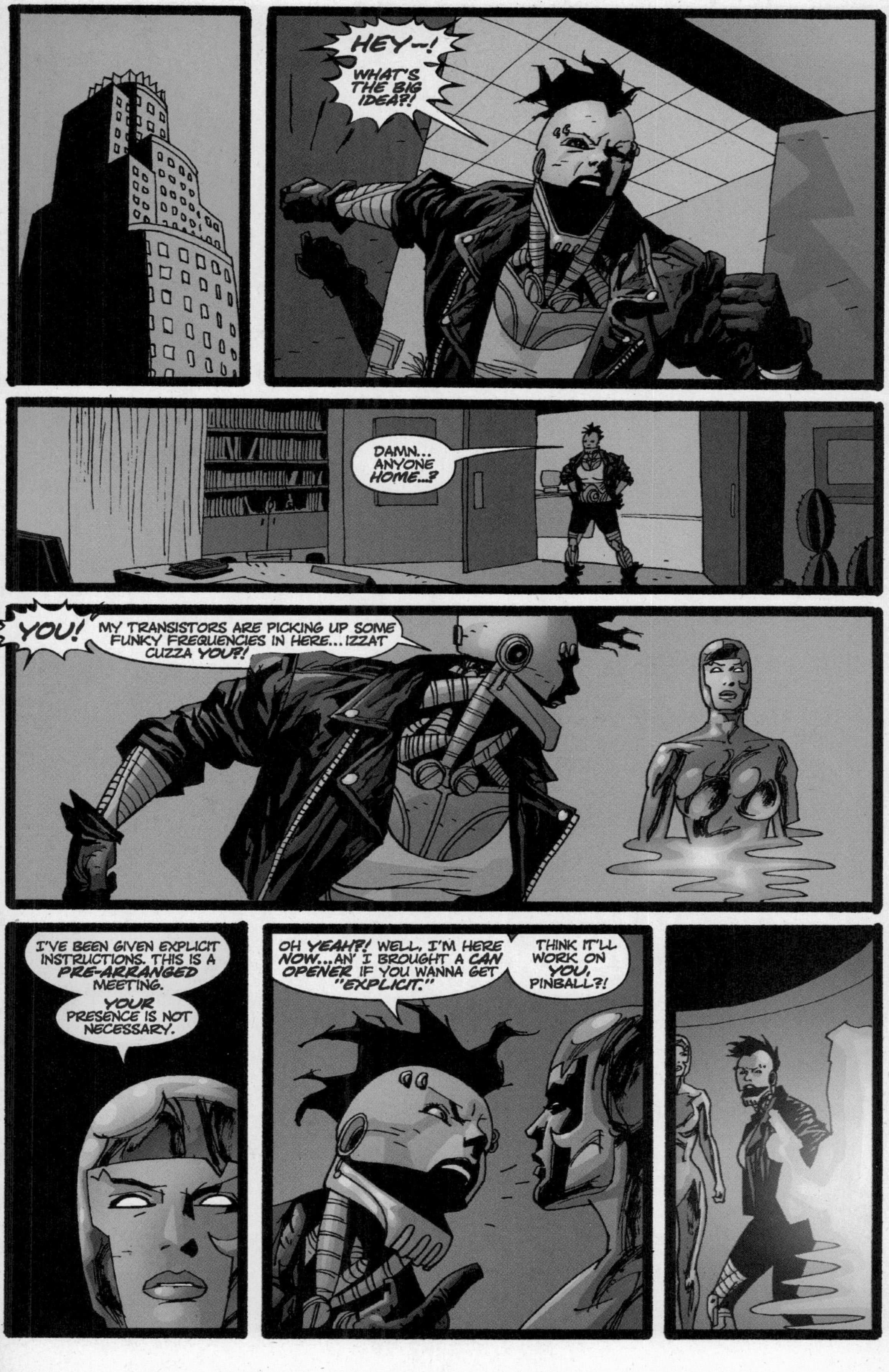
HEY--! WHAT'S THE BIG IDEA?!
DAMN... ANYONE HOME...?
YOU!
MY TRANSISTORS ARE PICKING UP SOME FUNKY FREQUENCIES IN HERE... IZZAT CUZZA YOU?!
I'VE BEEN GIVEN EXPLICIT INSTRUCTIONS. THIS IS A PRE-ARRANGED MEETING.
YOUR PRESENCE IS NOT NECESSARY.
OH YEAH?! WELL, I'M HERE NOW... AN' I BROUGHT A CAN OPENER IF YOU WANNA GET "EXPLICIT."
THINK IT'LL WORK ON YOU, PINBALL?!

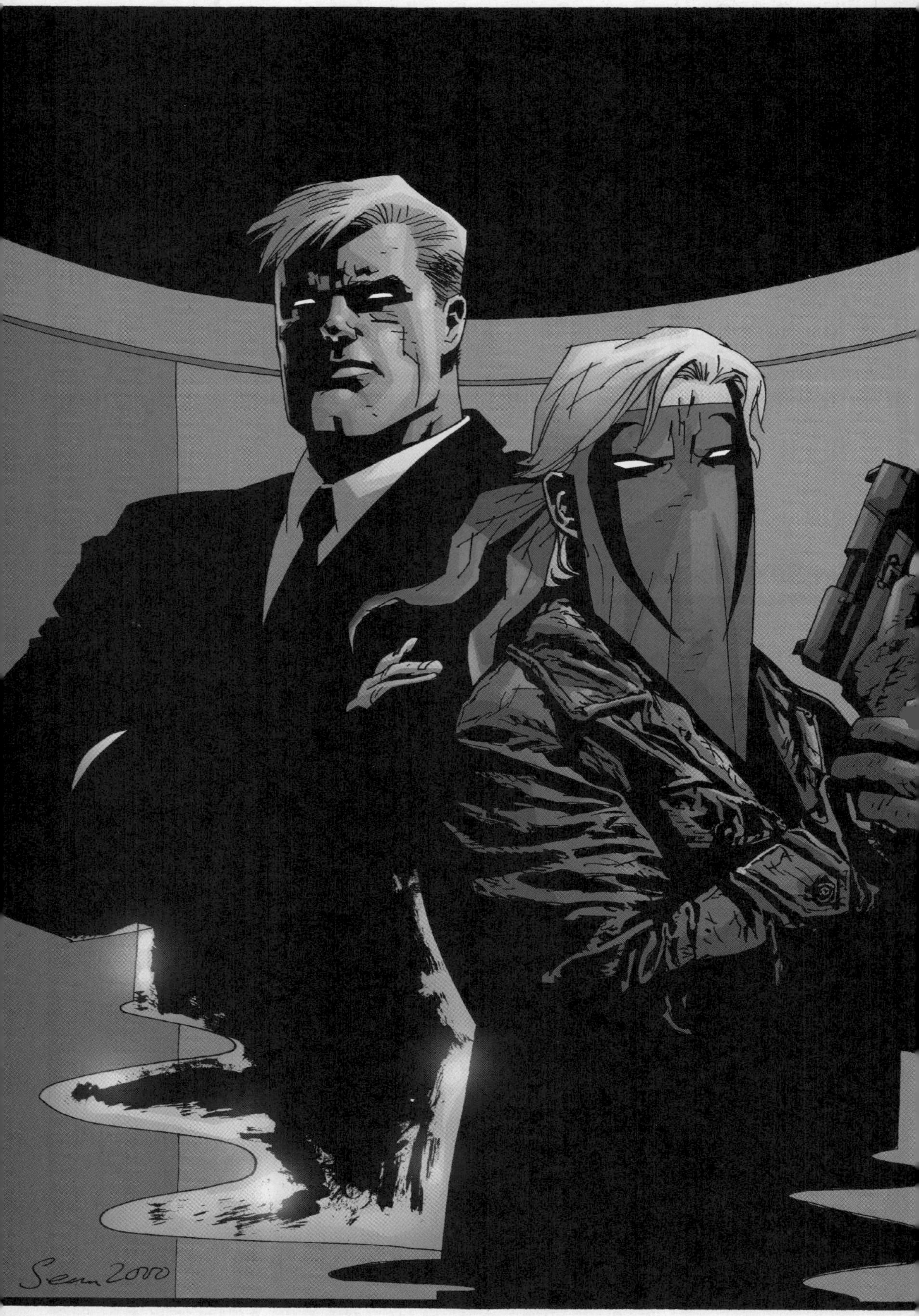
Sean 2000

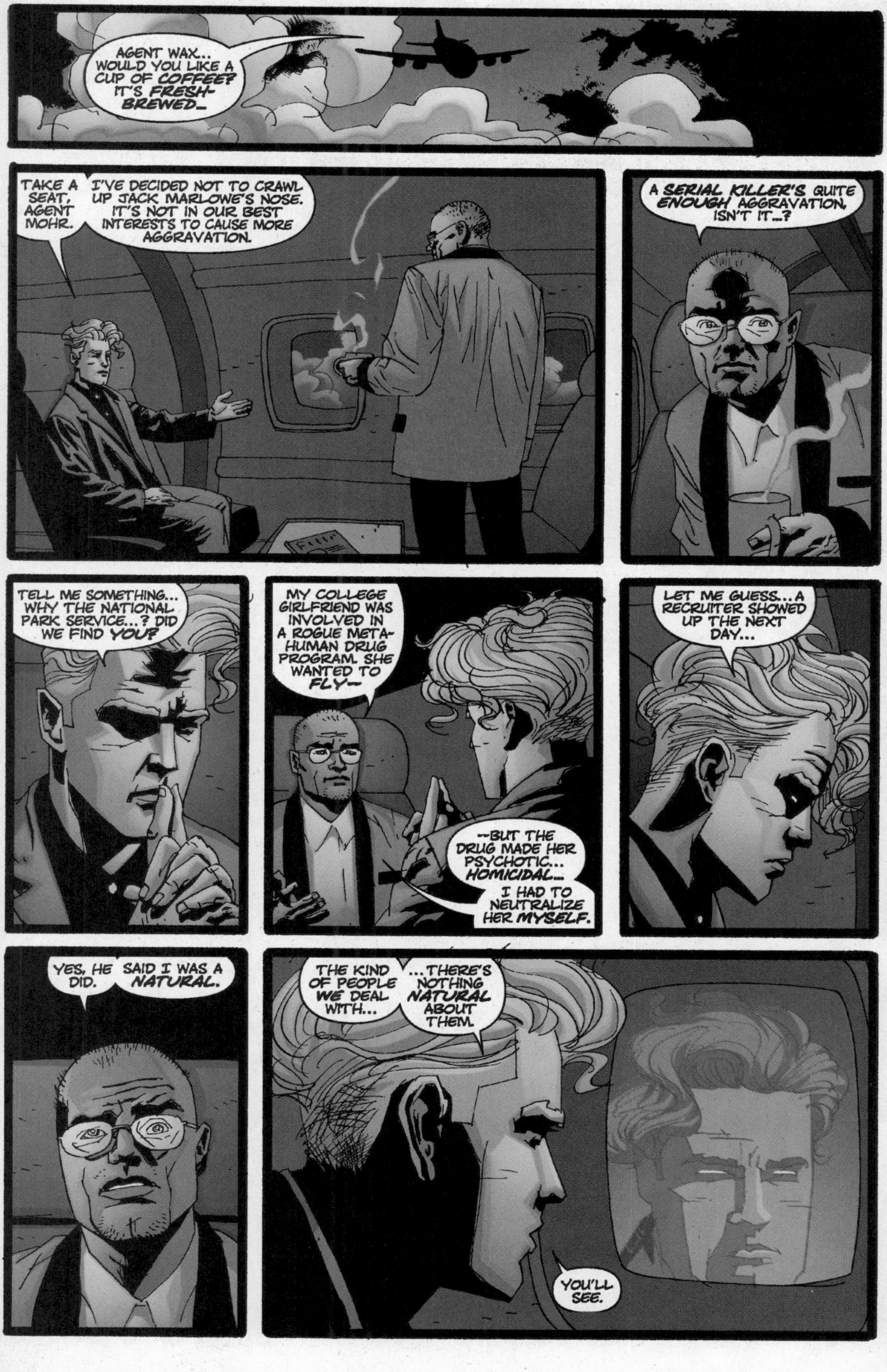
AGENT WAX... WOULD YOU LIKE A CUP OF COFFEE? IT'S FRESH-BREWED...
TAKE A SEAT, AGENT MOHR.
I'VE DECIDED NOT TO CRAWL UP JACK MARLOWE'S NOSE. IT'S NOT IN OUR BEST INTERESTS TO CAUSE MORE AGGRAVATION.
A SERIAL KILLER'S QUITE ENOUGH AGGRAVATION, ISN'T IT...?
TELL ME SOMETHING... WHY THE NATIONAL PARK SERVICE...? DID WE FIND YOU?
MY COLLEGE GIRLFRIEND WAS INVOLVED IN A ROGUE META-HUMAN DRUG PROGRAM. SHE WANTED TO FLY--
--BUT THE DRUG MADE HER PSYCHOTIC... HOMICIDAL...
I HAD TO NEUTRALIZE HER MYSELF.
LET ME GUESS... A RECRUITER SHOWED UP THE NEXT DAY...
YES, HE DID.
SAID I WAS A NATURAL.
THE KIND OF PEOPLE WE DEAL WITH...
...THERE'S NOTHING NATURAL ABOUT THEM.
YOU'LL SEE.

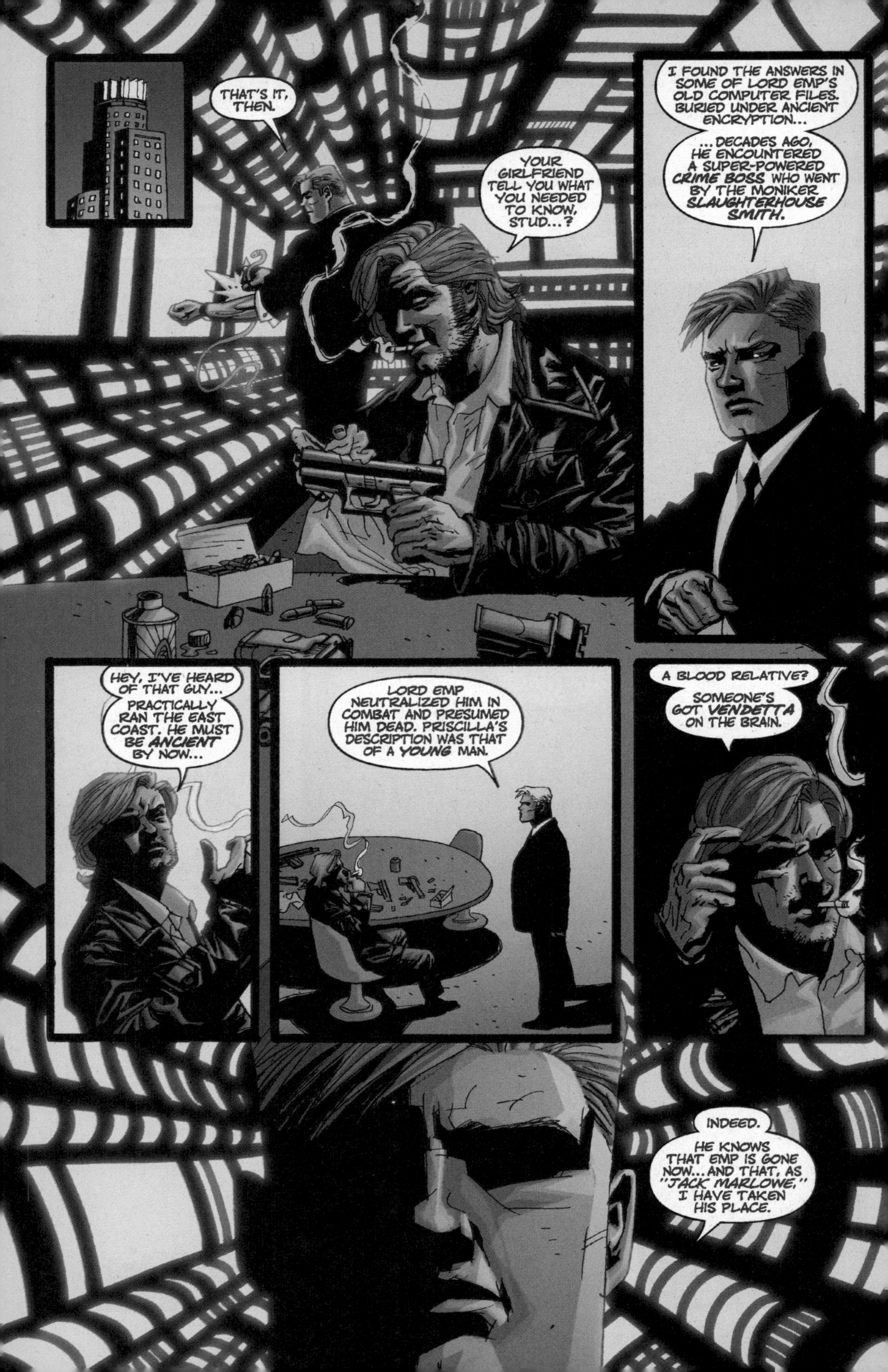

THAT'S IT, THEN.
YOUR GIRLFRIEND TELL YOU WHAT YOU NEEDED TO KNOW, STUD...?
I FOUND THE ANSWERS IN SOME OF LORD EMP'S OLD COMPUTER FILES. BURIED UNDER ANCIENT ENCRYPTION...
...DECADES AGO, HE ENCOUNTERED A SUPER-POWERED CRIME BOSS WHO WENT BY THE MONIKER SLAUGHTERHOUSE SMITH.
HEY, I'VE HEARD OF THAT GUY... PRACTICALLY RAN THE EAST COAST. HE MUST BE ANCIENT BY NOW...
LORD EMP NEUTRALIZED HIM IN COMBAT AND PRESUMED HIM DEAD. PRISCILLA'S DESCRIPTION WAS THAT OF A YOUNG MAN.
A BLOOD RELATIVE?
SOMEONE'S GOT VENDETTA ON THE BRAIN.
INDEED.
HE KNOWS THAT EMP IS GONE NOW...AND THAT, AS "JACK MARLOWE," I HAVE TAKEN HIS PLACE.

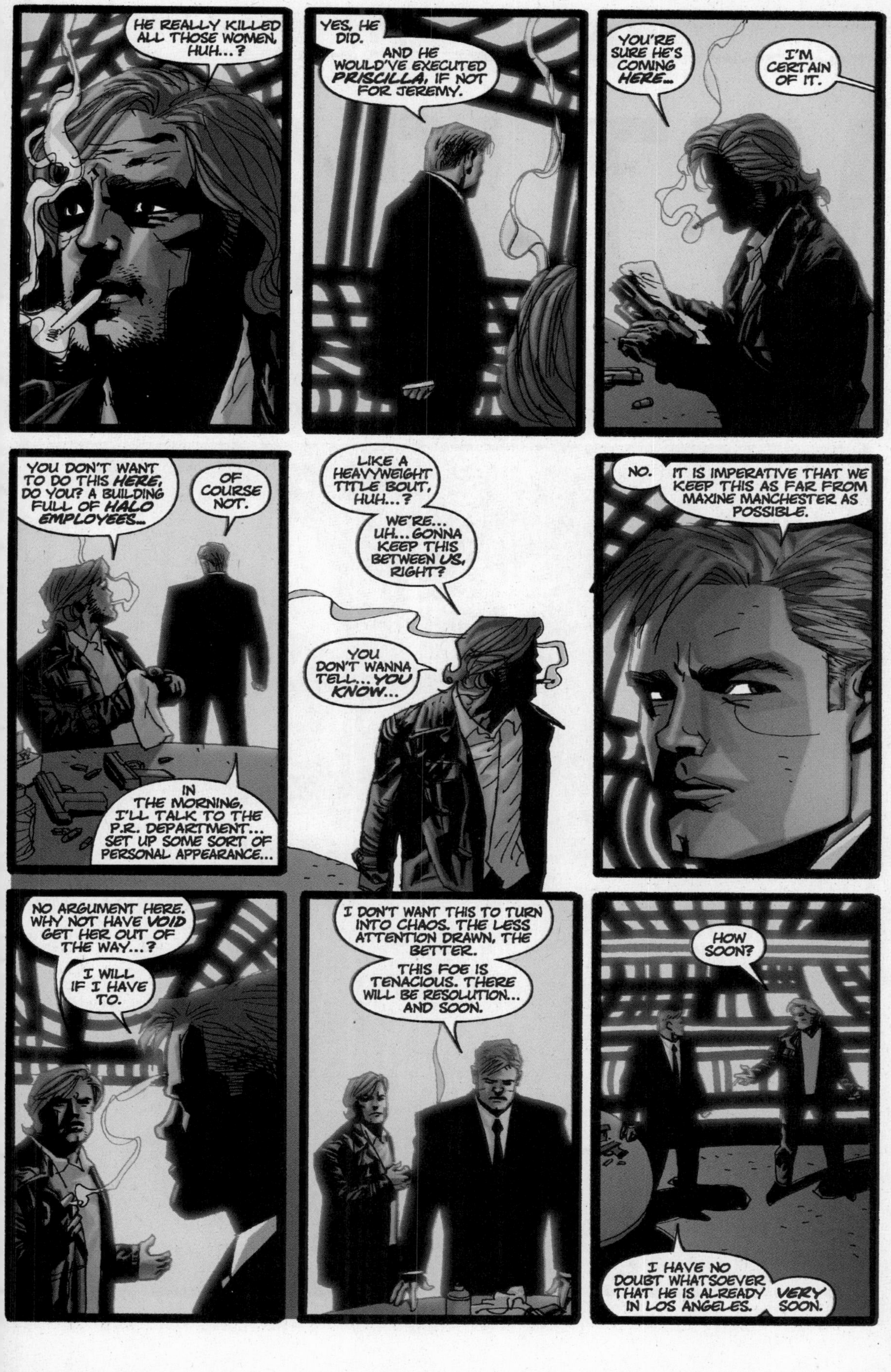
HE REALLY KILLED ALL THOSE WOMEN, HUH...?
YES, HE DID.
AND HE WOULD'VE EXECUTED PRISCILLA, IF NOT FOR JEREMY.
YOU'RE SURE HE'S COMING HERE...
I'M CERTAIN OF IT.
YOU DON'T WANT TO DO THIS HERE, DO YOU? A BUILDING FULL OF HALO EMPLOYEES...
OF COURSE NOT.
IN THE MORNING, I'LL TALK TO THE P.R. DEPARTMENT... SET UP SOME SORT OF PERSONAL APPEARANCE...
LIKE A HEAVYWEIGHT TITLE BOUT, HUH...?
WE'RE... UH... GONNA KEEP THIS BETWEEN US, RIGHT?
YOU DON'T WANNA TELL... YOU KNOW...
NO.
IT IS IMPERATIVE THAT WE KEEP THIS AS FAR FROM MAXINE MANCHESTER AS POSSIBLE.
NO ARGUMENT HERE. WHY NOT HAVE VOID GET HER OUT OF THE WAY...?
I WILL IF I HAVE TO.
I DON'T WANT THIS TO TURN INTO CHAOS. THE LESS ATTENTION DRAWN, THE BETTER.
THIS FOE IS TENACIOUS. THERE WILL BE RESOLUTION... AND SOON.
HOW SOON?
I HAVE NO DOUBT WHATSOEVER THAT HE IS ALREADY IN LOS ANGELES.
VERY SOON.

wired

JOE CASEY and **SEAN PHILLIPS** storytellers
wildstorm fx colors **richard starkings** and **comicraft's saida!** letters
scott dunbier editor **jim lee** and **brandon choi** wildcats creators

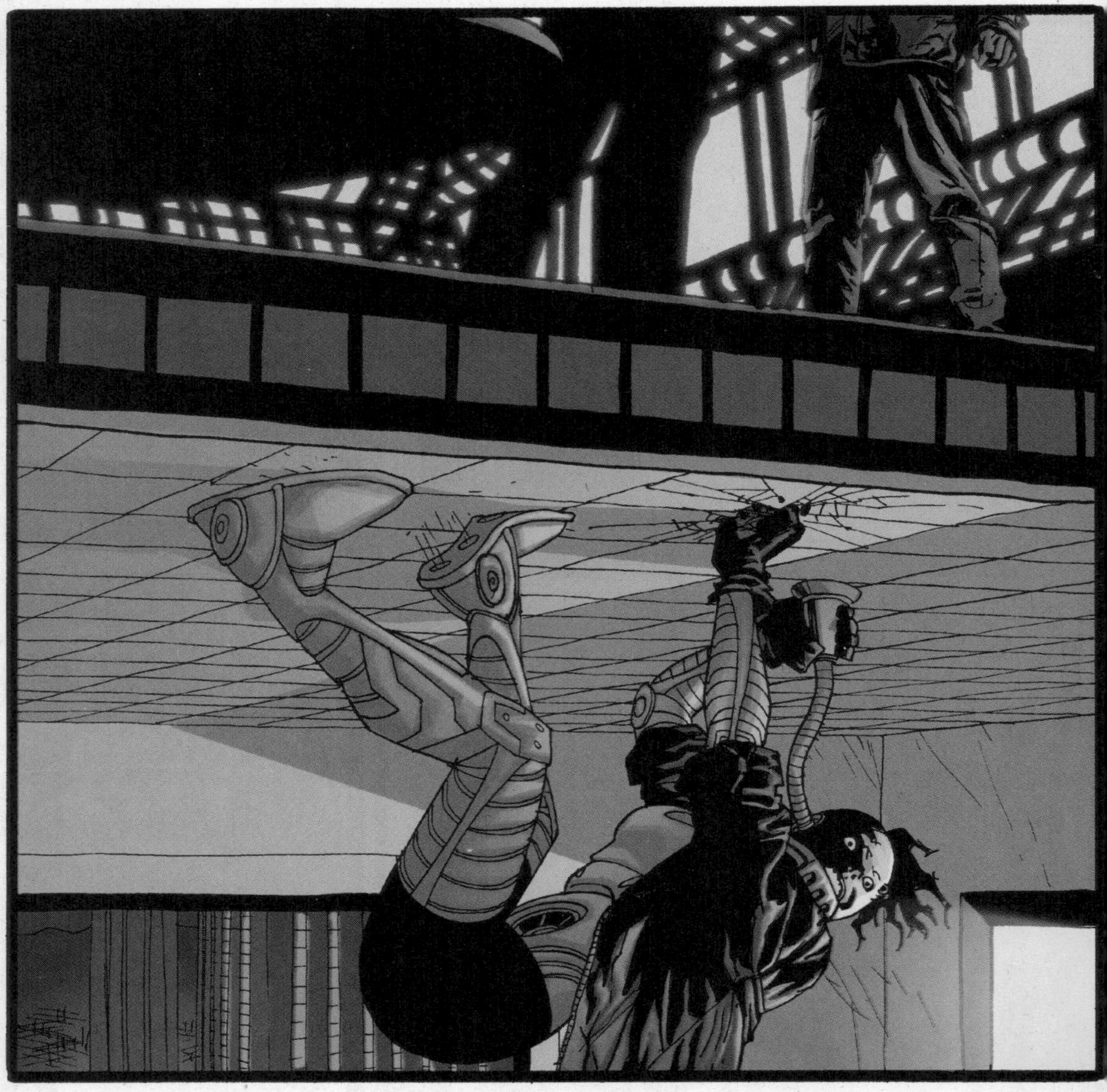

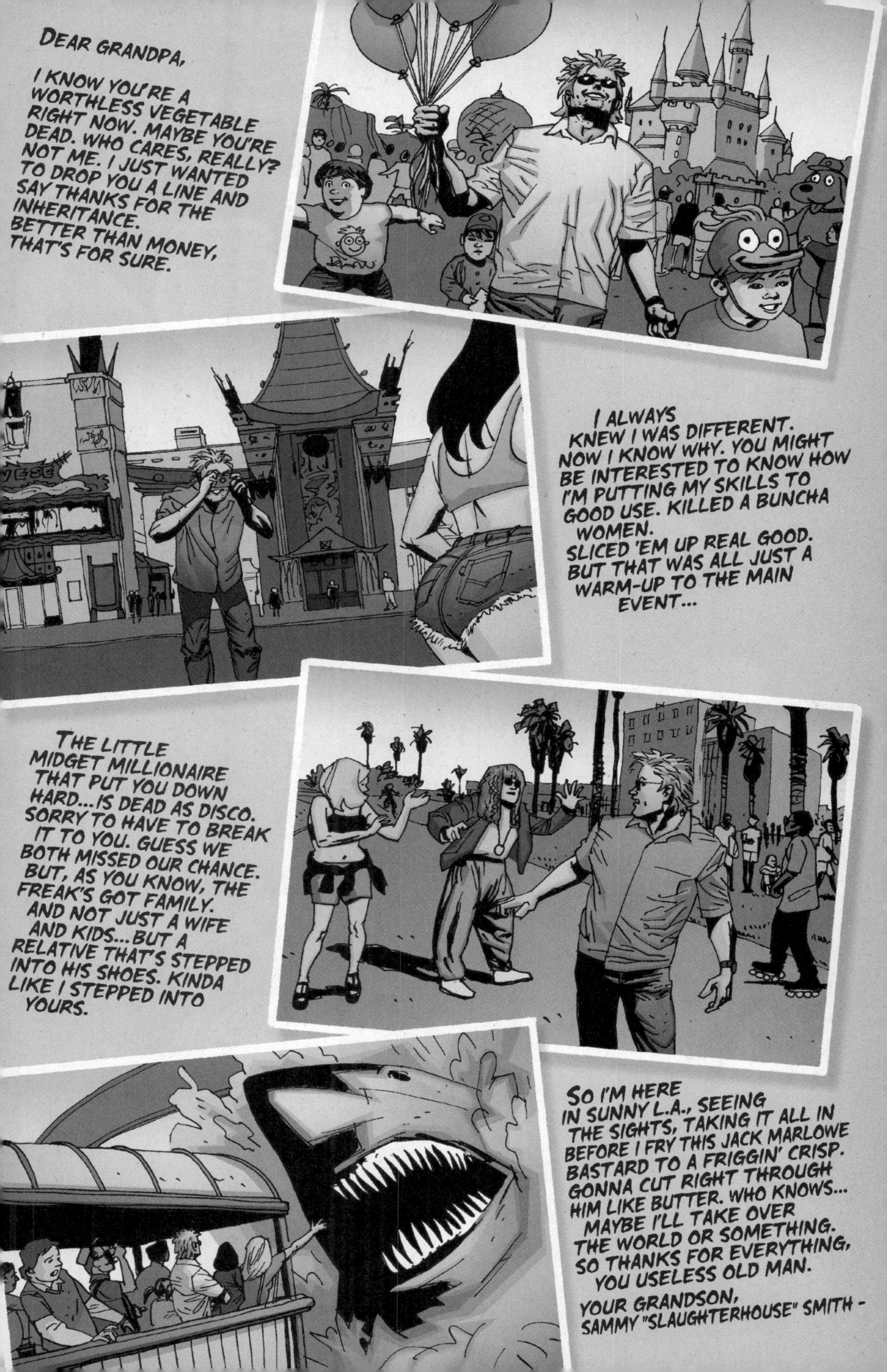
DEAR GRANDPA,
I KNOW YOU'RE A WORTHLESS VEGETABLE RIGHT NOW. MAYBE YOU'RE DEAD. WHO CARES, REALLY? NOT ME. I JUST WANTED TO DROP YOU A LINE AND SAY THANKS FOR THE INHERITANCE. BETTER THAN MONEY, THAT'S FOR SURE.
I ALWAYS KNEW I WAS DIFFERENT. NOW I KNOW WHY. YOU MIGHT BE INTERESTED TO KNOW HOW I'M PUTTING MY SKILLS TO GOOD USE. KILLED A BUNCHA WOMEN. SLICED 'EM UP REAL GOOD. BUT THAT WAS ALL JUST A WARM-UP TO THE MAIN EVENT...
THE LITTLE MIDGET MILLIONAIRE THAT PUT YOU DOWN HARD...IS DEAD AS DISCO. SORRY TO HAVE TO BREAK IT TO YOU. GUESS WE BOTH MISSED OUR CHANCE. BUT, AS YOU KNOW, THE FREAK'S GOT FAMILY. AND NOT JUST A WIFE AND KIDS...BUT A RELATIVE THAT'S STEPPED INTO HIS SHOES. KINDA LIKE I STEPPED INTO YOURS.
SO I'M HERE IN SUNNY L.A., SEEING THE SIGHTS, TAKING IT ALL IN BEFORE I FRY THIS JACK MARLOWE BASTARD TO A FRIGGIN' CRISP. GONNA CUT RIGHT THROUGH HIM LIKE BUTTER. WHO KNOWS... MAYBE I'LL TAKE OVER THE WORLD OR SOMETHING. SO THANKS FOR EVERYTHING, YOU USELESS OLD MAN.
YOUR GRANDSON,
SAMMY "SLAUGHTERHOUSE" SMITH -

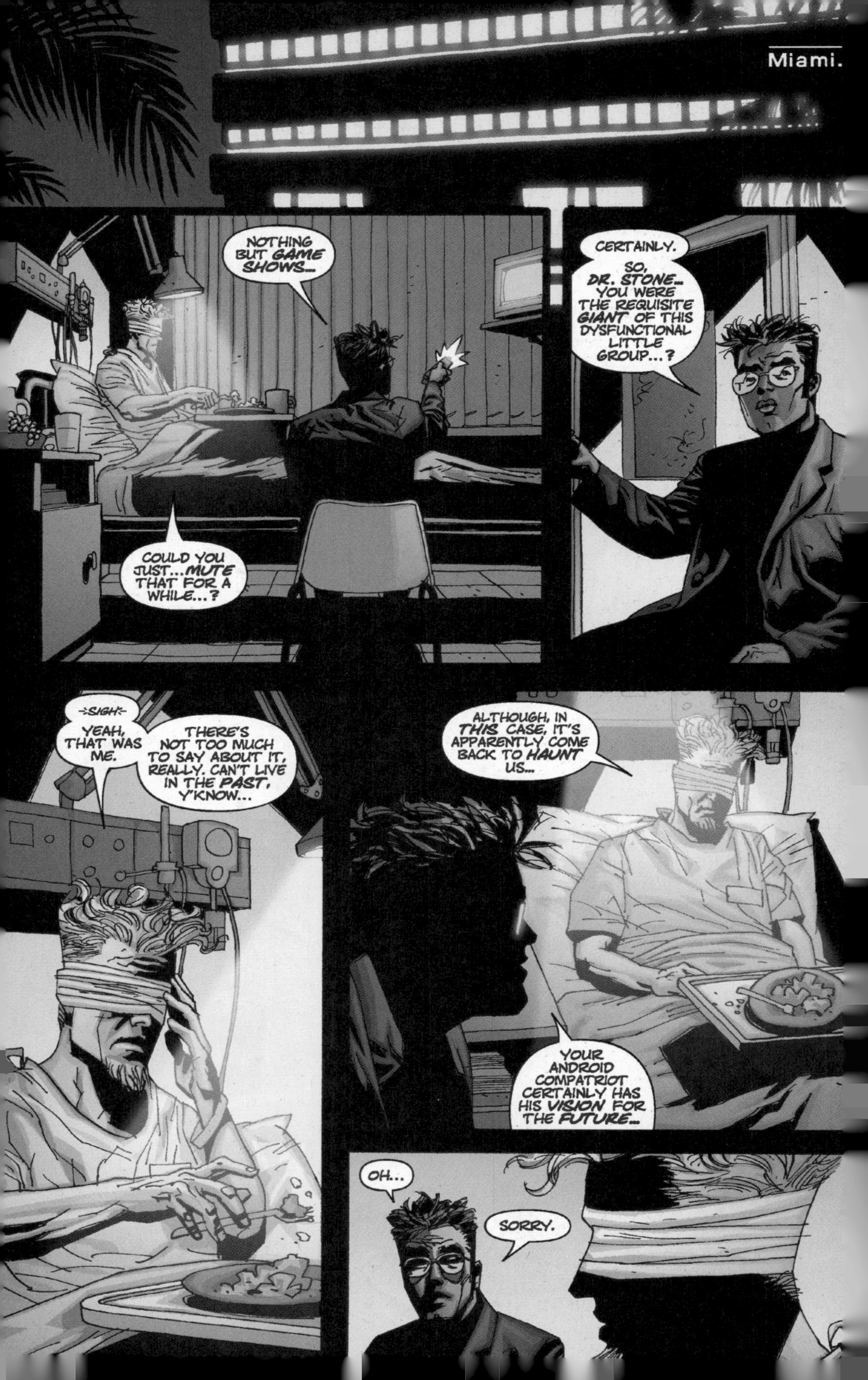
Miami.
NOTHING BUT GAME SHOWS...
COULD YOU JUST...MUTE THAT FOR A WHILE...?
CERTAINLY.
SO, DR. STONE... YOU WERE THE REQUISITE GIANT OF THIS DYSFUNCTIONAL LITTLE GROUP...?
-SIGH-
YEAH, THAT WAS ME.
THERE'S NOT TOO MUCH TO SAY ABOUT IT, REALLY. CAN'T LIVE IN THE PAST, Y'KNOW...
ALTHOUGH, IN THIS CASE, IT'S APPARENTLY COME BACK TO HAUNT US...
YOUR ANDROID COMPATRIOT CERTAINLY HAS HIS VISION FOR THE FUTURE...
OH...
SORRY.

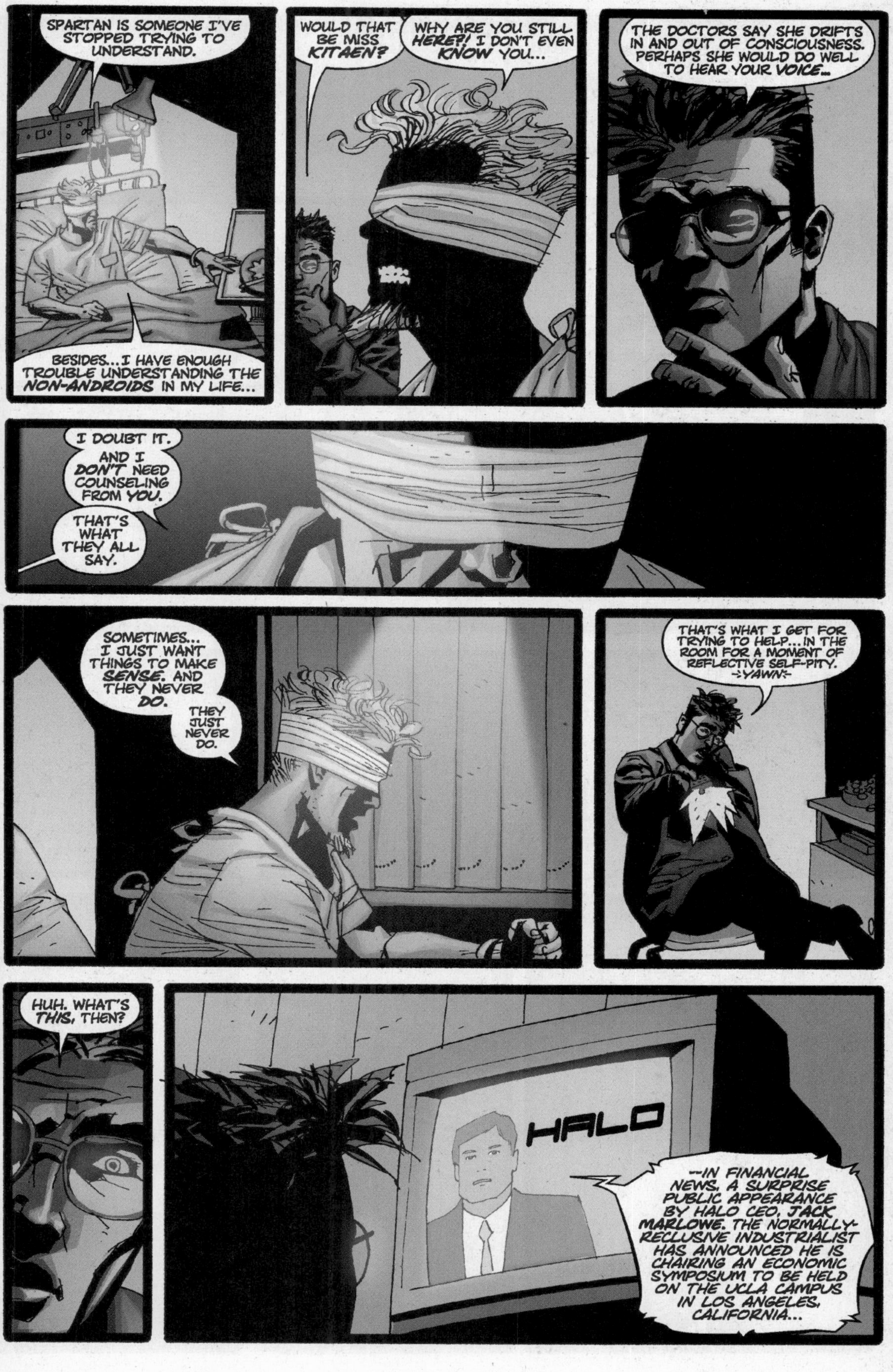
SPARTAN IS SOMEONE I'VE STOPPED TRYING TO UNDERSTAND.
BESIDES... I HAVE ENOUGH TROUBLE UNDERSTANDING THE NON-ANDROIDS IN MY LIFE...
WOULD THAT BE MISS KITAEN?
WHY ARE YOU STILL HERE?! I DON'T EVEN KNOW YOU...
THE DOCTORS SAY SHE DRIFTS IN AND OUT OF CONSCIOUSNESS. PERHAPS SHE WOULD DO WELL TO HEAR YOUR VOICE...
I DOUBT IT.
AND I DON'T NEED COUNSELING FROM YOU.
THAT'S WHAT THEY ALL SAY.
SOMETIMES... I JUST WANT THINGS TO MAKE SENSE. AND THEY NEVER DO.
THEY JUST NEVER DO.
THAT'S WHAT I GET FOR TRYING TO HELP... IN THE ROOM FOR A MOMENT OF REFLECTIVE SELF-PITY.
-YAWN-
HUH. WHAT'S THIS, THEN?
HALO
--IN FINANCIAL NEWS, A SURPRISE PUBLIC APPEARANCE BY HALO CEO, JACK MARLOWE. THE NORMALLY-RECLUSIVE INDUSTRIALIST HAS ANNOUNCED HE IS CHAIRING AN ECONOMIC SYMPOSIUM TO BE HELD ON THE UCLA CAMPUS IN LOS ANGELES, CALIFORNIA...

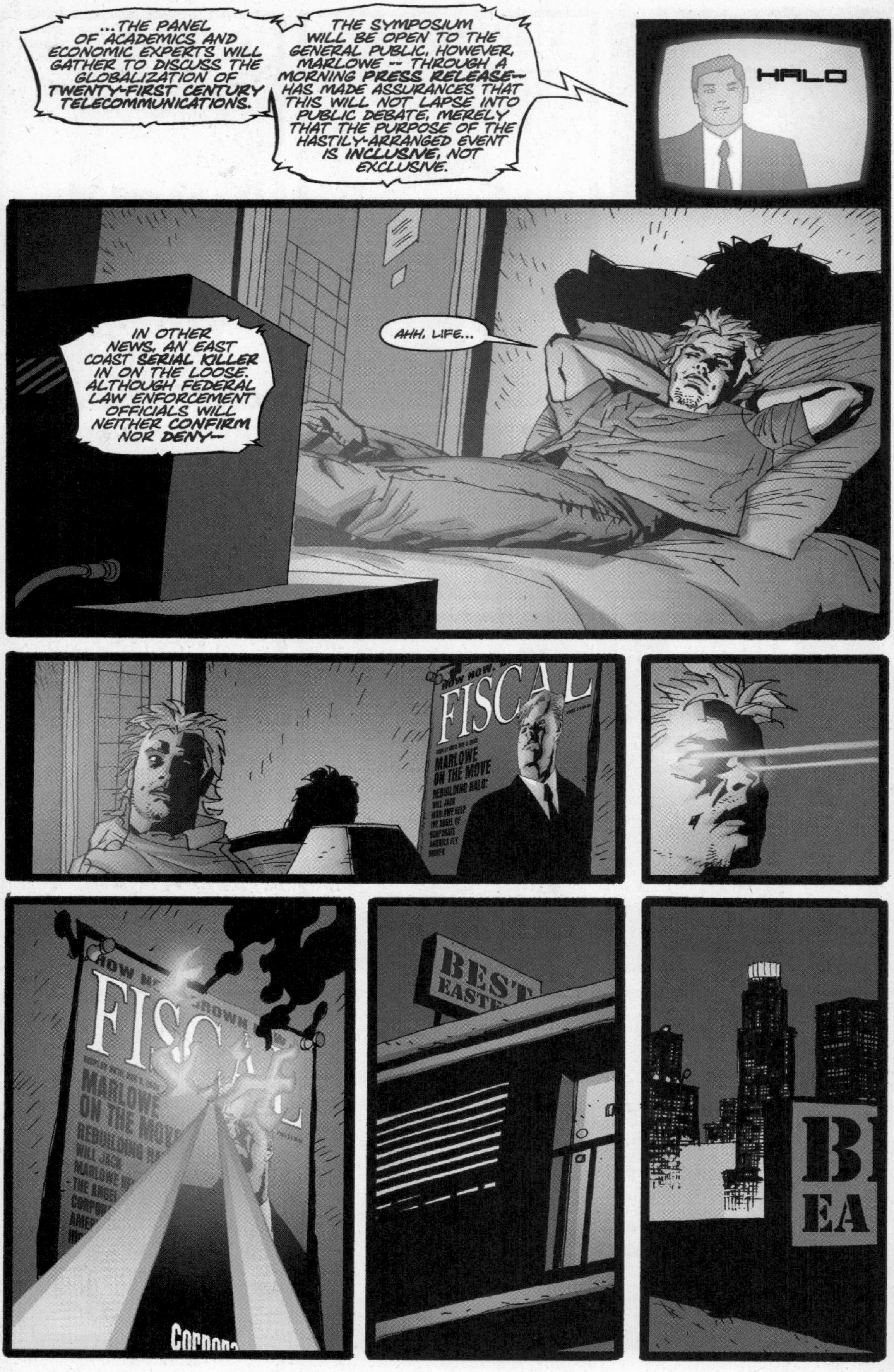
...THE PANEL OF ACADEMICS AND ECONOMIC EXPERTS WILL GATHER TO DISCUSS THE GLOBALIZATION OF TWENTY-FIRST CENTURY TELECOMMUNICATIONS.
THE SYMPOSIUM WILL BE OPEN TO THE GENERAL PUBLIC, HOWEVER, MARLOWE -- THROUGH A MORNING PRESS RELEASE-- HAS MADE ASSURANCES THAT THIS WILL NOT LAPSE INTO PUBLIC DEBATE, MERELY THAT THE PURPOSE OF THE HASTILY-ARRANGED EVENT IS INCLUSIVE, NOT EXCLUSIVE.
HALO
IN OTHER NEWS, AN EAST COAST SERIAL KILLER IN ON THE LOOSE. ALTHOUGH FEDERAL LAW ENFORCEMENT OFFICIALS WILL NEITHER CONFIRM NOR DENY--
AHH, LIFE...
FISCAL
MARLOWE ON THE MOVE
BEST

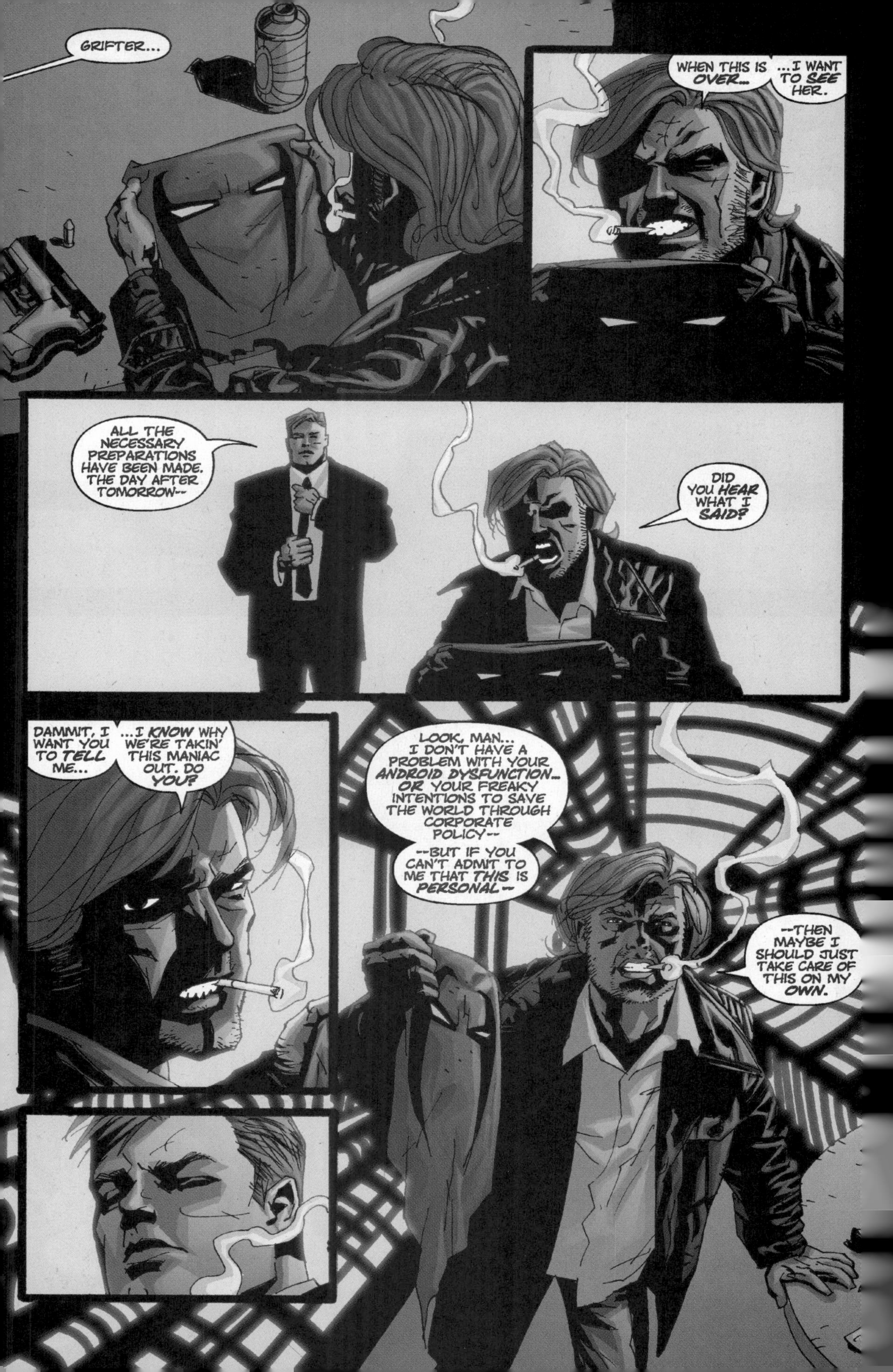
GRIFTER...
WHEN THIS IS OVER...
...I WANT TO SEE HER.
ALL THE NECESSARY PREPARATIONS HAVE BEEN MADE. THE DAY AFTER TOMORROW--
DID YOU HEAR WHAT I SAID?
DAMMIT, I WANT YOU TO TELL ME...
...I KNOW WHY WE'RE TAKIN' THIS MANIAC OUT. DO YOU?
LOOK, MAN... I DON'T HAVE A PROBLEM WITH YOUR ANDROID DYSFUNCTION... OR YOUR FREAKY INTENTIONS TO SAVE THE WORLD THROUGH CORPORATE POLICY--
--BUT IF YOU CAN'T ADMIT TO ME THAT THIS IS PERSONAL--
--THEN MAYBE I SHOULD JUST TAKE CARE OF THIS ON MY OWN.

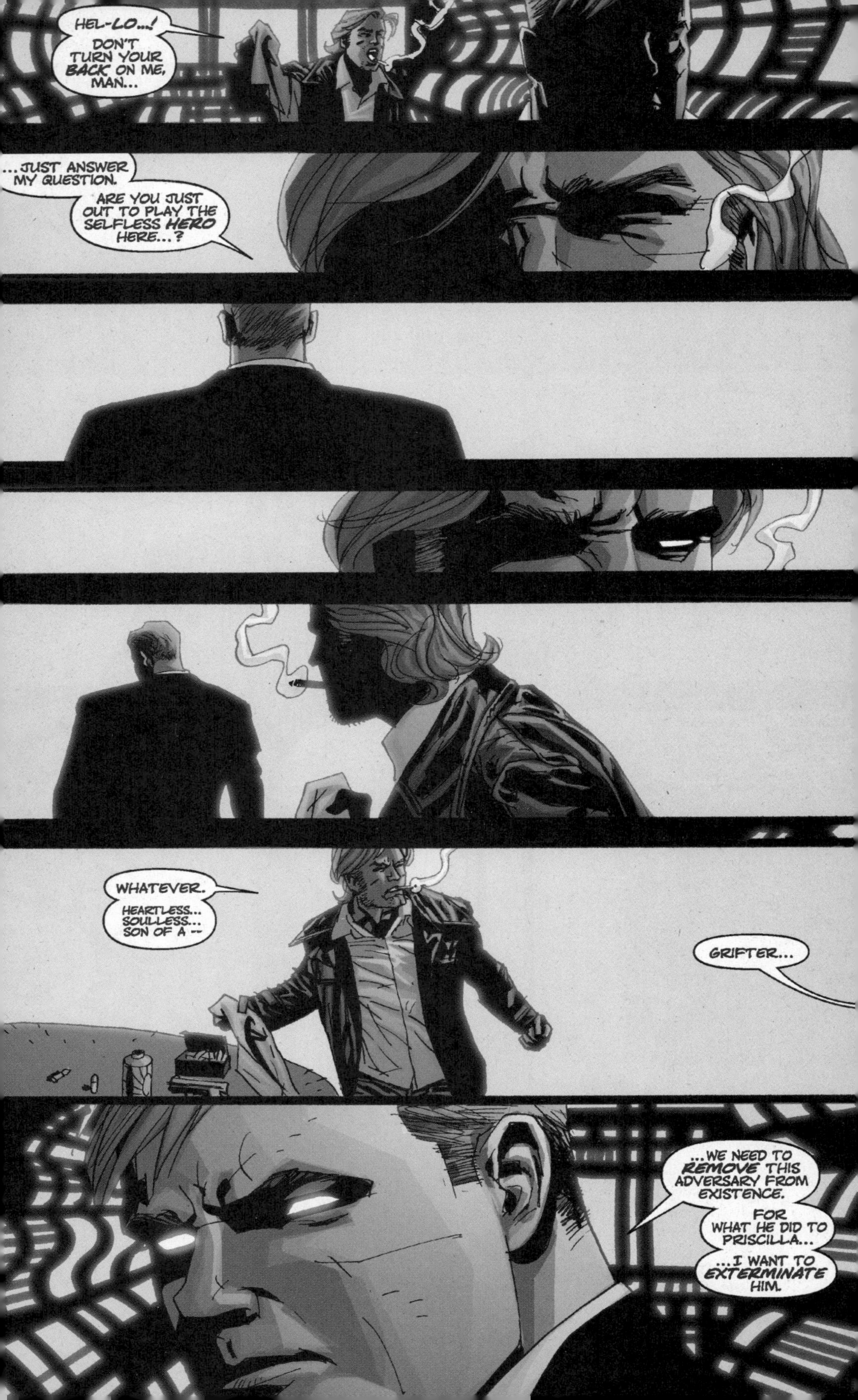
HEL-LO...! DON'T TURN YOUR BACK ON ME, MAN...
...JUST ANSWER MY QUESTION.
ARE YOU JUST OUT TO PLAY THE SELFLESS HERO HERE...?
WHATEVER.
HEARTLESS... SOULLESS... SON OF A --
GRIFTER...
...WE NEED TO REMOVE THIS ADVERSARY FROM EXISTENCE.
FOR WHAT HE DID TO PRISCILLA...
...I WANT TO EXTERMINATE HIM.

FIREWALL ONLINE DIRECTORY
SEARCH | DISCOUNTS | LINKS | CONTACT
COMFORTABLE INN
"We put you in the zone"
HOLLYWOOD HOTELS
MARINA BAY Hotels & Suites
"The Pacific at your window"
Wyatt Hotels & Resorts
WYATT Hotels & Resorts
"Feel the WYATT touch"
FIREWALL ONLINE DIRECTORY
SEARCH | DISCOUNTS | LINKS | CONTACT
BEST EASTERN
BEST EASTERN
Los Angeles County>
Guest Registration>
Search:
Smith, S.
SEARCHING
ZZZZ
ZZZZZZZT
KRAK KRAK

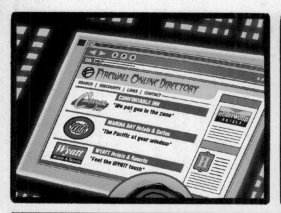

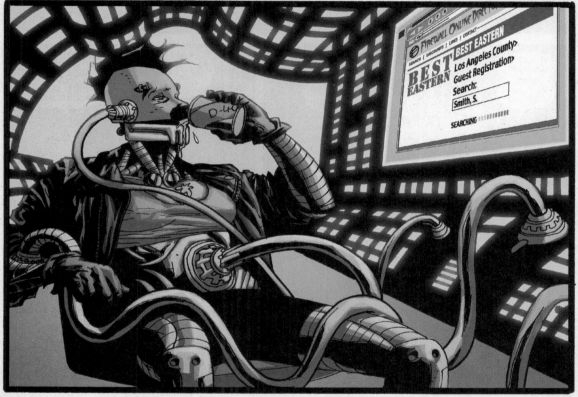

HERE WE ARE... THE HONEYMOON SUITE...

HMMM...

BIG SPENDER. BEEN IN TOWN LONG...?

COUPLA DAYS. L.A.'S BIG IN MY SALES REGION.

HEY... ...THIS DUMP AIN'T REALLY WHERE YOU'RE STAYING, IS IT...?

HELL, NO. I'M AT THE AIRPORT HILTON. I GOT THIS PLACE YESTERDAY UNDER ANOTHER NAME... FOR JUST SUCH AN OCCASION.

WELL, SINCE WE'VE ALREADY SET THE PRICE...SHALL WE GET ON WITH IT, BIG MAN...?

WELL SAID.

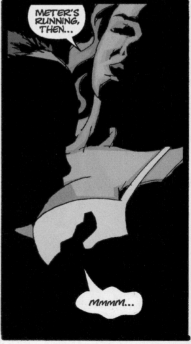

METER'S RUNNING, THEN...

MMMM...

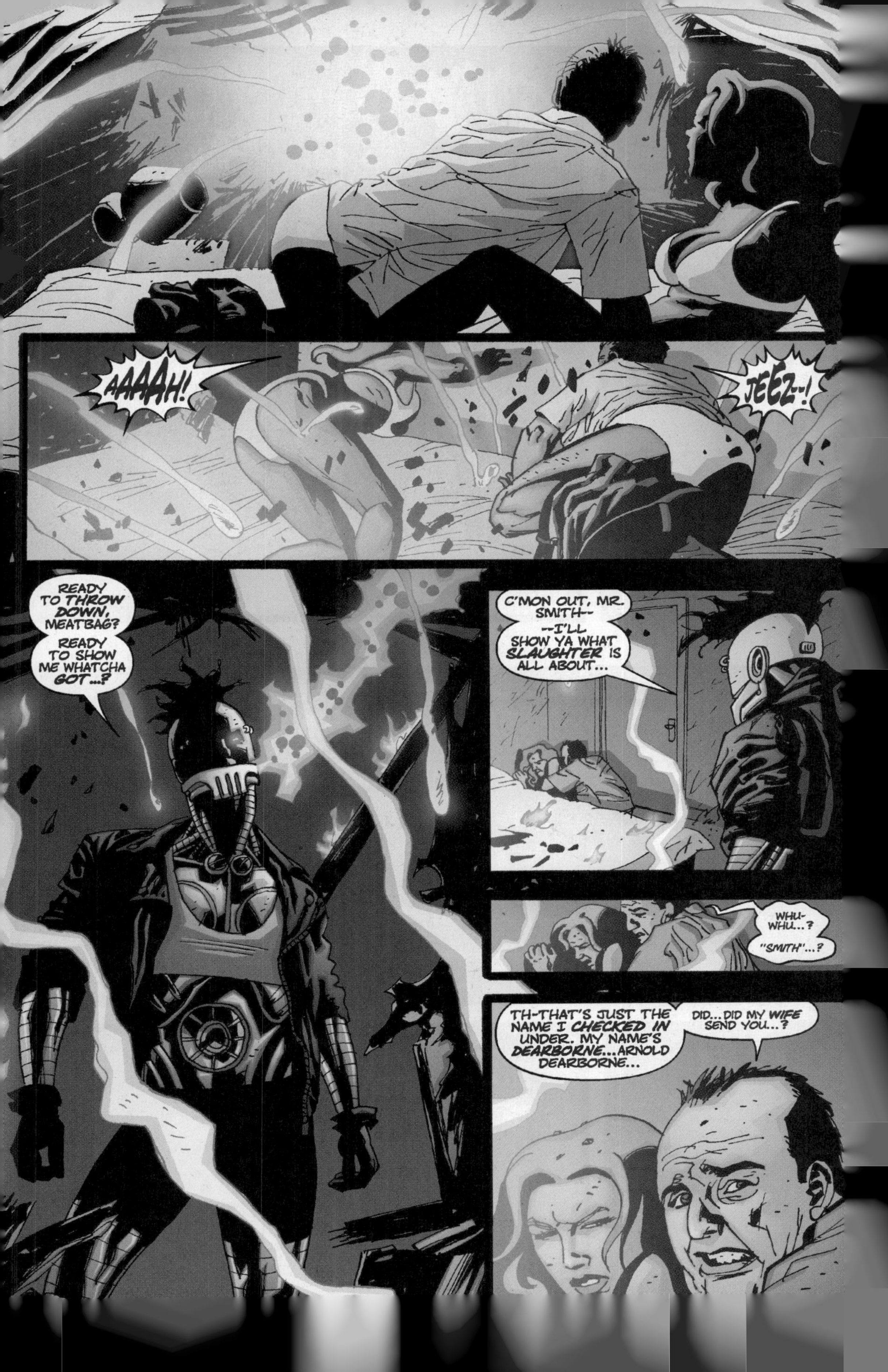
AAAAH!
JEEZ--!
READY TO THROW DOWN, MEATBAG?
READY TO SHOW ME WHATCHA GOT...?
C'MON OUT, MR. SMITH--
--I'LL SHOW YA WHAT SLAUGHTER IS ALL ABOUT...
WHU-WHU...?
"SMITH"...?
TH-THAT'S JUST THE NAME I CHECKED IN UNDER. MY NAME'S DEARBORNE...ARNOLD DEARBORNE...
DID...DID MY WIFE SEND YOU...?

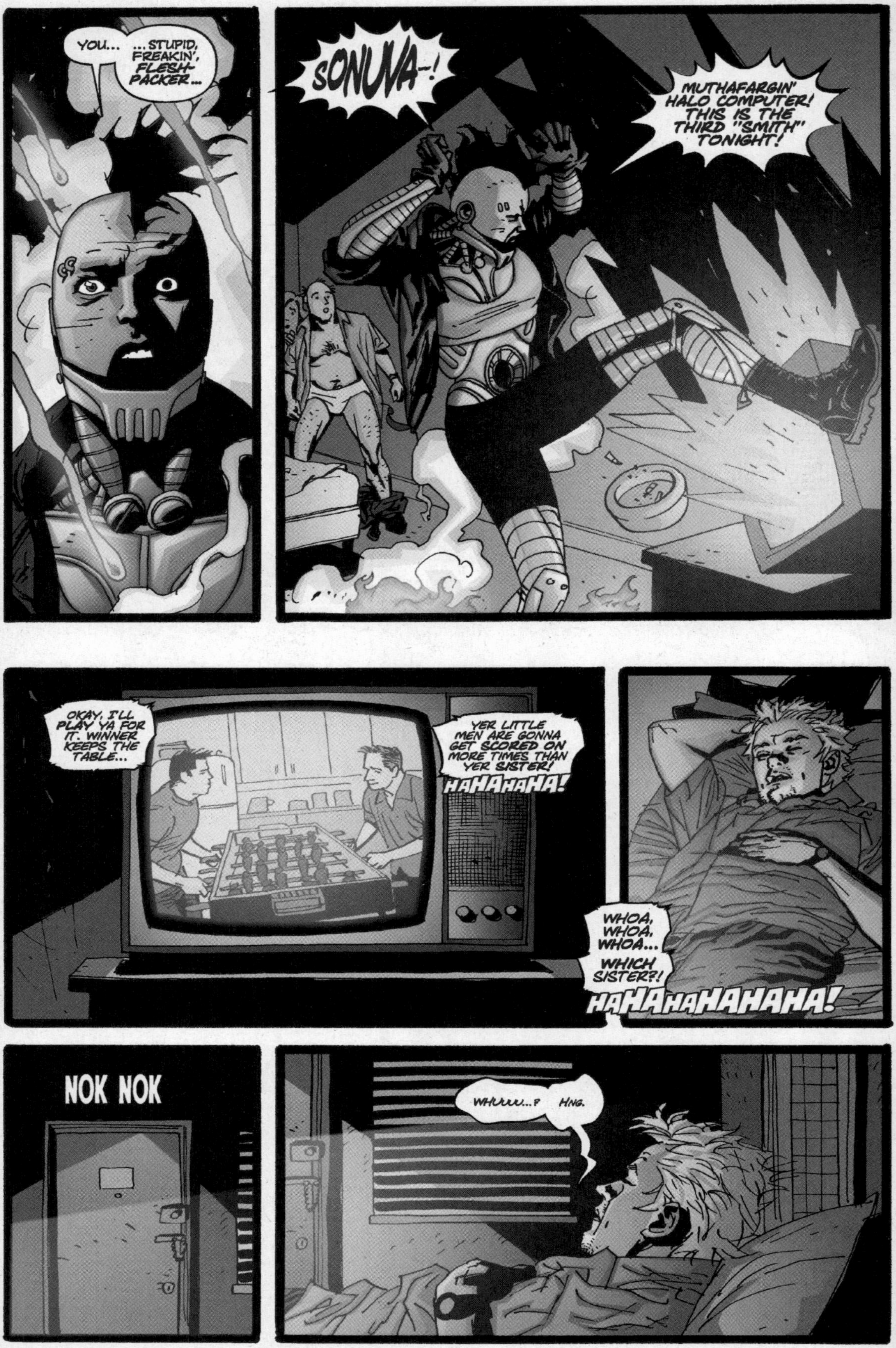
YOU... ...STUPID, FREAKIN', FLESH-PACKER...
SONUVA-!
MUTHAFARGIN' HALO COMPUTER! THIS IS THE THIRD "SMITH" TONIGHT!
OKAY, I'LL PLAY YA FOR IT. WINNER KEEPS THE TABLE...
YER LITTLE MEN ARE GONNA GET SCORED ON MORE TIMES THAN YER SISTER!
HAHAHAHA!
WHOA, WHOA, WHOA... WHICH SISTER?!
HAHAHAHAHAHA!
NOK NOK
WHUUU...? HNG.

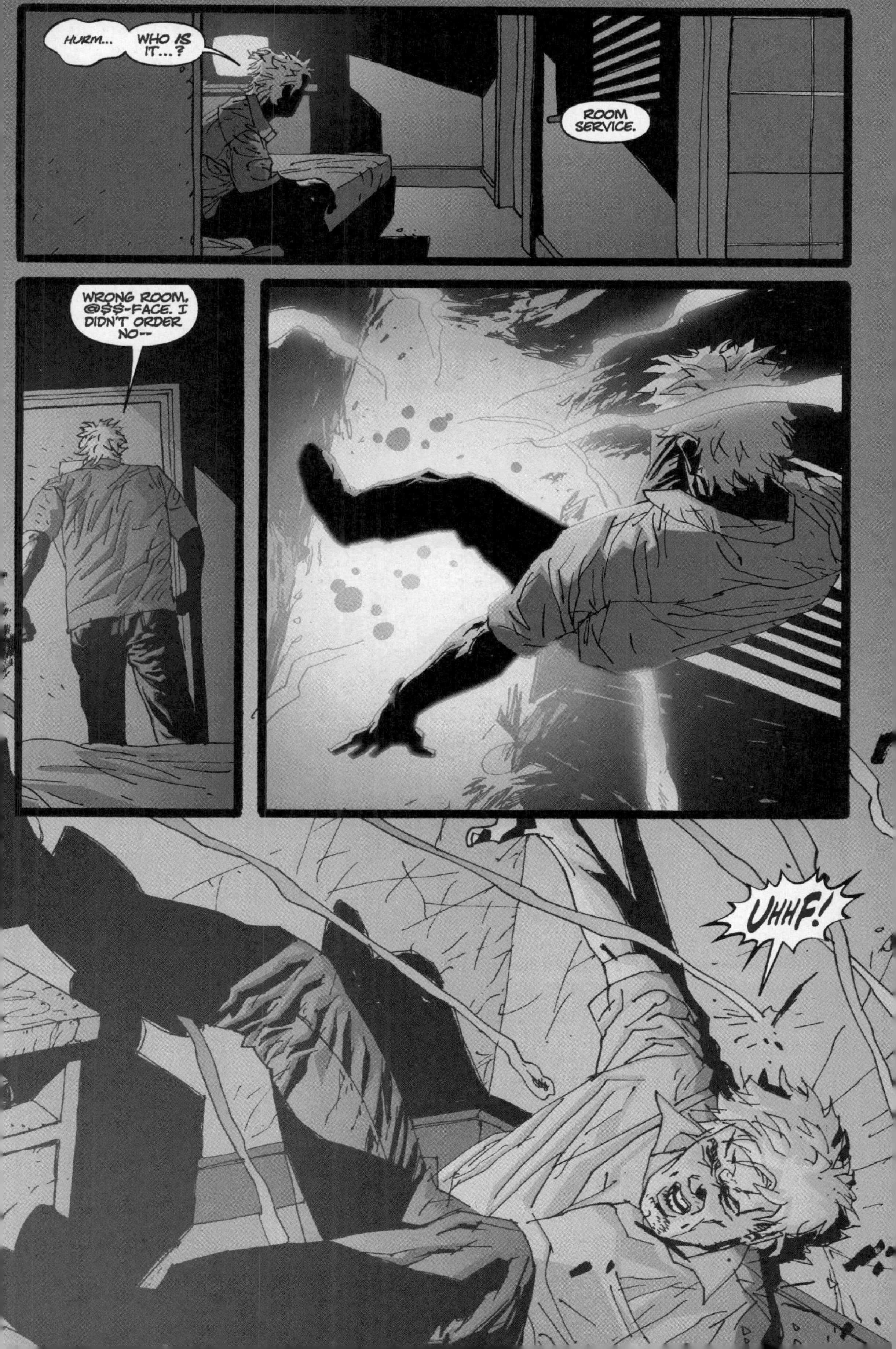
HURM...
WHO IS IT...?
ROOM SERVICE.
WRONG ROOM, @$$-FACE. I DIDN'T ORDER NO--
UHHF!

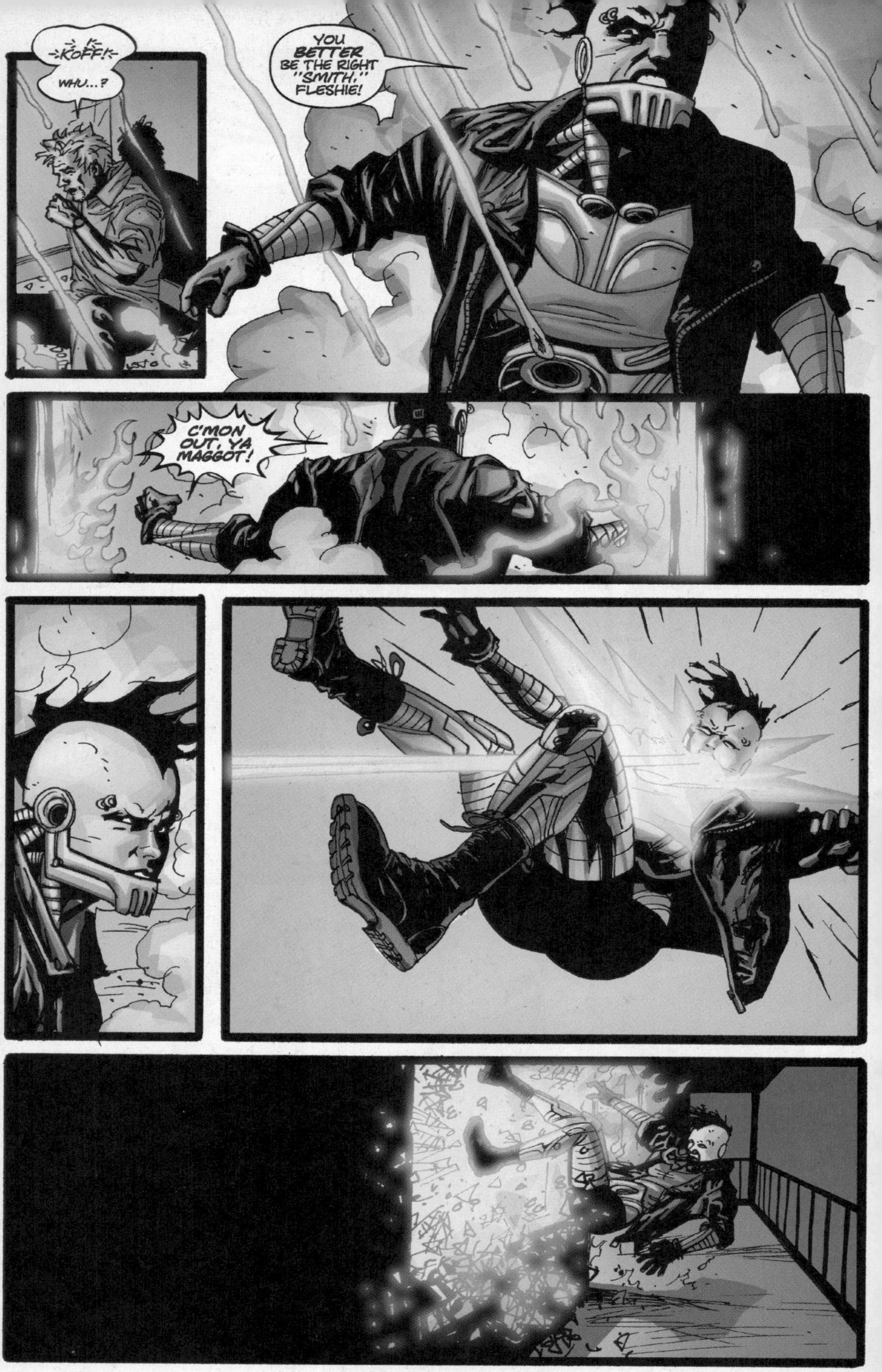

-KOFF!-
WHU...?
YOU BETTER BE THE RIGHT "SMITH," FLESHIE!
C'MON OUT, YA MAGGOT!

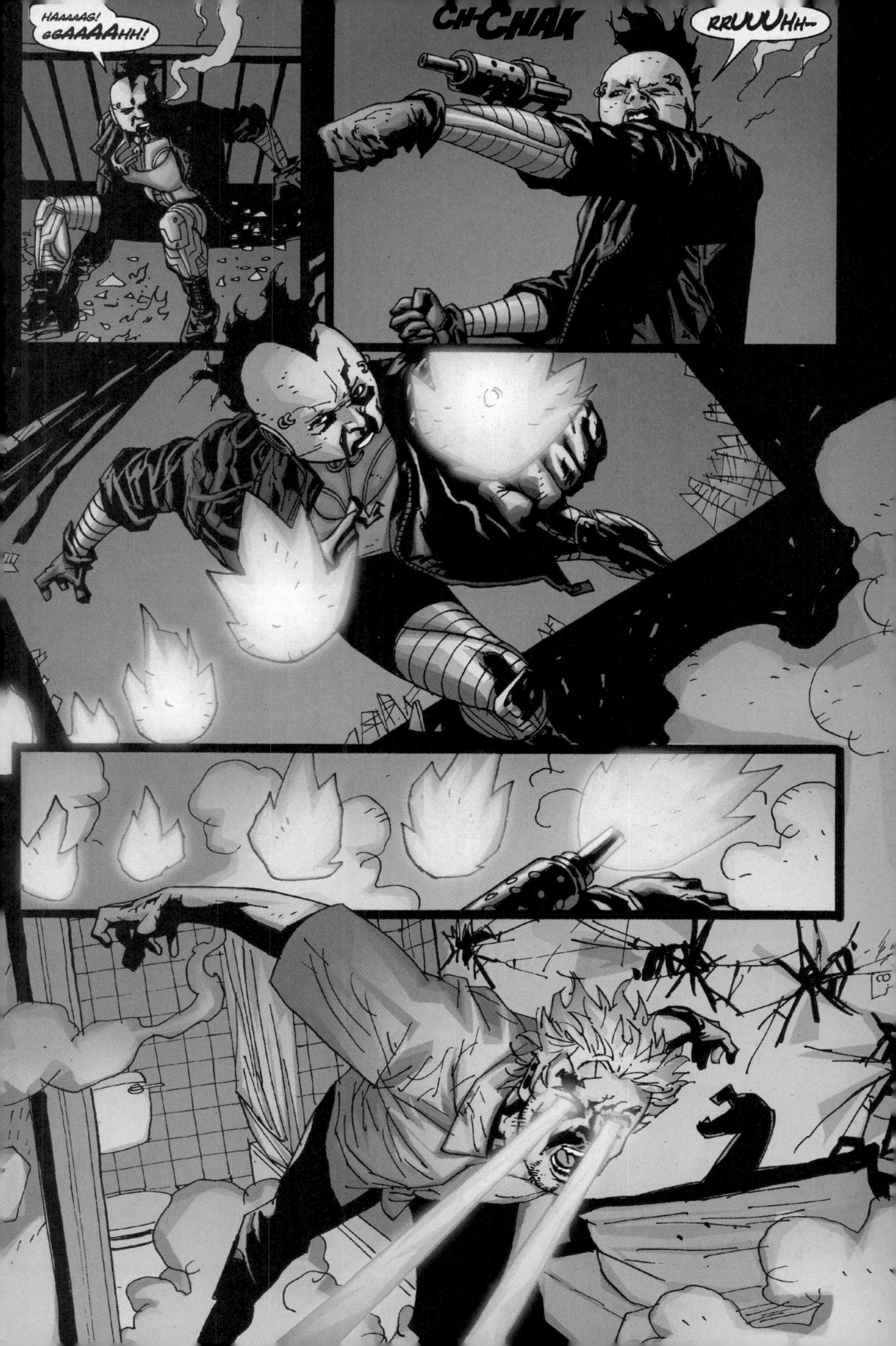

HAAAAAG! GGAAAAAHH!
CH-CHAK
RRUUUHH--

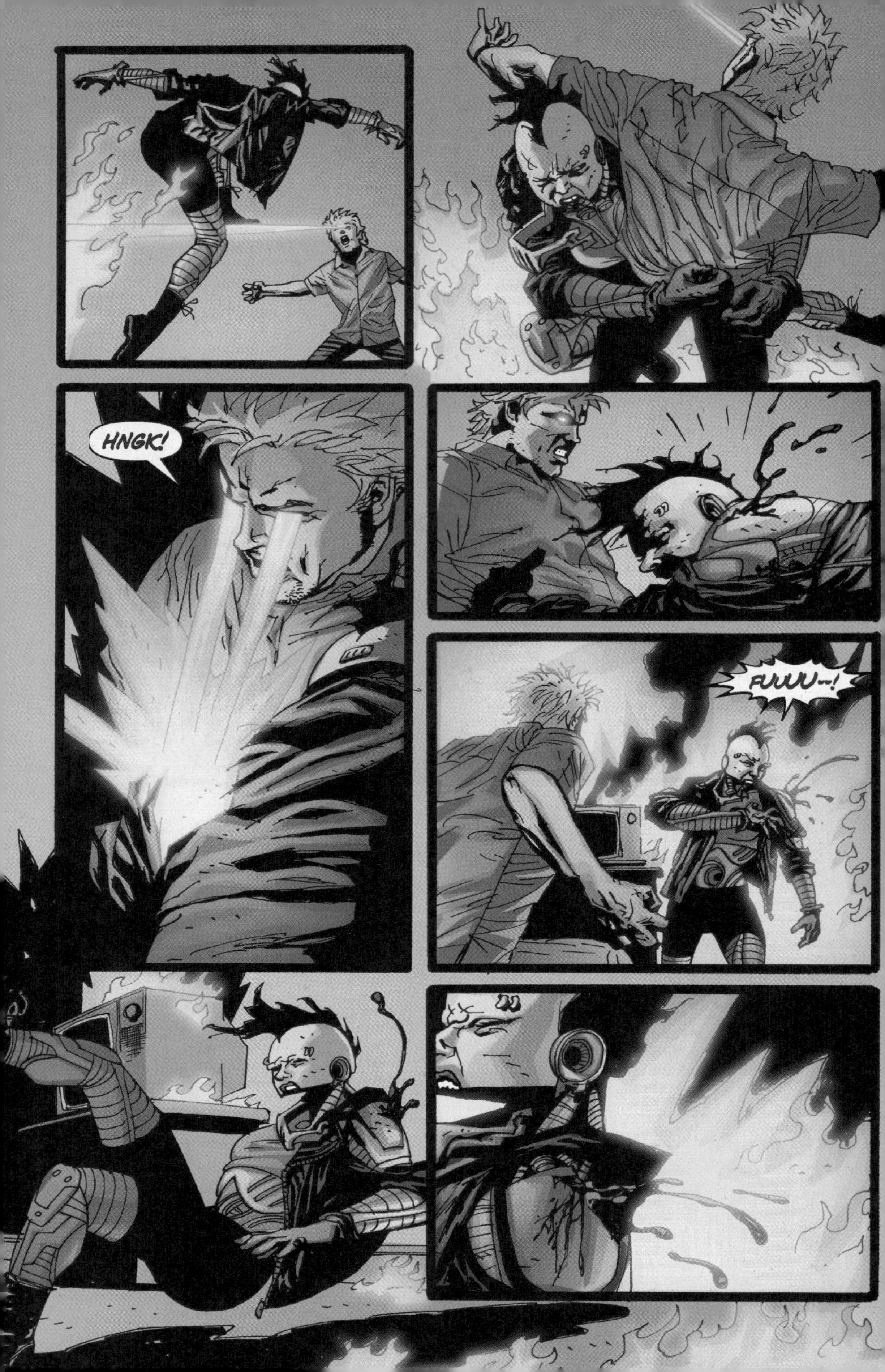
HNGK!
FUUUU--!

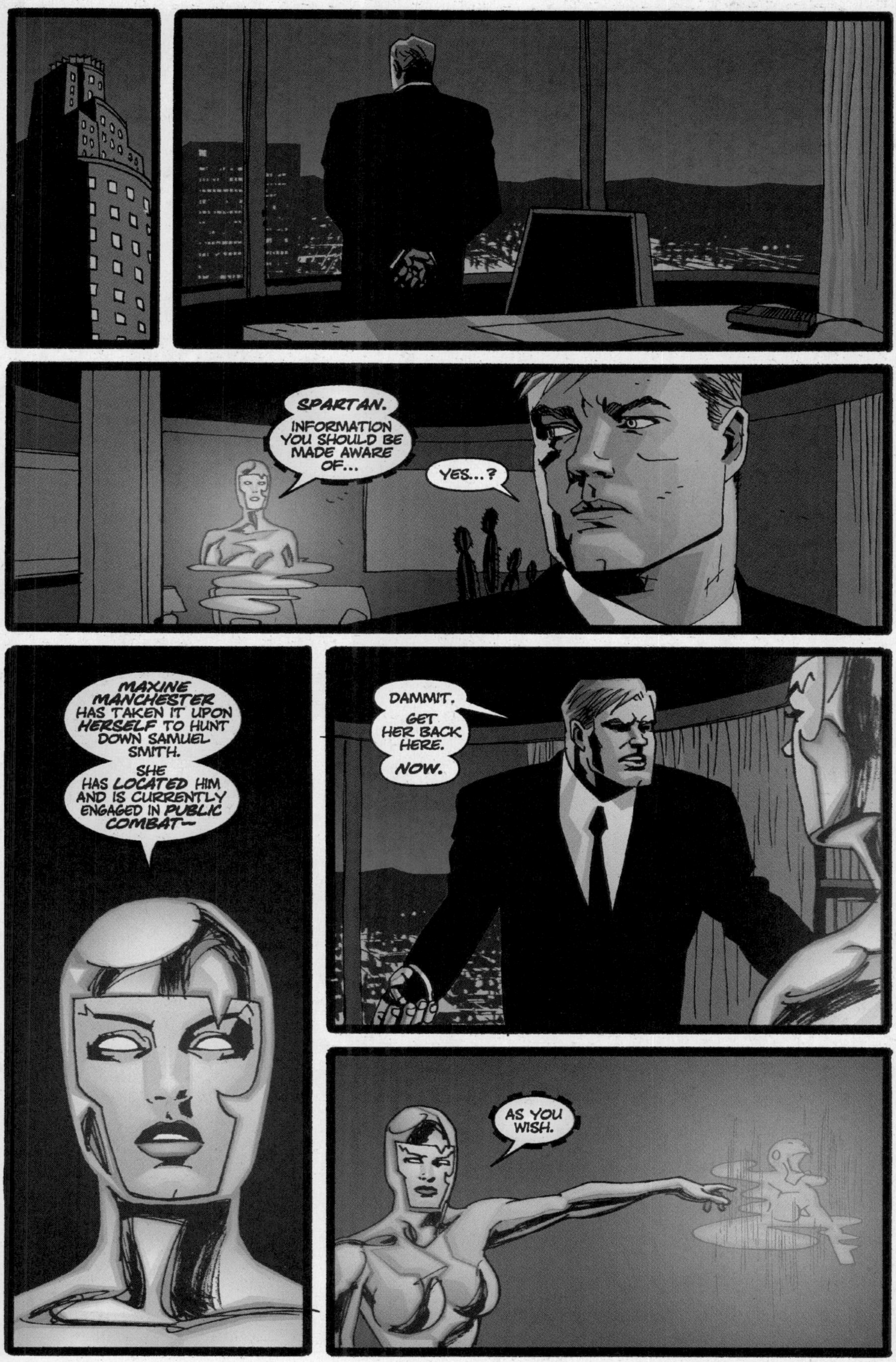

SPARTAN.
INFORMATION YOU SHOULD BE MADE AWARE OF...
YES...?
MAXINE MANCHESTER HAS TAKEN IT UPON HERSELF TO HUNT DOWN SAMUEL SMITH.
SHE HAS LOCATED HIM AND IS CURRENTLY ENGAGED IN PUBLIC COMBAT--
DAMMIT.
GET HER BACK HERE.
NOW.
AS YOU WISH.

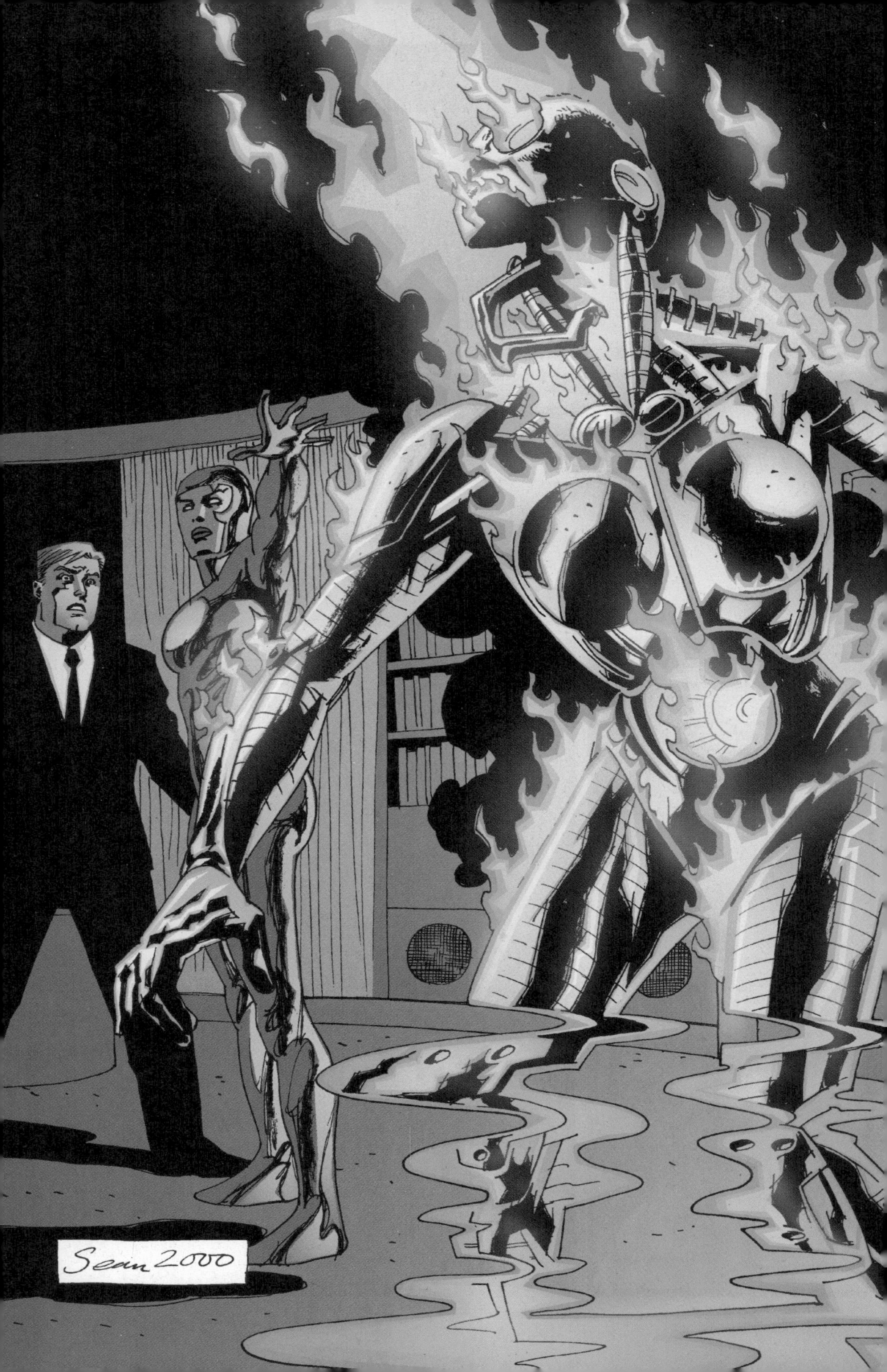
Sean 2000

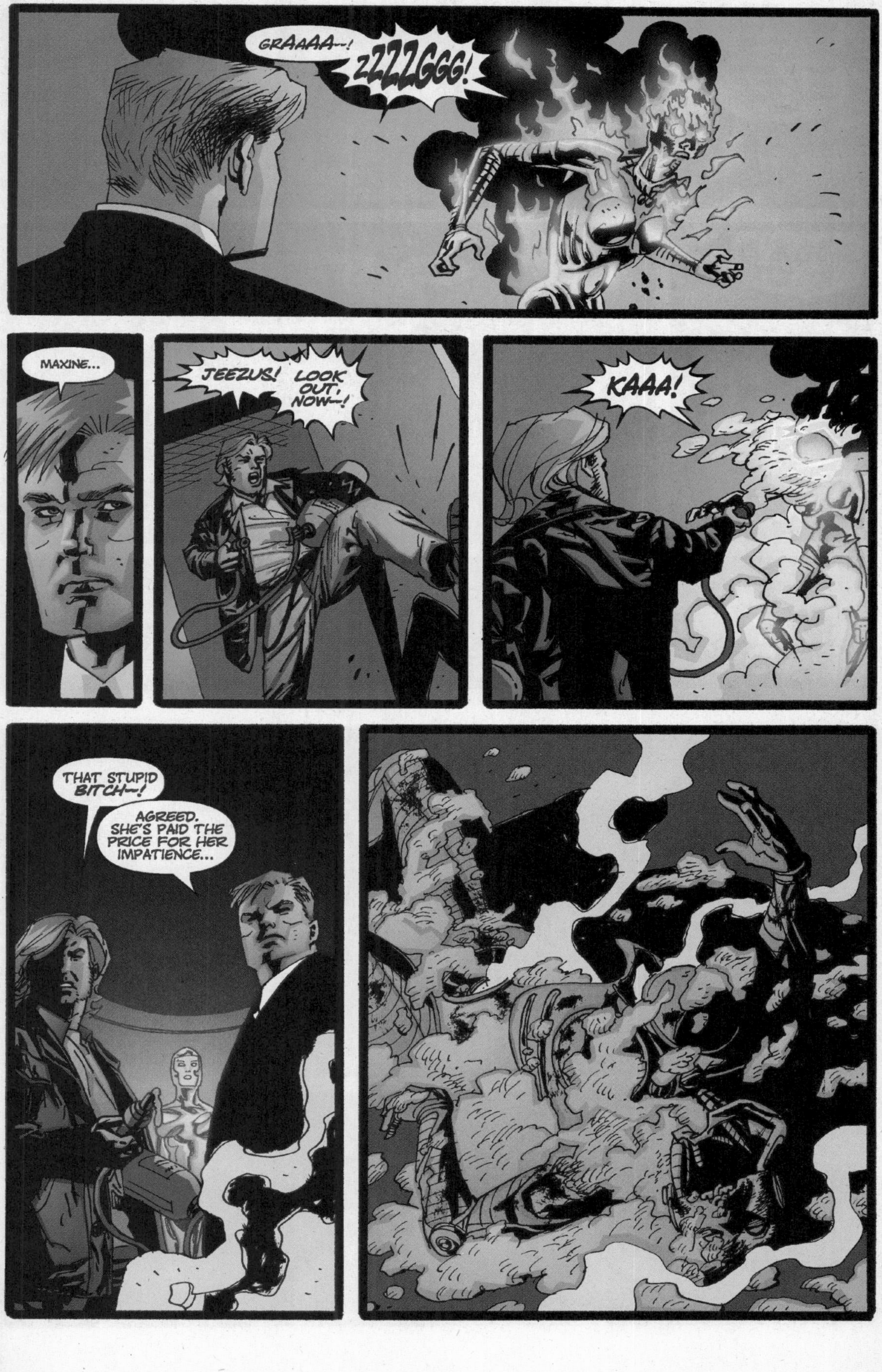
GRAAAA--!
ZZZZGGG!
MAXINE...
JEEZUS!
LOOK OUT. NOW--!
KAAA!
THAT STUPID BITCH--!
AGREED. SHE'S PAID THE PRICE FOR HER IMPATIENCE...

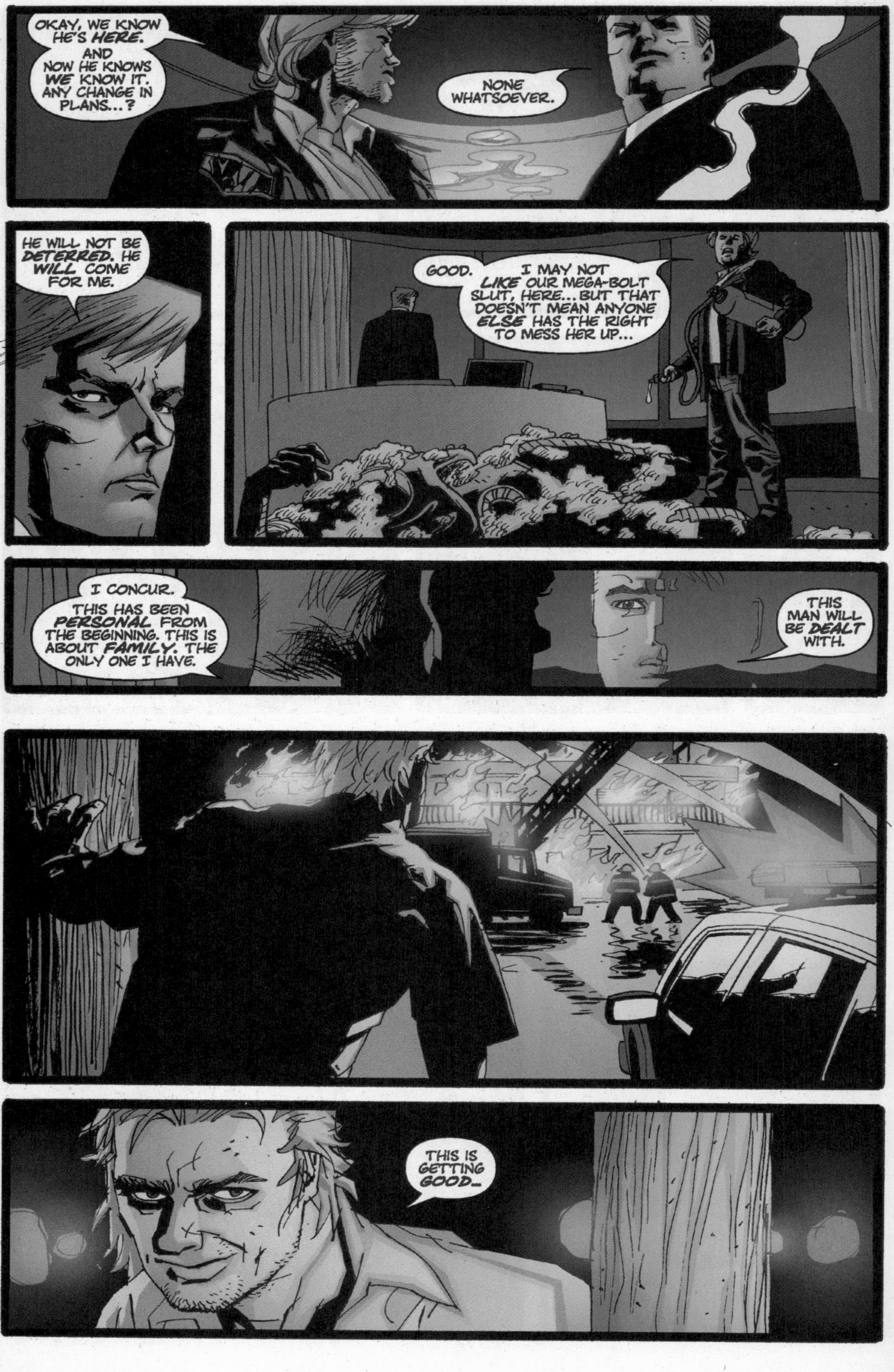
OKAY, WE KNOW HE'S HERE. AND NOW HE KNOWS WE KNOW IT. ANY CHANGE IN PLANS...?
NONE WHATSOEVER.
HE WILL NOT BE DETERRED. HE WILL COME FOR ME.
GOOD.
I MAY NOT LIKE OUR MEGA-BOLT SLUT, HERE... BUT THAT DOESN'T MEAN ANYONE ELSE HAS THE RIGHT TO MESS HER UP...
I CONCUR.
THIS HAS BEEN PERSONAL FROM THE BEGINNING. THIS IS ABOUT FAMILY. THE ONLY ONE I HAVE.
THIS MAN WILL BE DEALT WITH.
THIS IS GETTING GOOD...

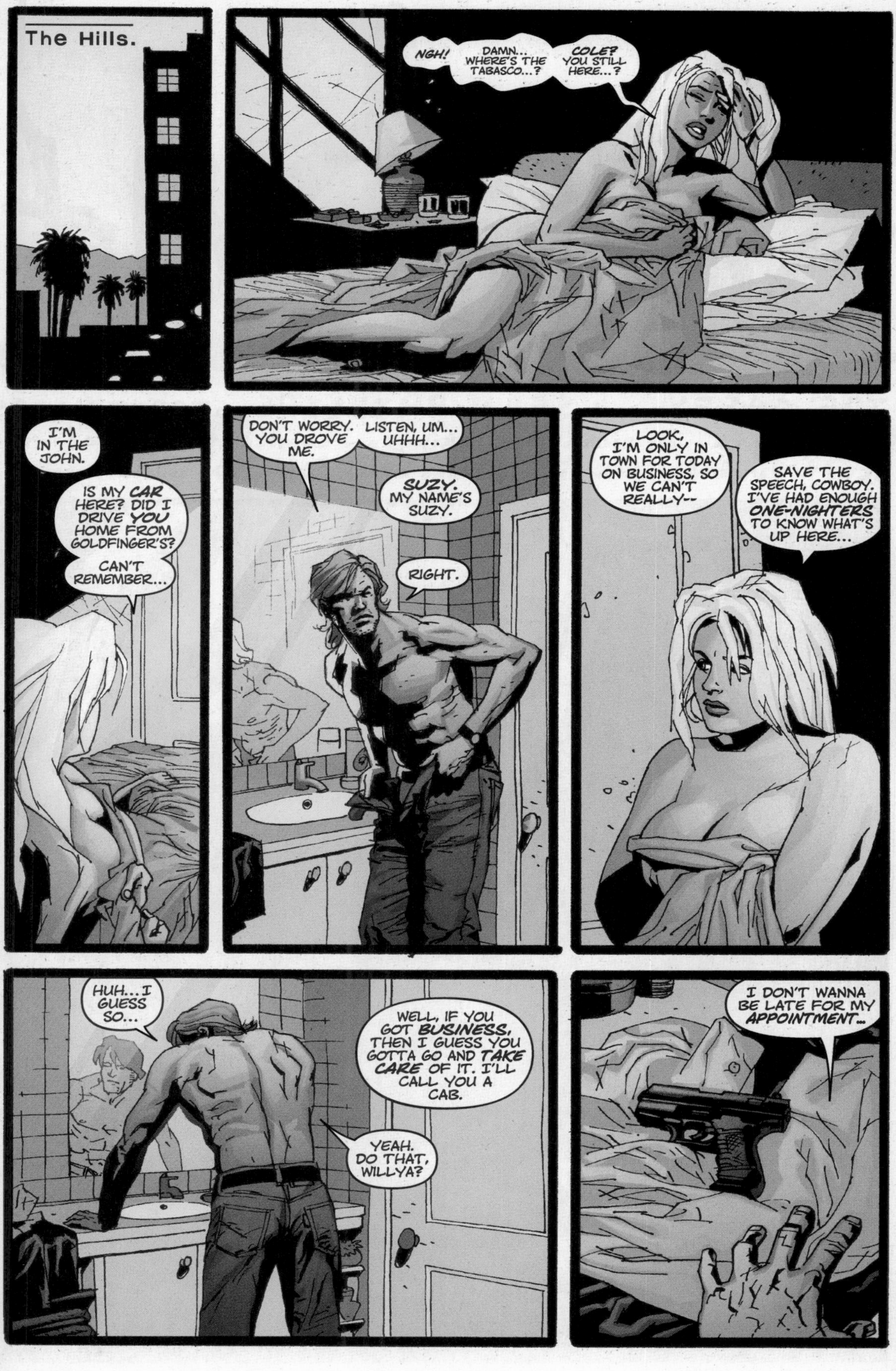
The Hills.
NGH!
DAMN... WHERE'S THE TABASCO...?
COLE? YOU STILL HERE...?
I'M IN THE JOHN.
IS MY CAR HERE? DID I DRIVE YOU HOME FROM GOLDFINGER'S?
CAN'T REMEMBER...
DON'T WORRY. YOU DROVE ME.
LISTEN, UM... UHHH...
SUZY. MY NAME'S SUZY.
RIGHT.
LOOK, I'M ONLY IN TOWN FOR TODAY ON BUSINESS, SO WE CAN'T REALLY--
SAVE THE SPEECH, COWBOY. I'VE HAD ENOUGH ONE-NIGHTERS TO KNOW WHAT'S UP HERE...
HUH... I GUESS SO...
WELL, IF YOU GOT BUSINESS, THEN I GUESS YOU GOTTA GO AND TAKE CARE OF IT. I'LL CALL YOU A CAB.
YEAH. DO THAT, WILLYA?
I DON'T WANNA BE LATE FOR MY APPOINTMENT...

Blowout

JOE CASEY and SEAN PHILLIPS storytellers
wildstorm fx colors Richard Starkings and Comicraft's Saida! letters
Scott Dunbier editor Jim Lee and Brandon Choi wildcats creators

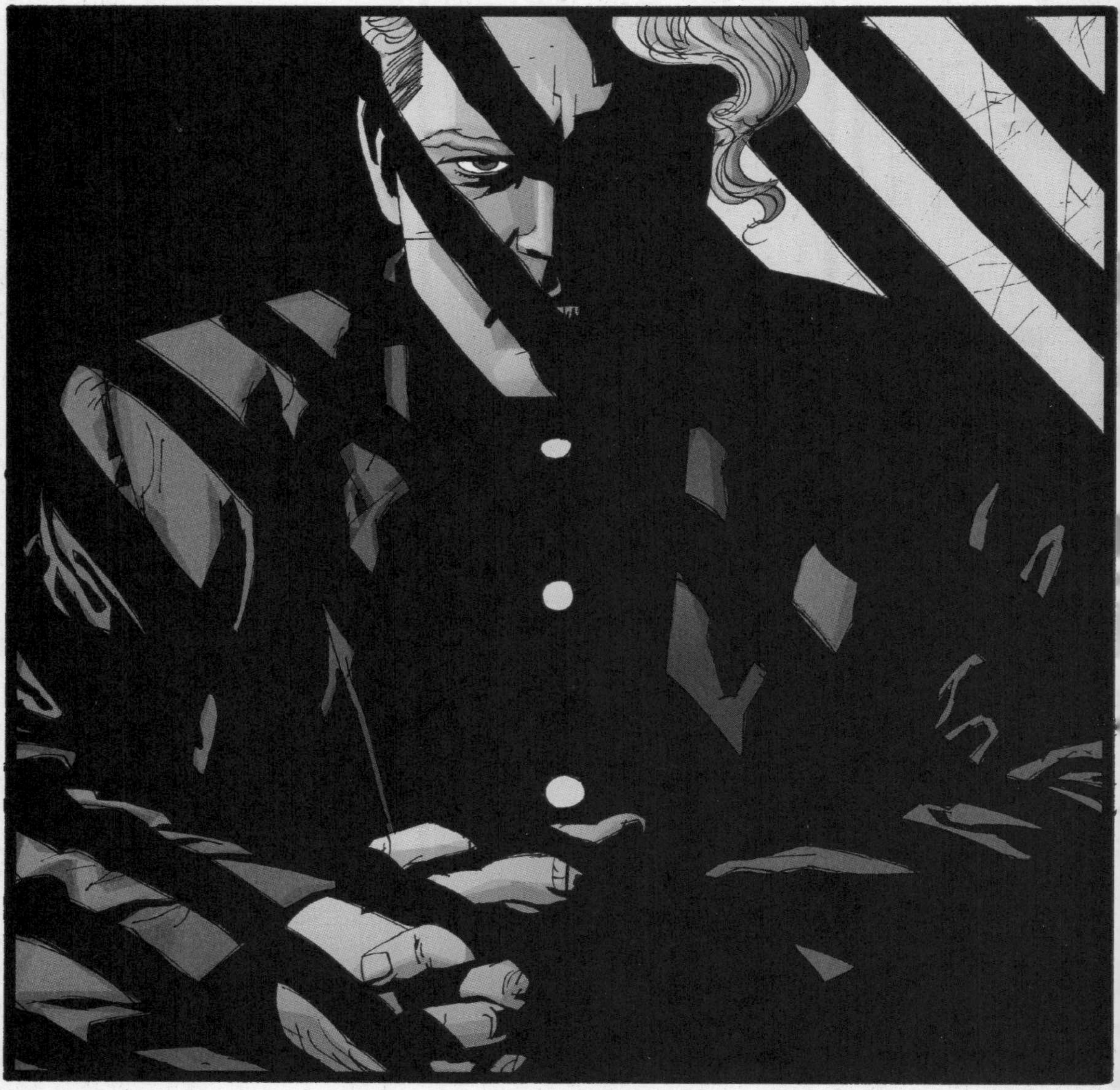

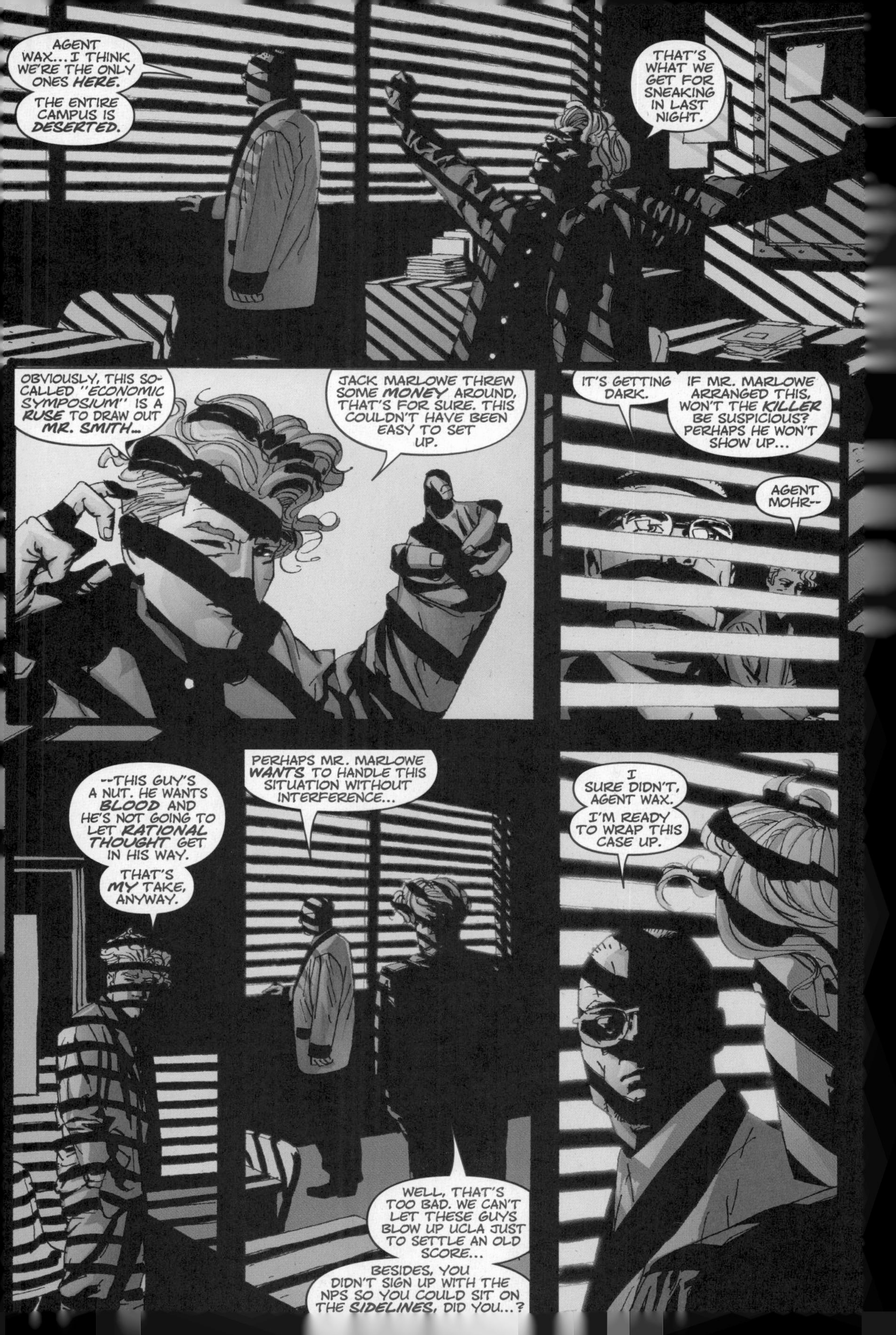
AGENT WAX... I THINK WE'RE THE ONLY ONES HERE.
THE ENTIRE CAMPUS IS DESERTED.
THAT'S WHAT WE GET FOR SNEAKING IN LAST NIGHT.
OBVIOUSLY, THIS SO-CALLED "ECONOMIC SYMPOSIUM" IS A RUSE TO DRAW OUT MR. SMITH...
JACK MARLOWE THREW SOME MONEY AROUND, THAT'S FOR SURE. THIS COULDN'T HAVE BEEN EASY TO SET UP.
IT'S GETTING DARK.
IF MR. MARLOWE ARRANGED THIS, WON'T THE KILLER BE SUSPICIOUS? PERHAPS HE WON'T SHOW UP...
AGENT MOHR--
--THIS GUY'S A NUT. HE WANTS BLOOD AND HE'S NOT GOING TO LET RATIONAL THOUGHT GET IN HIS WAY.
THAT'S MY TAKE, ANYWAY.
PERHAPS MR. MARLOWE WANTS TO HANDLE THIS SITUATION WITHOUT INTERFERENCE...
WELL, THAT'S TOO BAD. WE CAN'T LET THESE GUYS BLOW UP UCLA JUST TO SETTLE AN OLD SCORE...
BESIDES, YOU DIDN'T SIGN UP WITH THE NPS SO YOU COULD SIT ON THE SIDELINES, DID YOU...?
I SURE DIDN'T, AGENT WAX.
I'M READY TO WRAP THIS CASE UP.

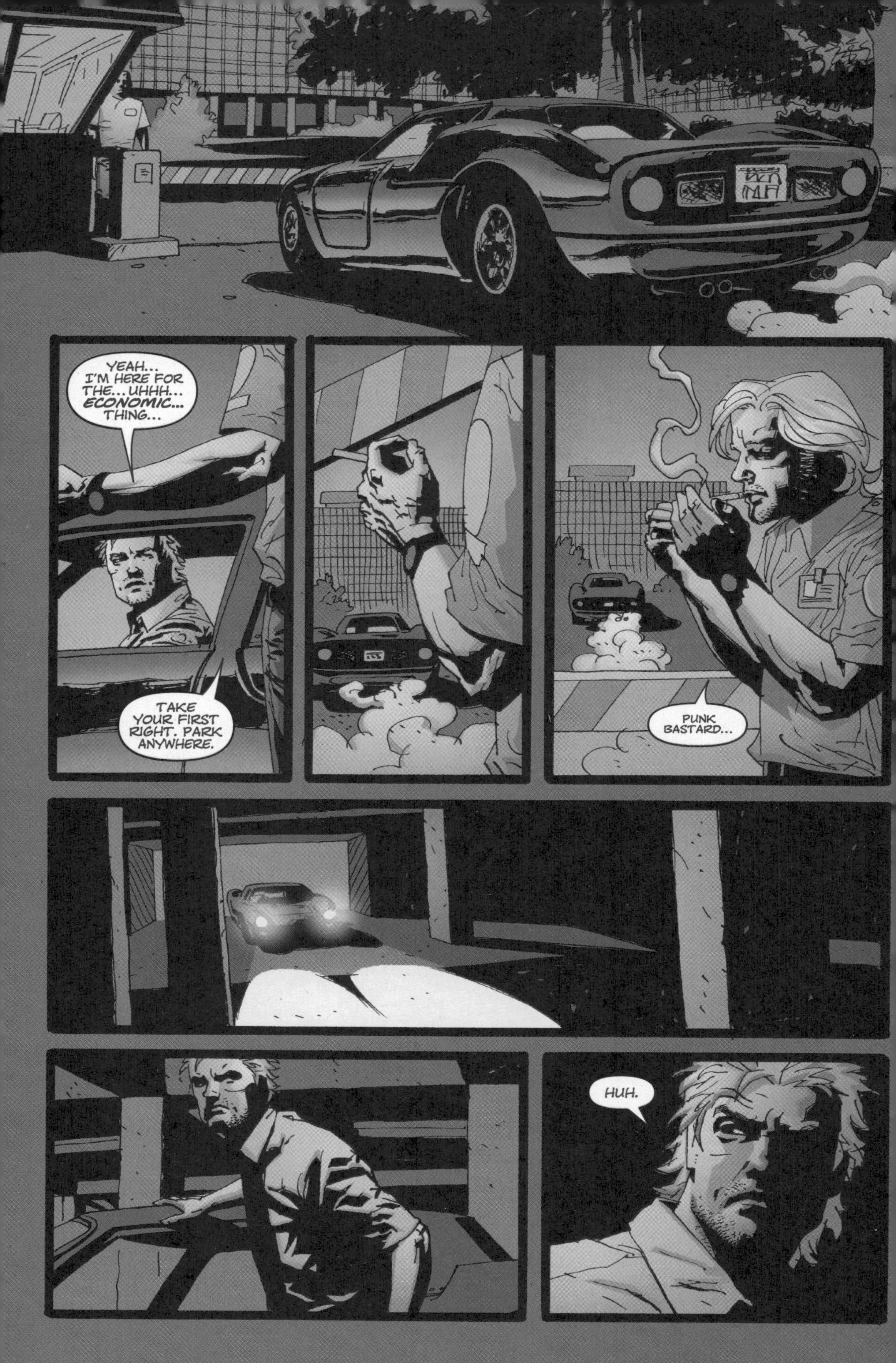
YEAH... I'M HERE FOR THE... UHHH... ECONOMIC... THING...
TAKE YOUR FIRST RIGHT. PARK ANYWHERE.
PUNK BASTARD...
HUH.

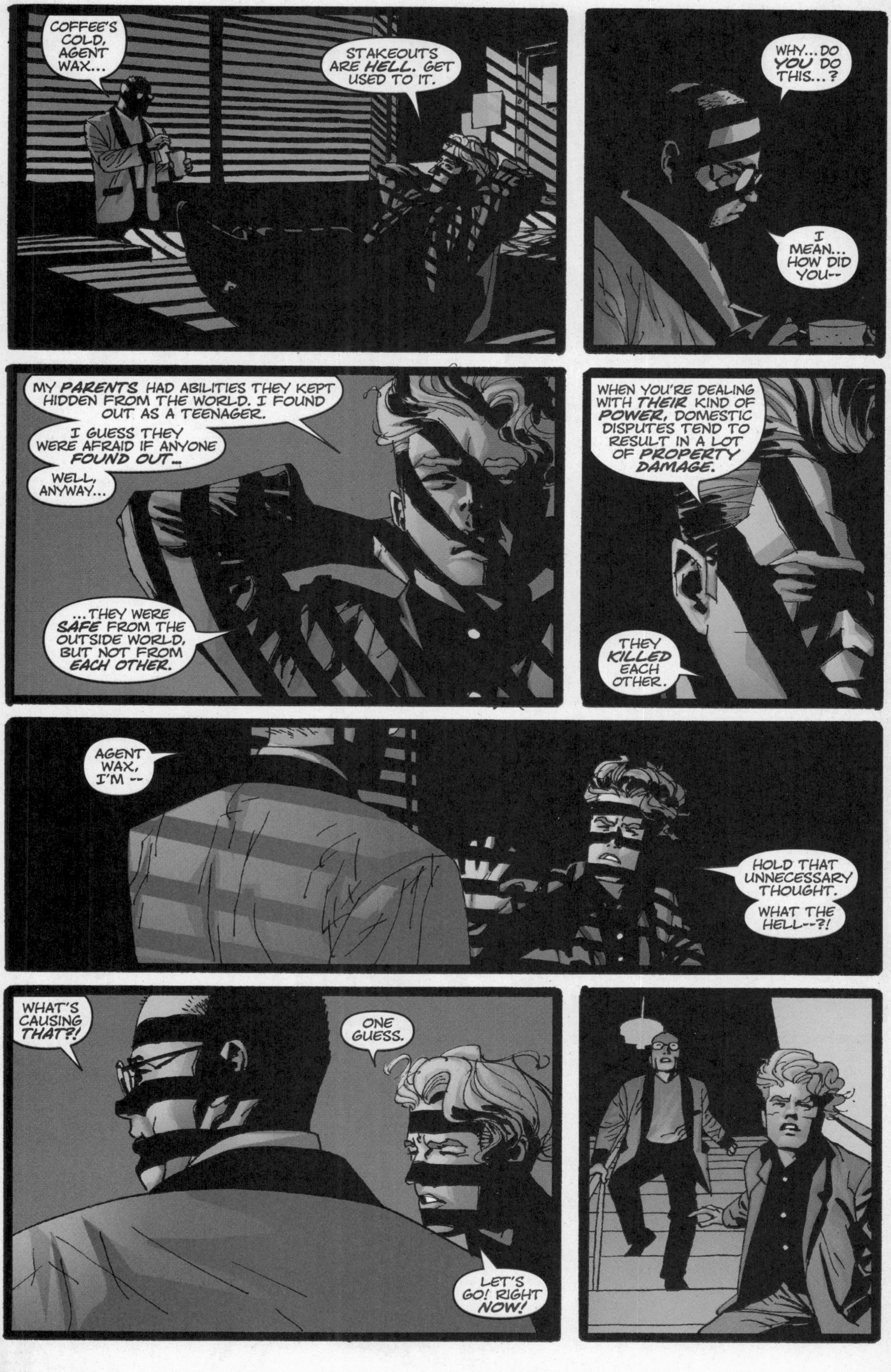
COFFEE'S COLD, AGENT WAX...
STAKEOUTS ARE HELL. GET USED TO IT.
WHY... DO YOU DO THIS...?
I MEAN... HOW DID YOU--
MY PARENTS HAD ABILITIES THEY KEPT HIDDEN FROM THE WORLD. I FOUND OUT AS A TEENAGER.
I GUESS THEY WERE AFRAID IF ANYONE FOUND OUT...
WELL, ANYWAY...
...THEY WERE SAFE FROM THE OUTSIDE WORLD, BUT NOT FROM EACH OTHER.
WHEN YOU'RE DEALING WITH THEIR KIND OF POWER, DOMESTIC DISPUTES TEND TO RESULT IN A LOT OF PROPERTY DAMAGE.
THEY KILLED EACH OTHER.
AGENT WAX, I'M --
HOLD THAT UNNECESSARY THOUGHT.
WHAT THE HELL--?!
WHAT'S CAUSING THAT?!
ONE GUESS.
LET'S GO! RIGHT NOW!

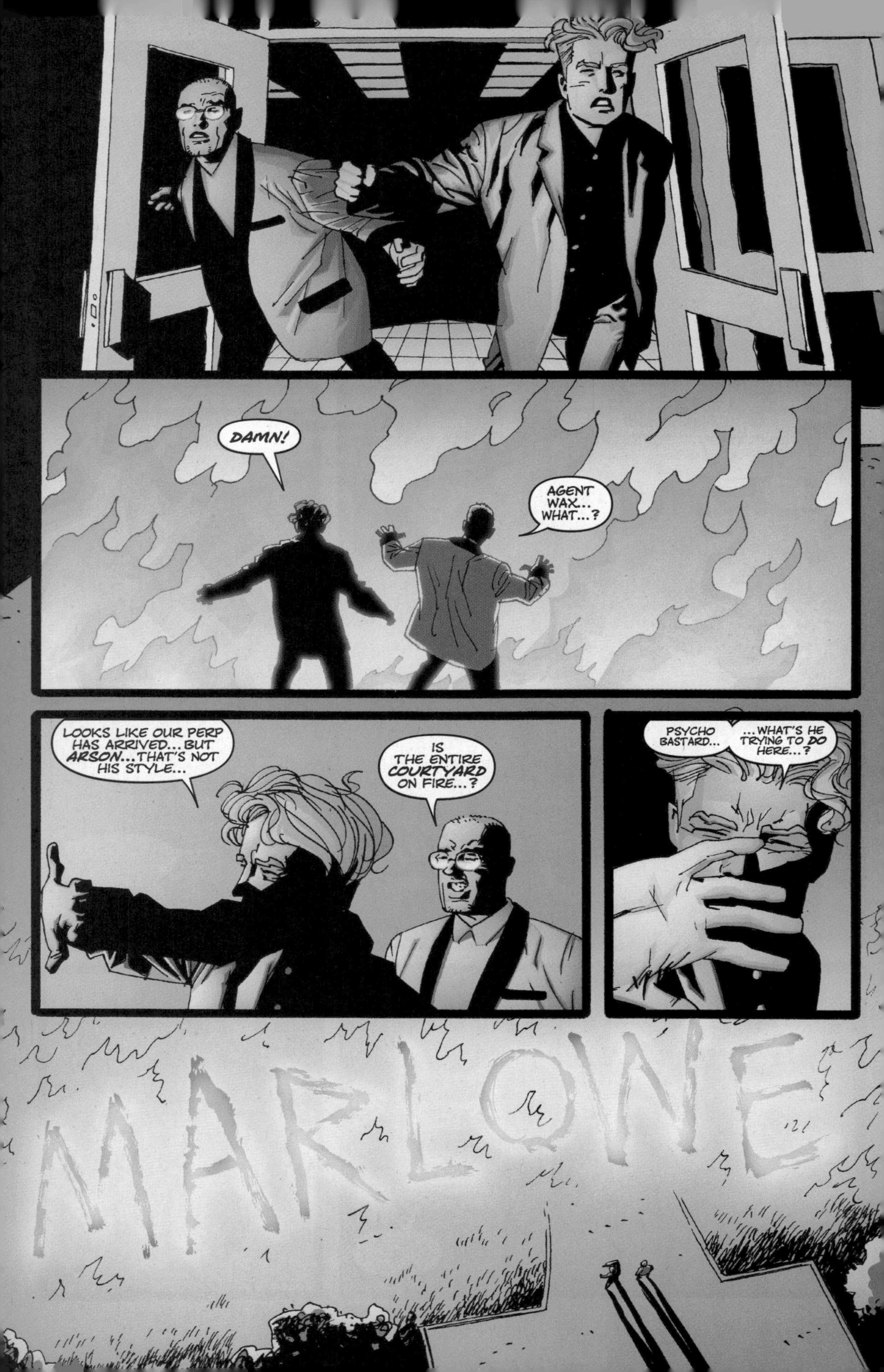

DAMN!
AGENT WAX... WHAT...?
LOOKS LIKE OUR PERP HAS ARRIVED... BUT ARSON... THAT'S NOT HIS STYLE...
IS THE ENTIRE COURTYARD ON FIRE...?
PSYCHO BASTARD...
...WHAT'S HE TRYING TO DO HERE...?
MARLOWE

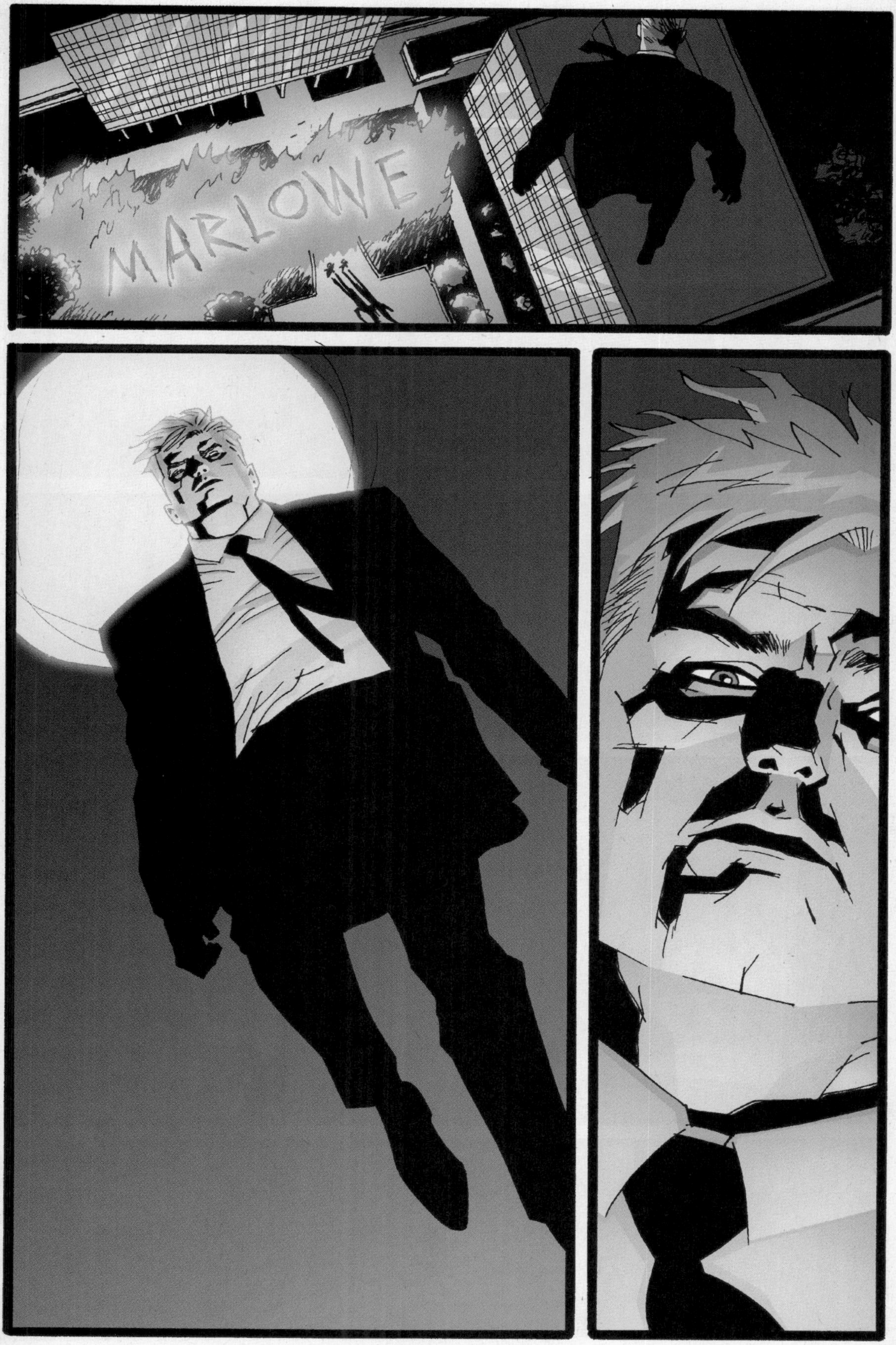
MARLOWE

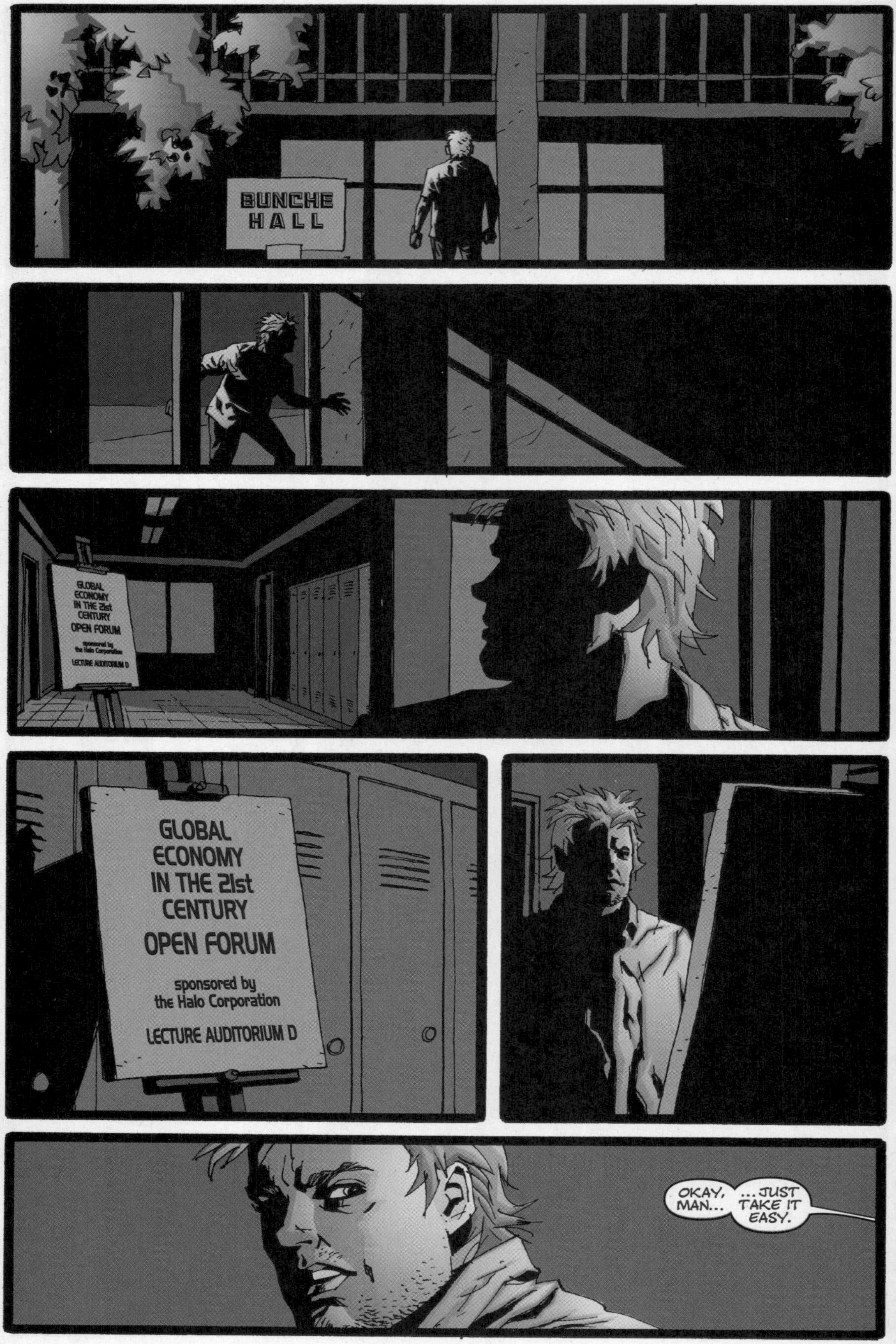
BUNCHE HALL
GLOBAL ECONOMY IN THE 21st CENTURY
OPEN FORUM
sponsored by the Halo Corporation
LECTURE AUDITORIUM D
GLOBAL ECONOMY IN THE 21st CENTURY
OPEN FORUM
sponsored by the Halo Corporation
LECTURE AUDITORIUM D
OKAY, MAN...
...JUST TAKE IT EASY.

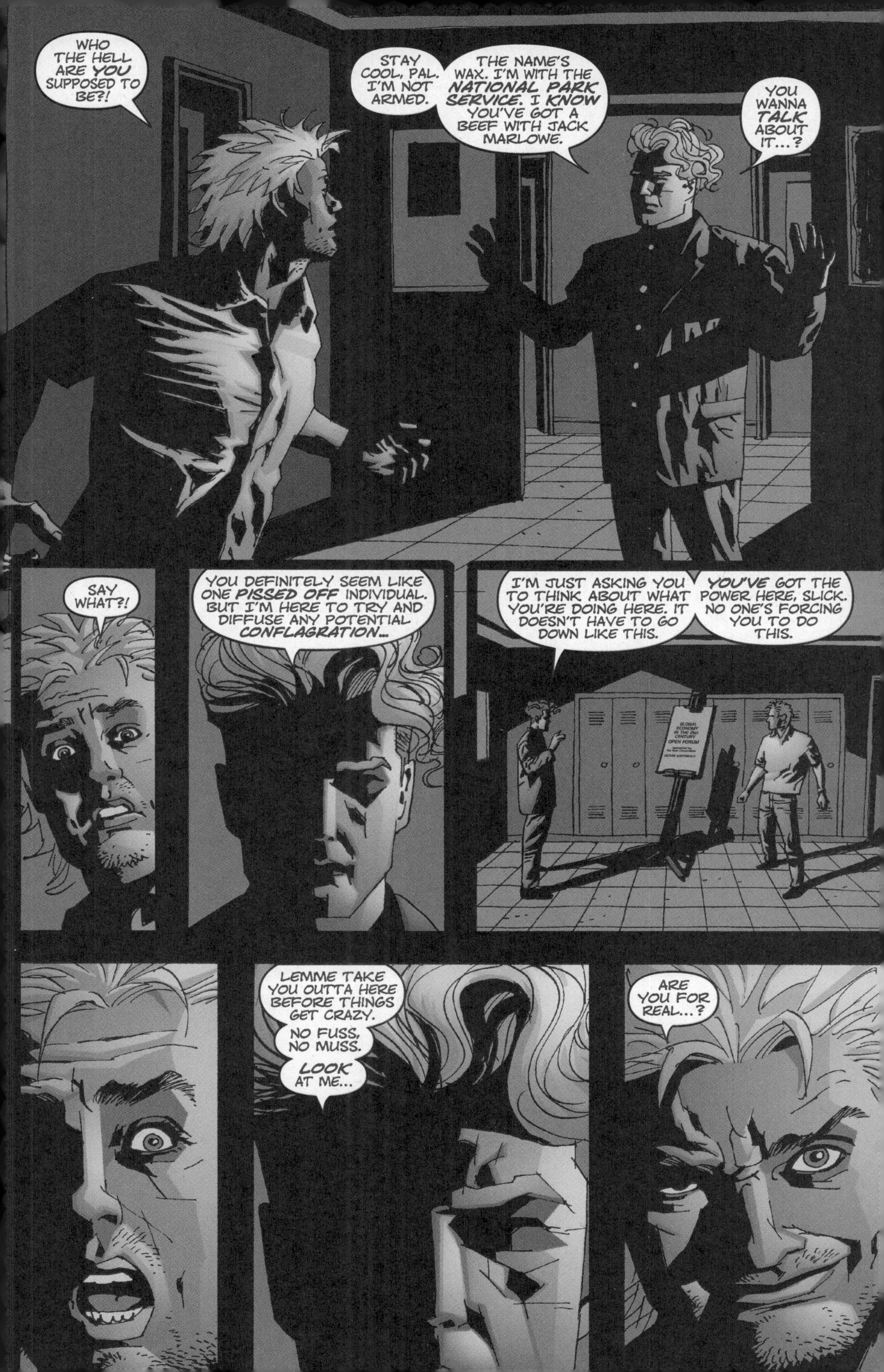
WHO THE HELL ARE YOU SUPPOSED TO BE?!
STAY COOL, PAL. I'M NOT ARMED.
THE NAME'S WAX. I'M WITH THE NATIONAL PARK SERVICE. I KNOW YOU'VE GOT A BEEF WITH JACK MARLOWE.
YOU WANNA TALK ABOUT IT...?
SAY WHAT?!
YOU DEFINITELY SEEM LIKE ONE PISSED OFF INDIVIDUAL. BUT I'M HERE TO TRY AND DIFFUSE ANY POTENTIAL CONFLAGRATION...
I'M JUST ASKING YOU TO THINK ABOUT WHAT YOU'RE DOING HERE. IT DOESN'T HAVE TO GO DOWN LIKE THIS.
YOU'VE GOT THE POWER HERE, SLICK. NO ONE'S FORCING YOU TO DO THIS.
LEMME TAKE YOU OUTTA HERE BEFORE THINGS GET CRAZY.
NO FUSS, NO MUSS.
LOOK AT ME...
ARE YOU FOR REAL...?

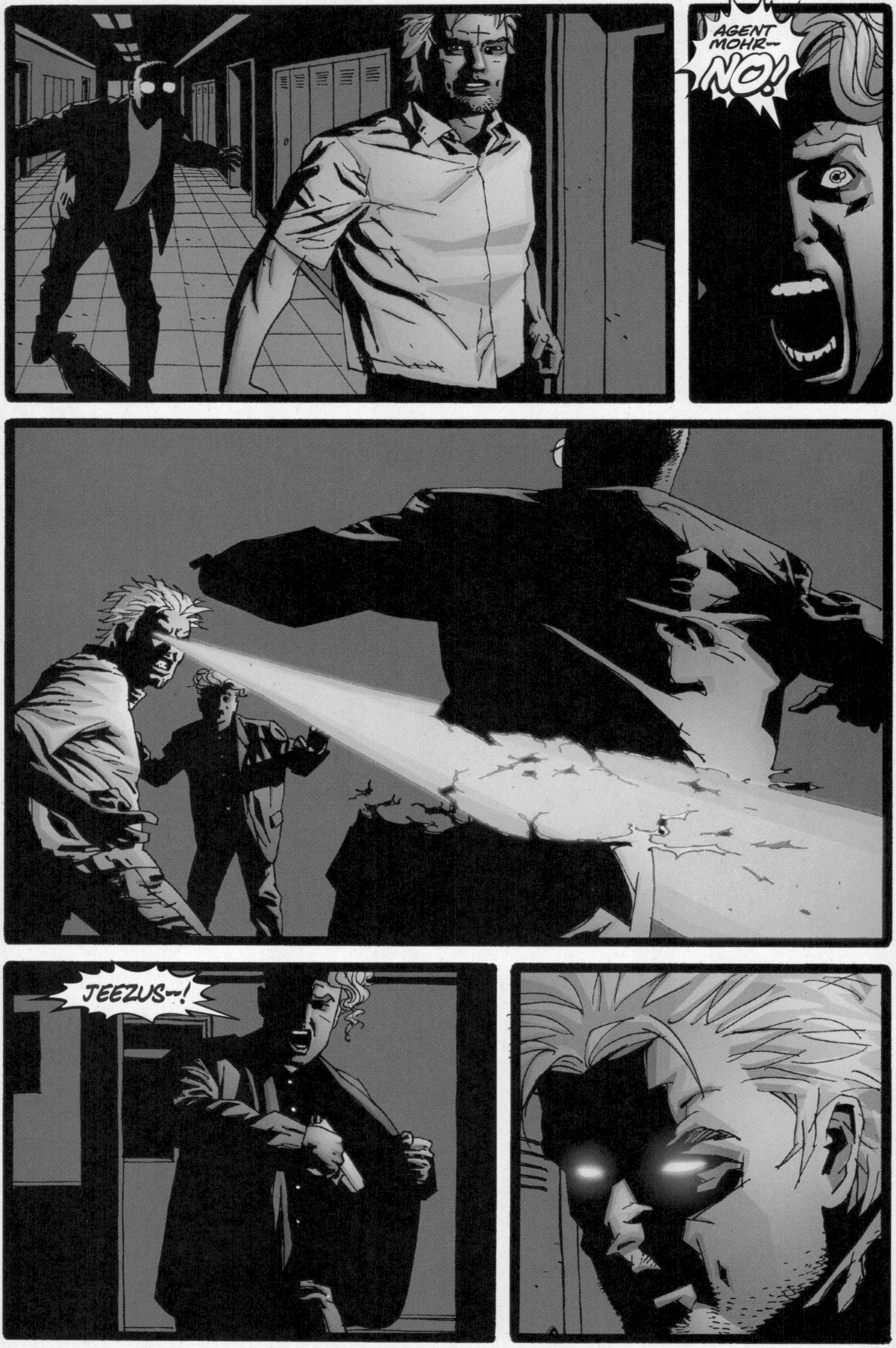

AGENT MOHR-- NO!
JEEZUS--!

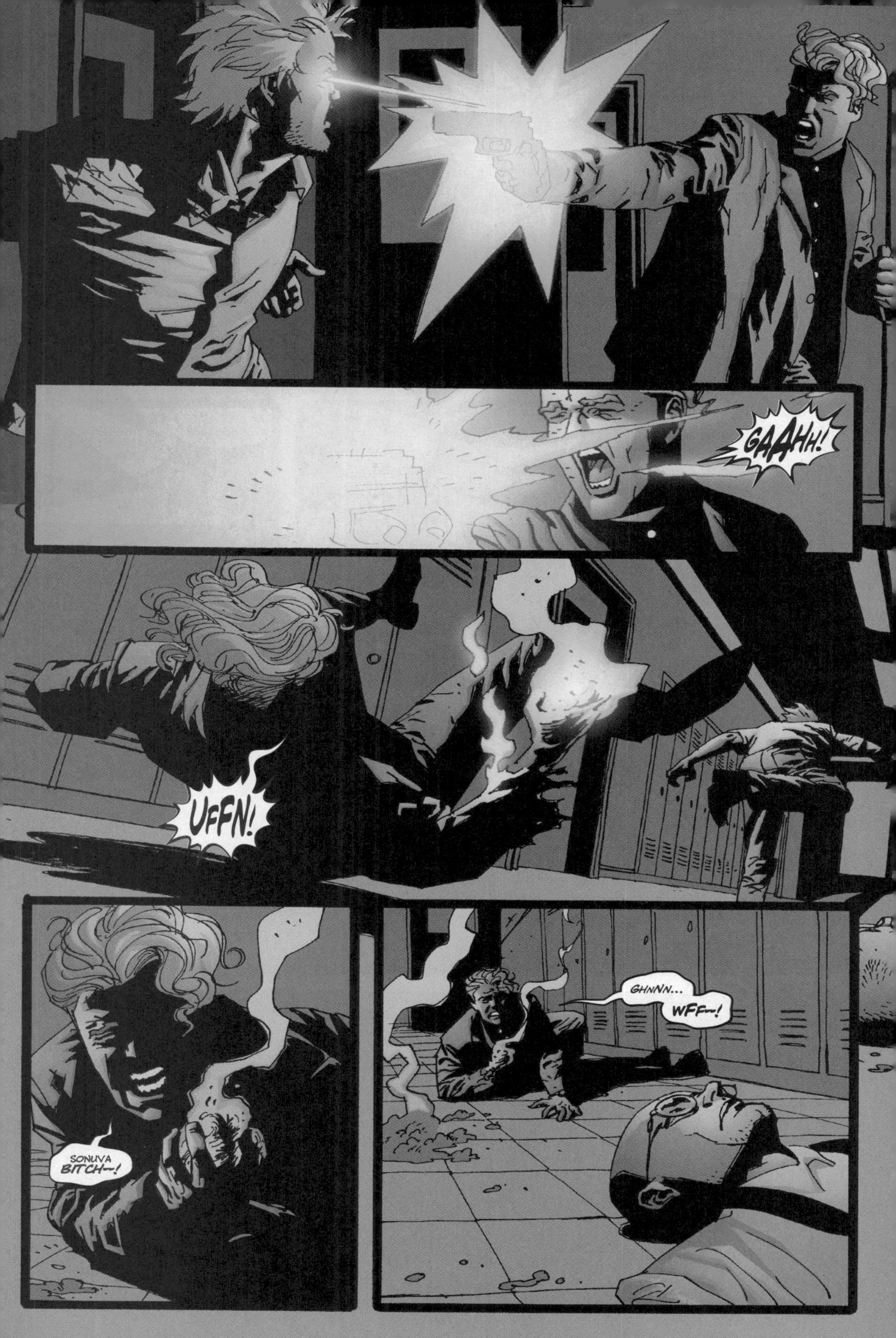
GAAHH!
UFFN!
SONUVA BITCH--!
GHNNN...
WFF--!

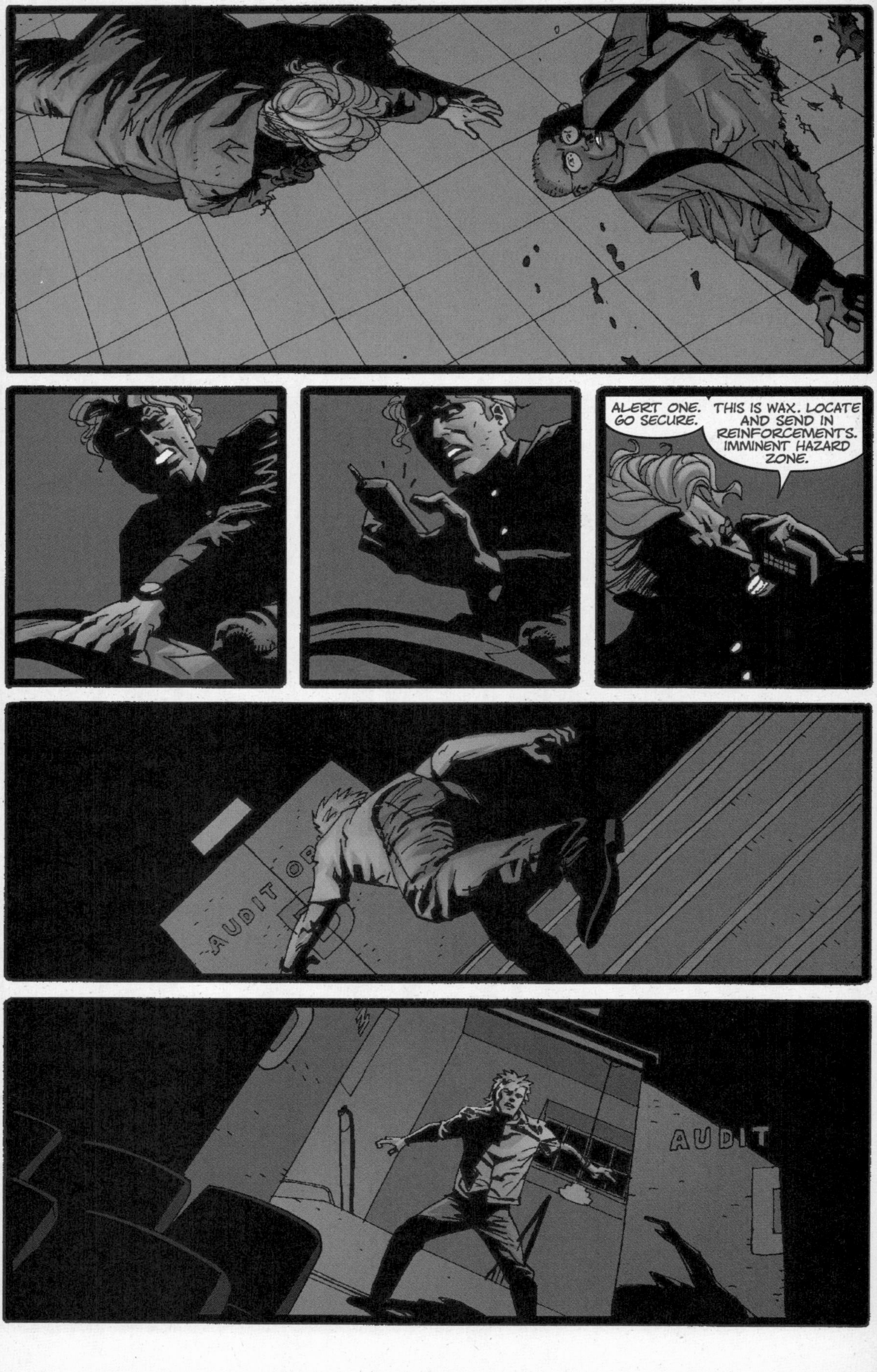
ALERT ONE. GO SECURE.
THIS IS WAX. LOCATE AND SEND IN REINFORCEMENTS. IMMINENT HAZARD ZONE.
AUDIT OF
AUDIT

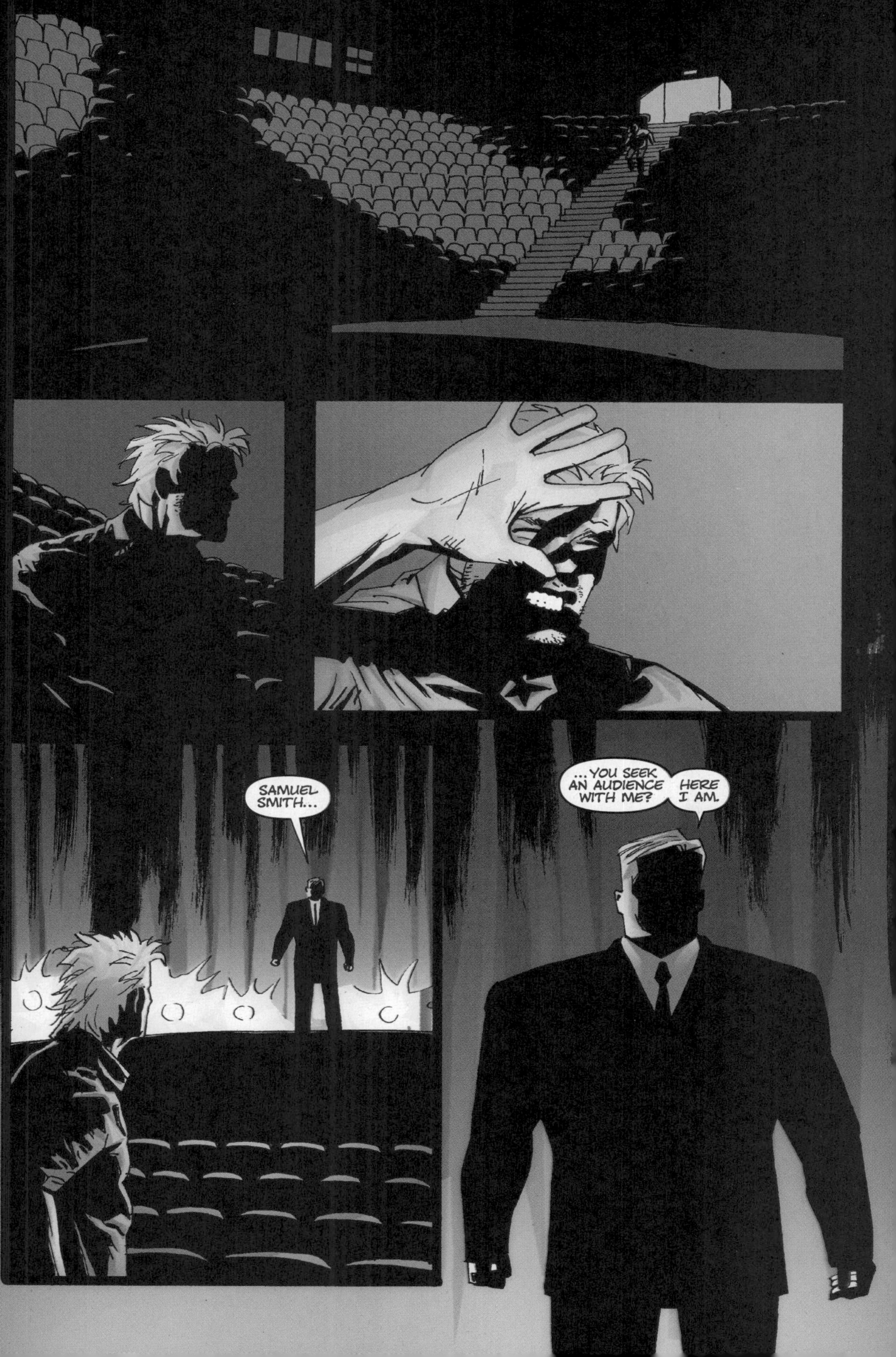
SAMUEL SMITH...
...YOU SEEK AN AUDIENCE WITH ME?
HERE I AM.

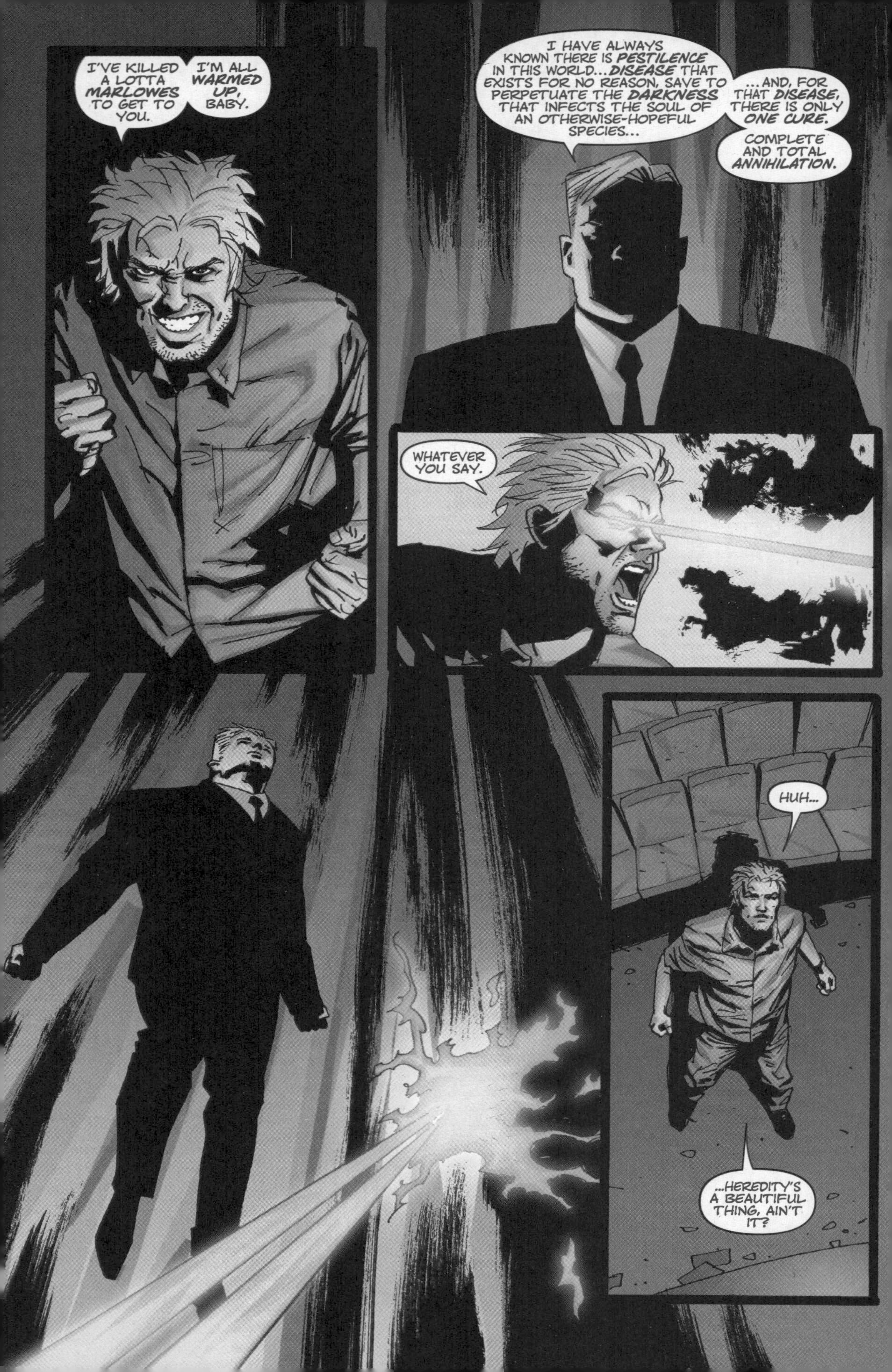
I'VE KILLED A LOTTA MARLOWES TO GET TO YOU.
I'M ALL WARMED UP, BABY.
I HAVE ALWAYS KNOWN THERE IS PESTILENCE IN THIS WORLD...DISEASE THAT EXISTS FOR NO REASON, SAVE TO PERPETUATE THE DARKNESS THAT INFECTS THE SOUL OF AN OTHERWISE-HOPEFUL SPECIES...
...AND, FOR THAT DISEASE, THERE IS ONLY ONE CURE.
COMPLETE AND TOTAL ANNIHILATION.
WHATEVER YOU SAY.
HUH...
...HEREDITY'S A BEAUTIFUL THING, AIN'T IT?

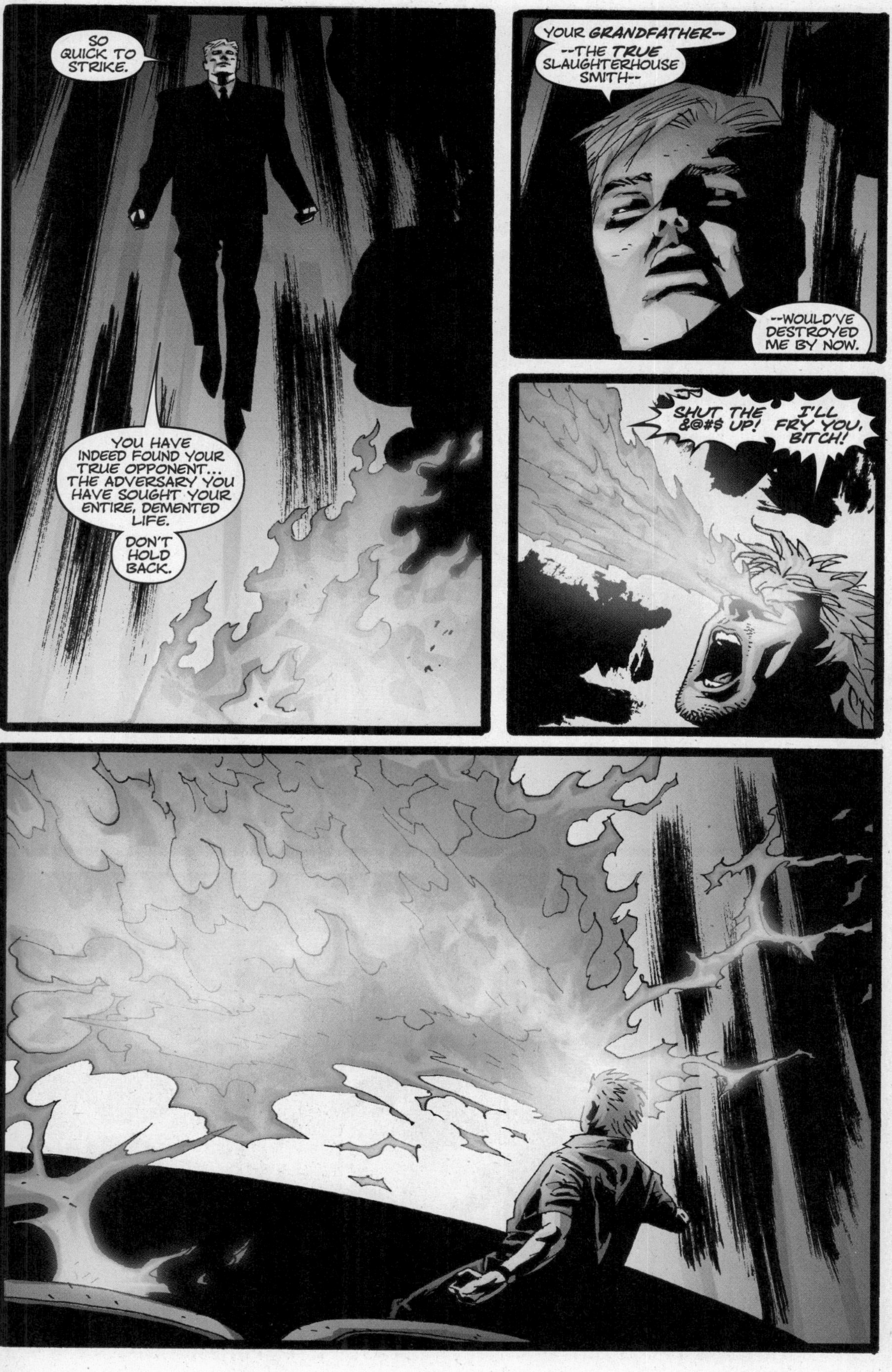
SO QUICK TO STRIKE.
YOU HAVE INDEED FOUND YOUR TRUE OPPONENT... THE ADVERSARY YOU HAVE SOUGHT YOUR ENTIRE, DEMENTED LIFE.
DON'T HOLD BACK.
YOUR GRANDFATHER--
--THE TRUE SLAUGHTERHOUSE SMITH--
--WOULD'VE DESTROYED ME BY NOW.
SHUT THE &@#$ UP!
I'LL FRY YOU, BITCH!

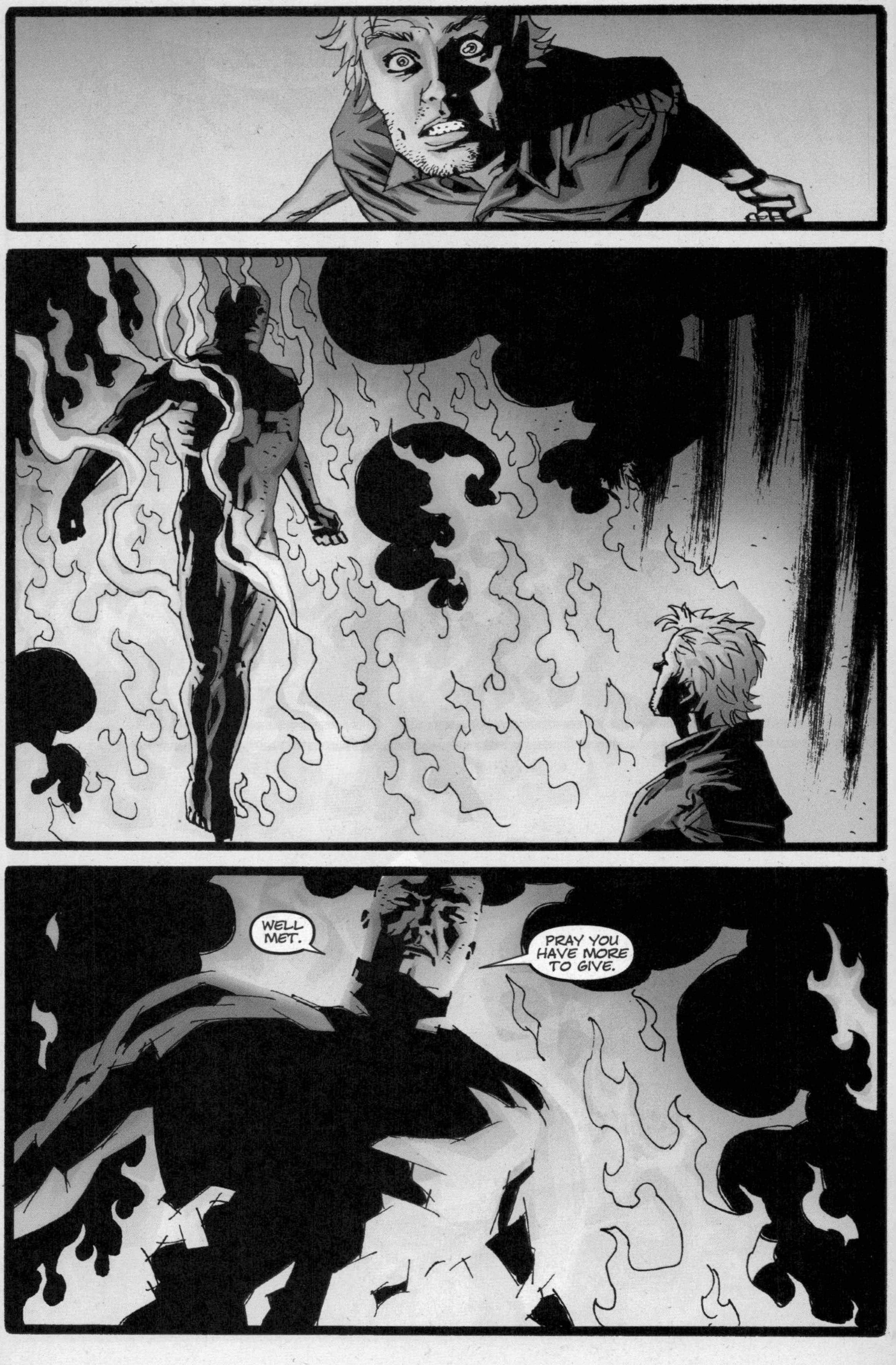
WELL MET.
PRAY YOU HAVE MORE TO GIVE.

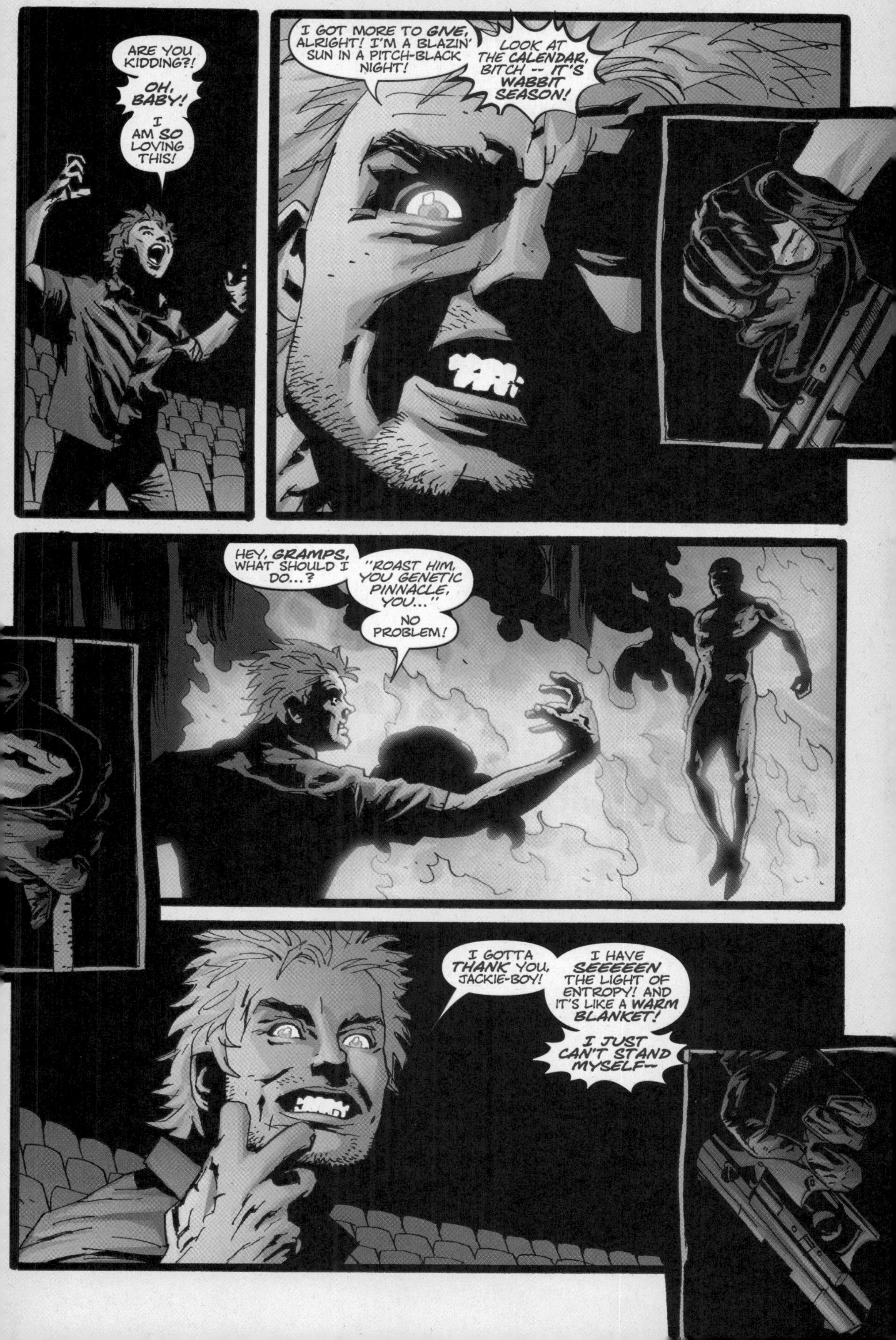
ARE YOU KIDDING?!
OH, BABY!
I AM SO LOVING THIS!
I GOT MORE TO GIVE, ALRIGHT! I'M A BLAZIN' SUN IN A PITCH-BLACK NIGHT!
LOOK AT THE CALENDAR, BITCH -- IT'S WABBIT SEASON!
HEY, GRAMPS, WHAT SHOULD I DO...?
"ROAST HIM, YOU GENETIC PINNACLE, YOU..."
NO PROBLEM!
I GOTTA THANK YOU, JACKIE-BOY!
I HAVE SEEEEEEN THE LIGHT OF ENTROPY! AND IT'S LIKE A WARM BLANKET!
I JUST CAN'T STAND MYSELF--

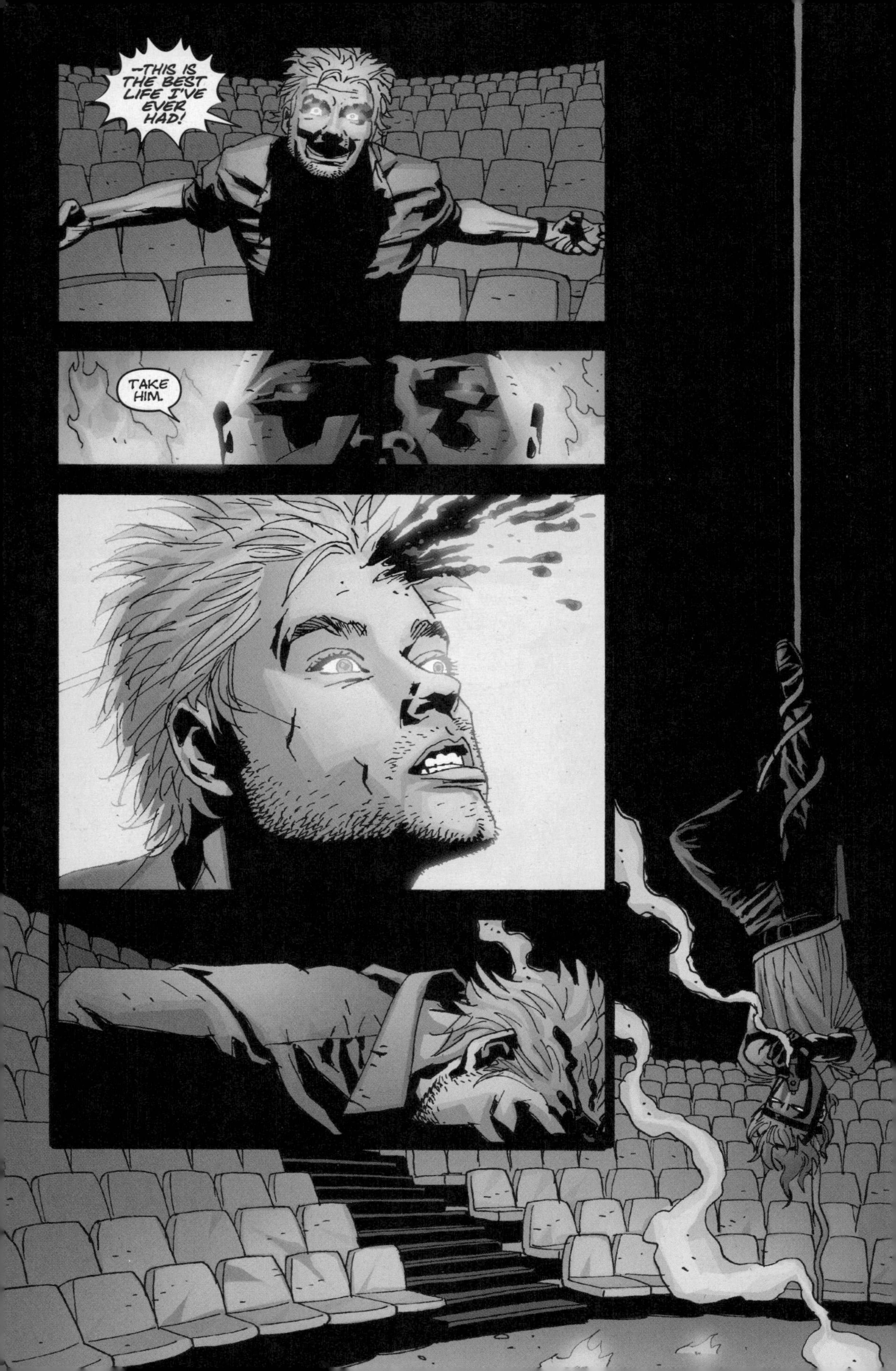
--THIS IS THE BEST LIFE I'VE EVER HAD!
TAKE HIM.

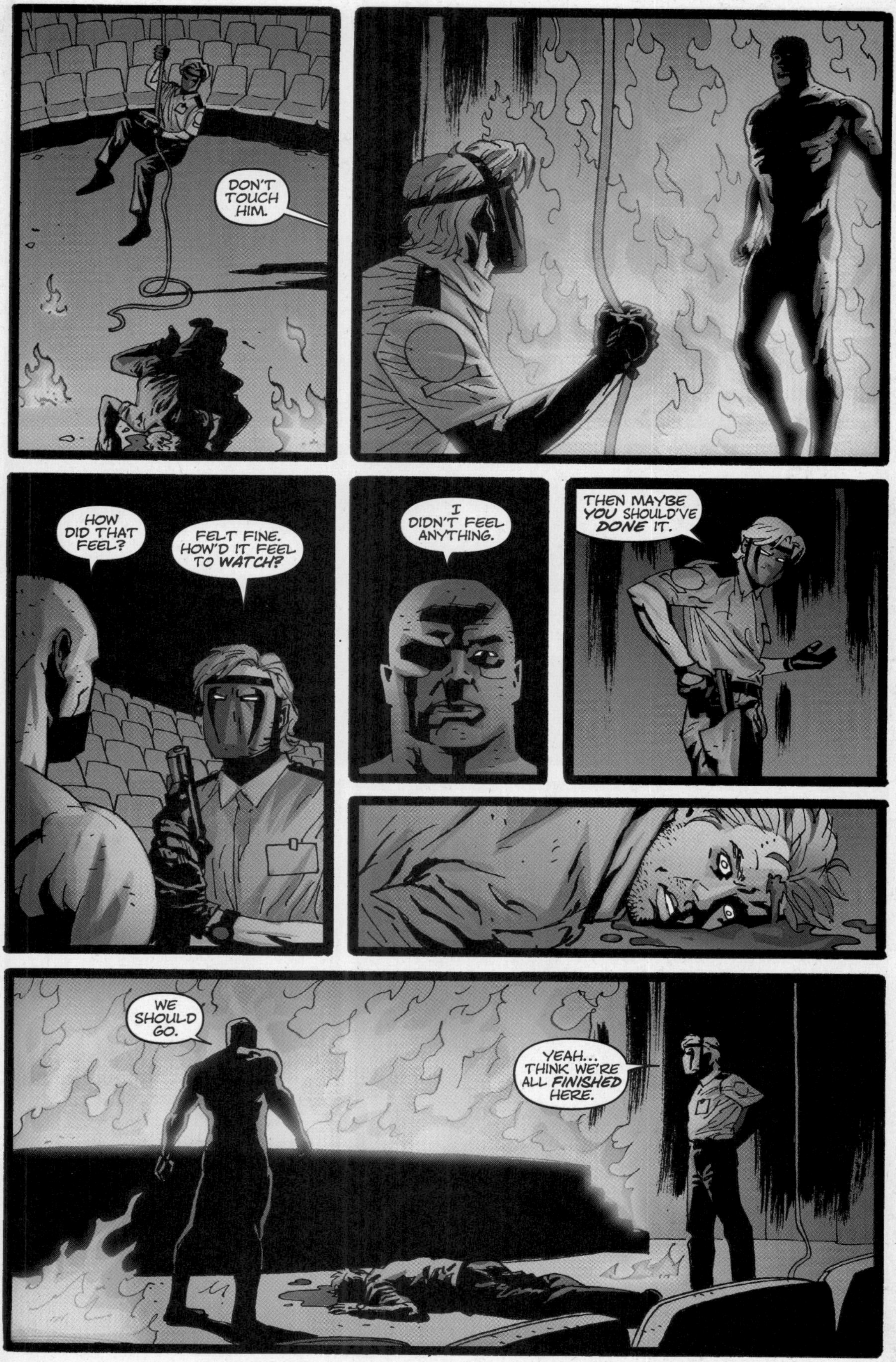
DON'T TOUCH HIM.
HOW DID THAT FEEL?
FELT FINE. HOW'D IT FEEL TO WATCH?
I DIDN'T FEEL ANYTHING.
THEN MAYBE YOU SHOULD'VE DONE IT.
WE SHOULD GO.
YEAH... THINK WE'RE ALL FINISHED HERE.

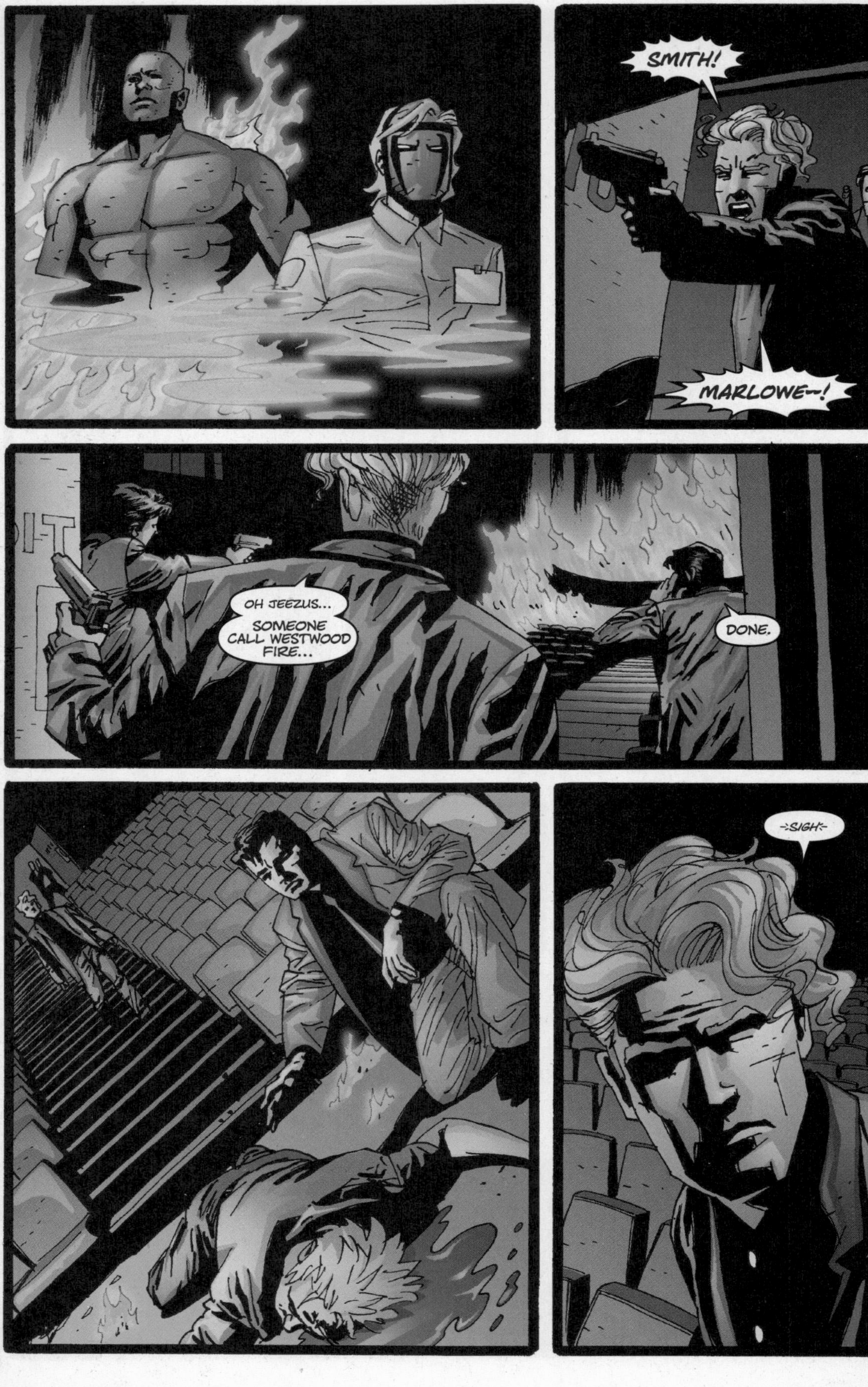

SMITH!
MARLOWE~!
OH JEEZUS... SOMEONE CALL WESTWOOD FIRE...
DONE.
-:SIGH:-

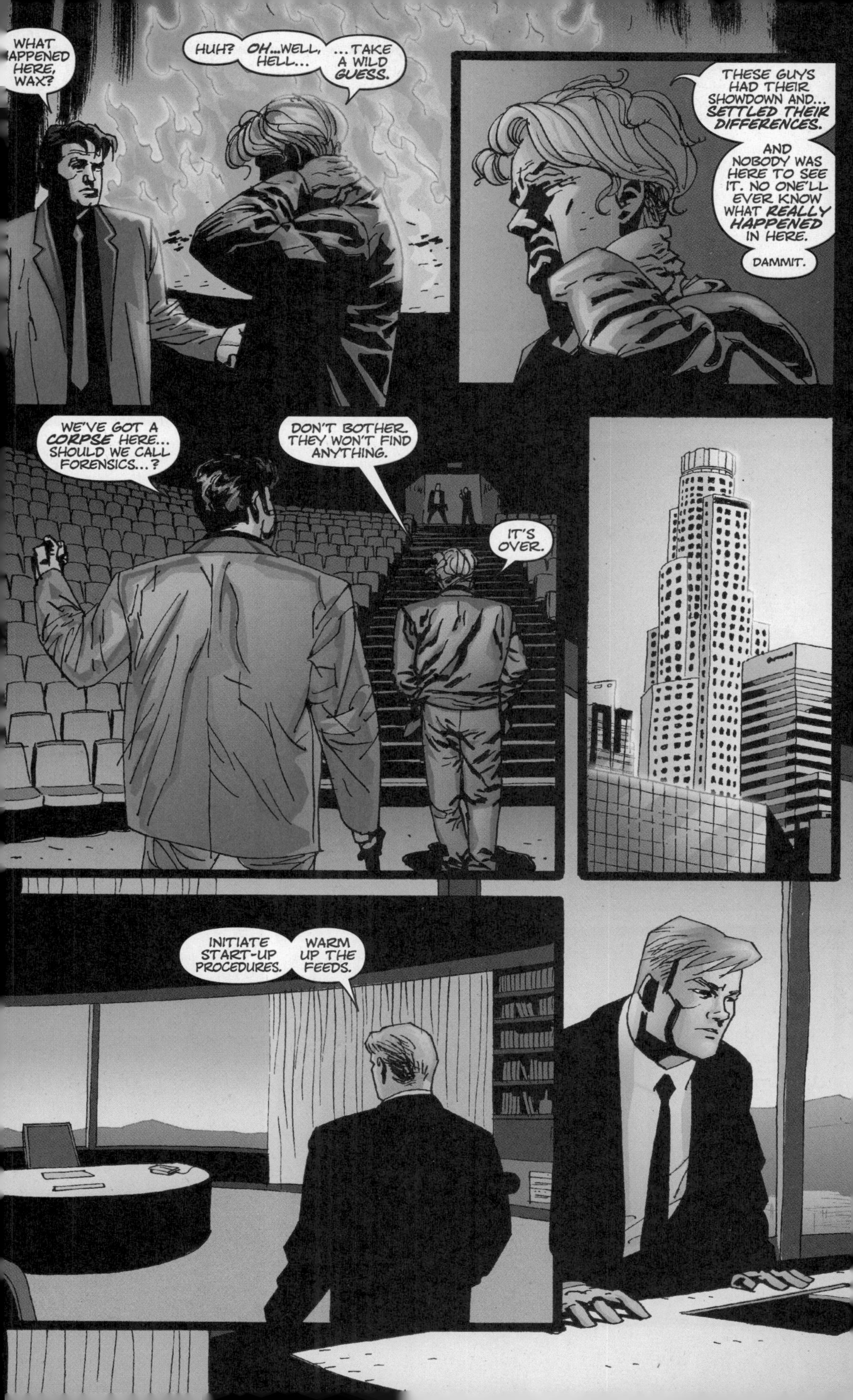
WHAT HAPPENED HERE, WAX?
HUH? OH...WELL, HELL...
...TAKE A WILD GUESS.
THESE GUYS HAD THEIR SHOWDOWN AND... SETTLED THEIR DIFFERENCES.
AND NOBODY WAS HERE TO SEE IT. NO ONE'LL EVER KNOW WHAT REALLY HAPPENED IN HERE.
DAMMIT.
WE'VE GOT A CORPSE HERE... SHOULD WE CALL FORENSICS...?
DON'T BOTHER. THEY WON'T FIND ANYTHING.
IT'S OVER.
INITIATE START-UP PROCEDURES.
WARM UP THE FEEDS.

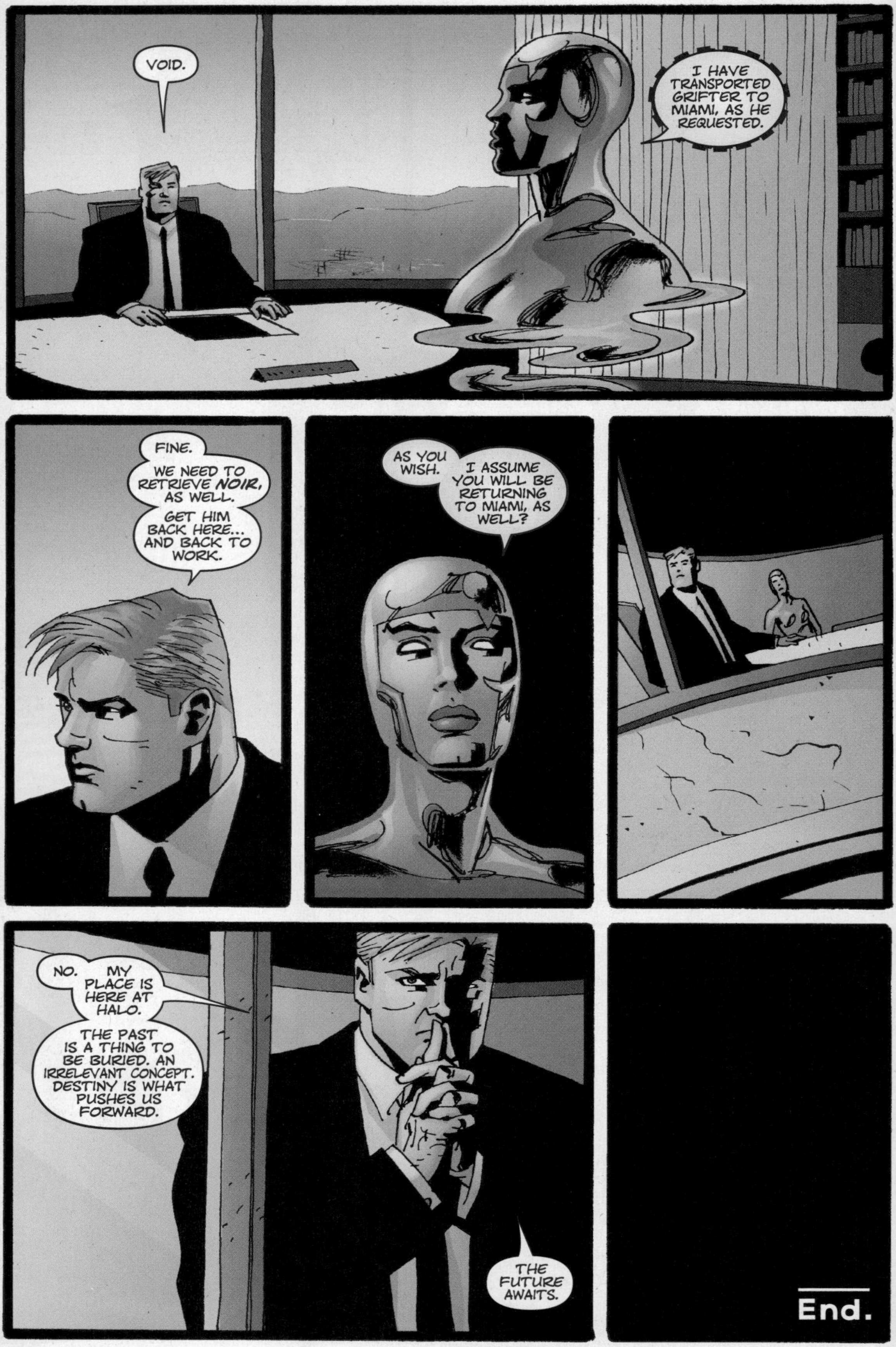
VOID.
I HAVE TRANSPORTED GRIFTER TO MIAMI, AS HE REQUESTED.
FINE.
WE NEED TO RETRIEVE NOIR, AS WELL.
GET HIM BACK HERE... AND BACK TO WORK.
AS YOU WISH.
I ASSUME YOU WILL BE RETURNING TO MIAMI, AS WELL?
NO. MY PLACE IS HERE AT HALO.
THE PAST IS A THING TO BE BURIED. AN IRRELEVANT CONCEPT. DESTINY IS WHAT PUSHES US FORWARD.
THE FUTURE AWAITS.
End.

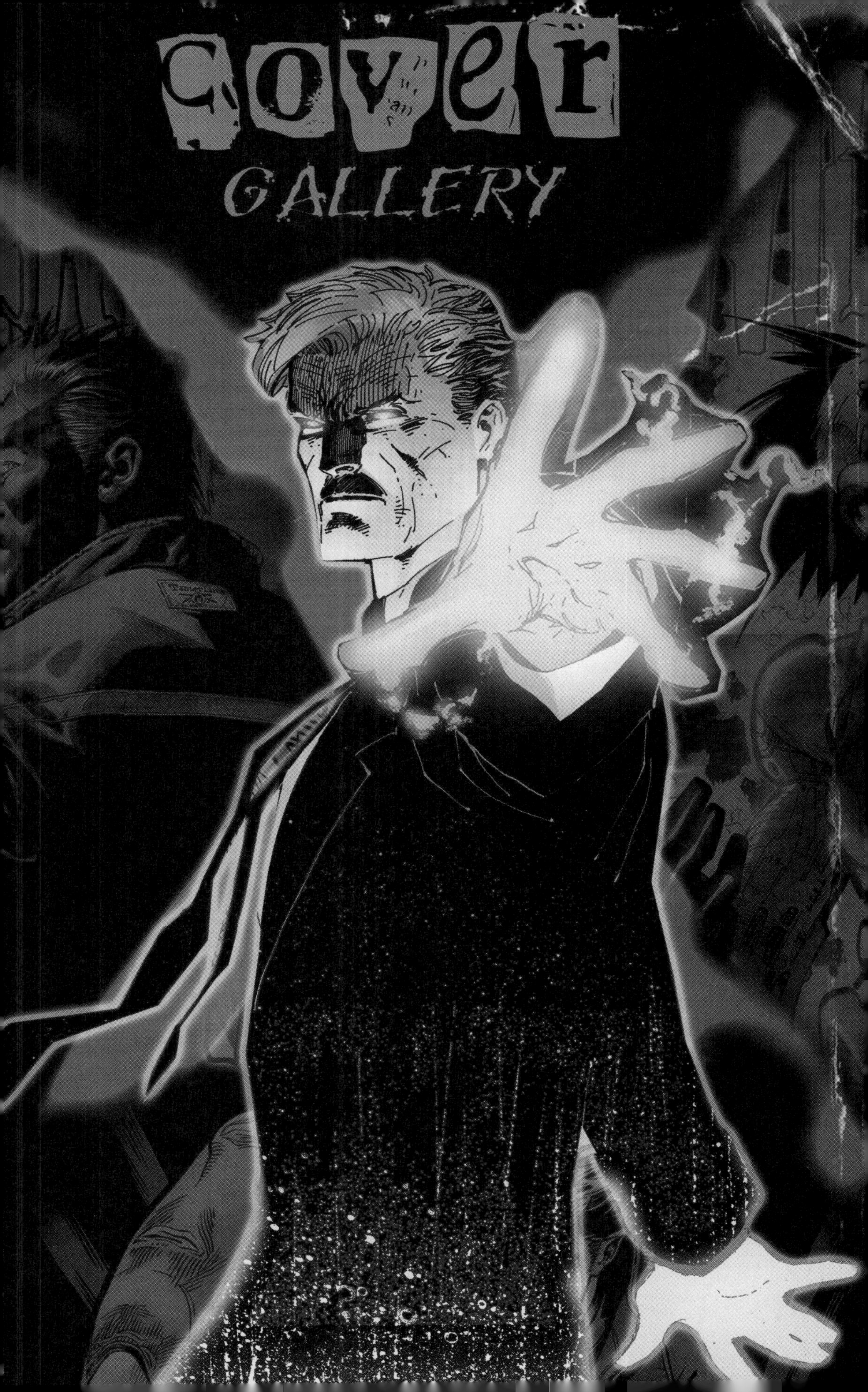
cover
GALLERY

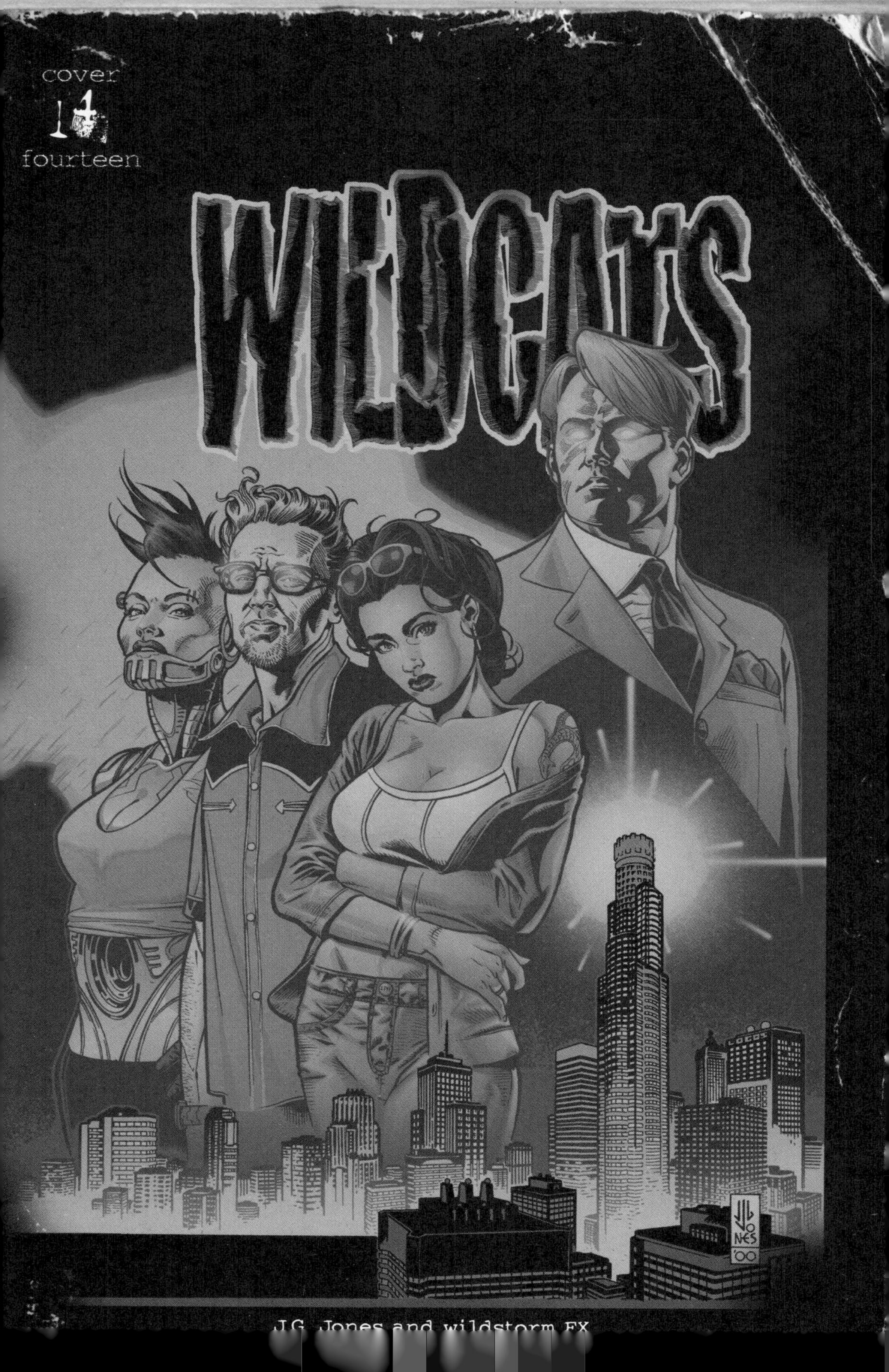
cover
14
fourteen
WILDCATS

J.G. Jones and wildstorm FX

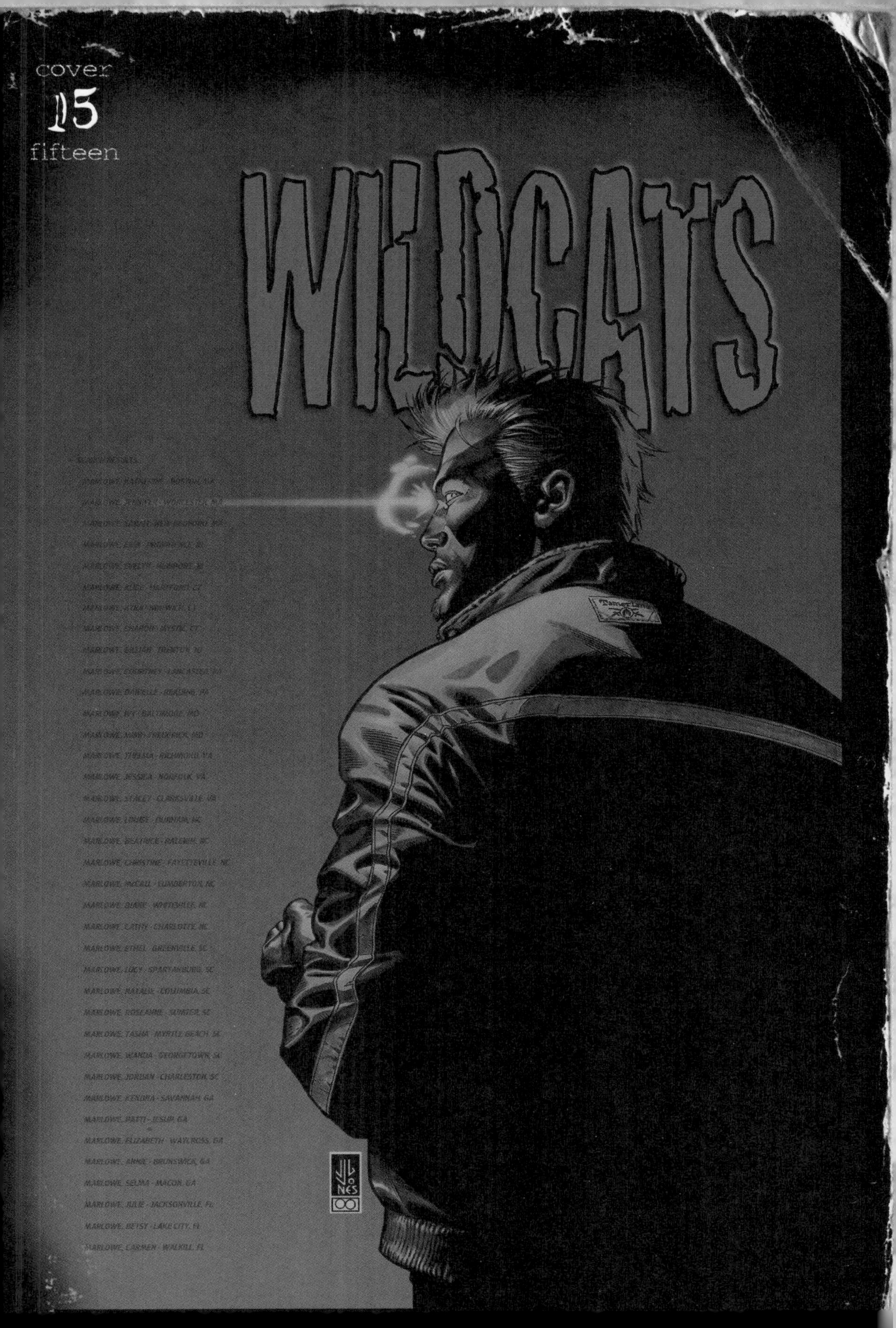
cover
15
fifteen
WILDCATS

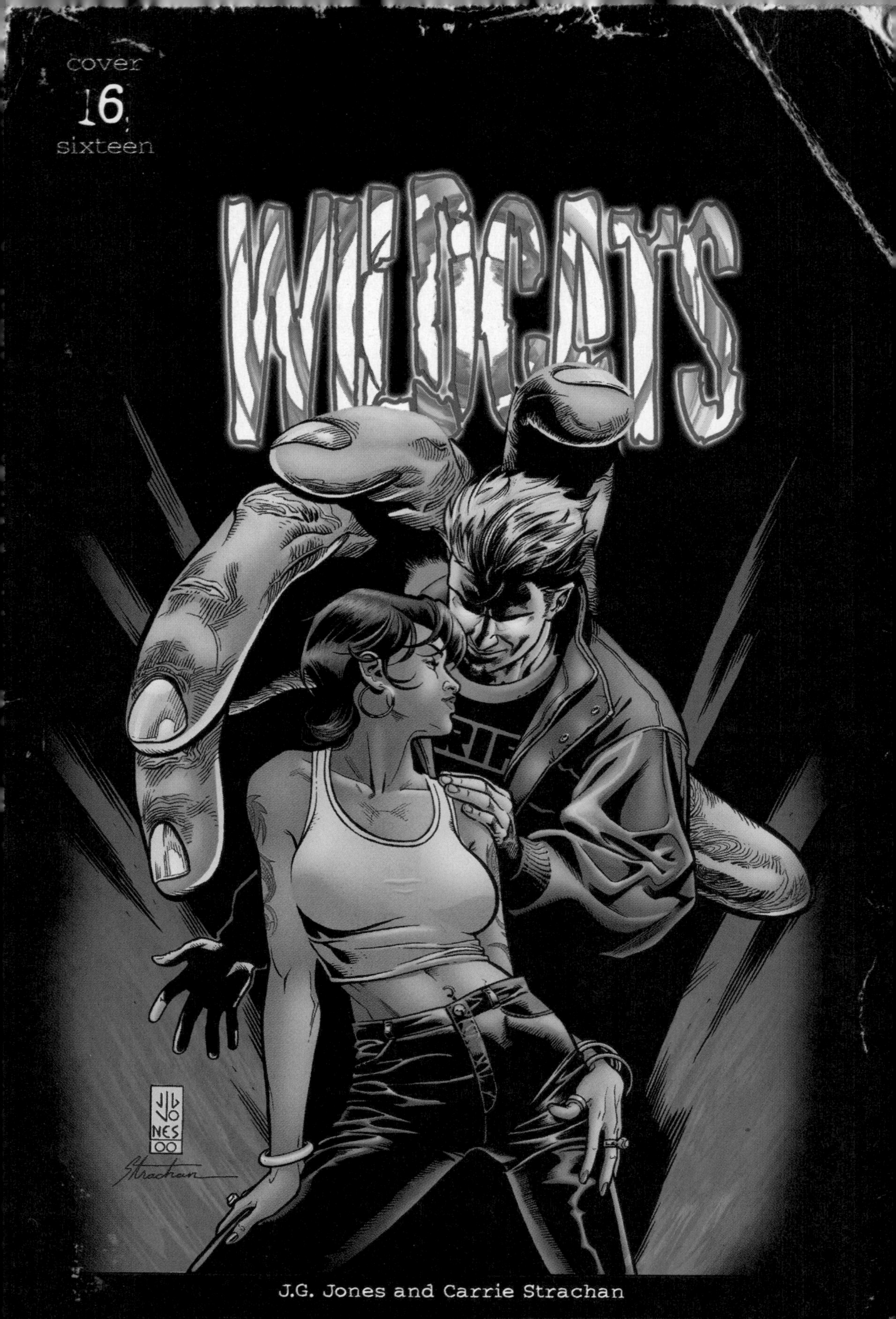
cover
16
sixteen
WILDC.A.T.S

J.G. Jones and Carrie Strachan

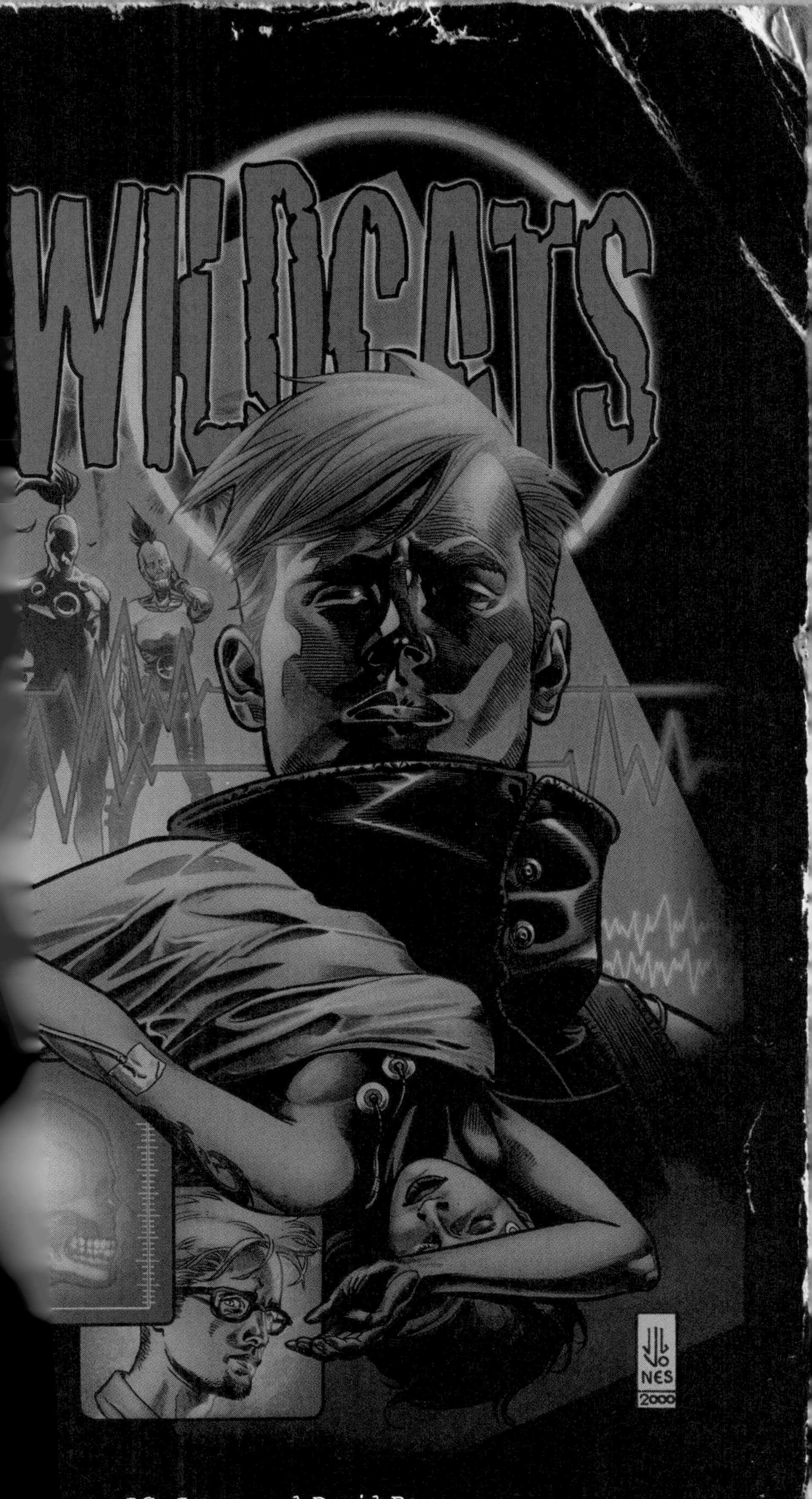
WILDCATS
JONES 2000

J.G. Jones and David Baron

cover
18
eighteen

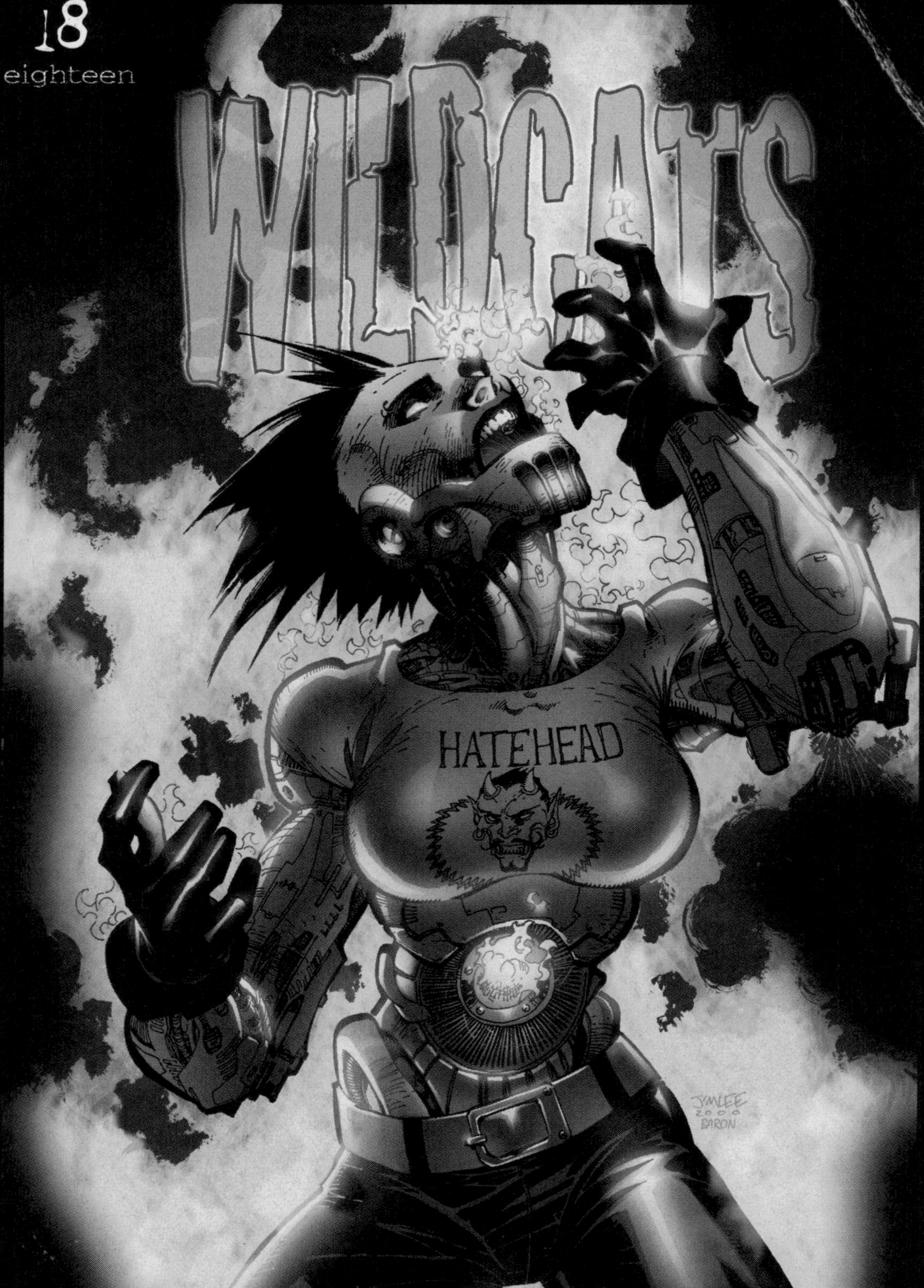
WILDCATS
HATEHEAD
JIMLEE
2000
BARON

Jim Lee and David Baron

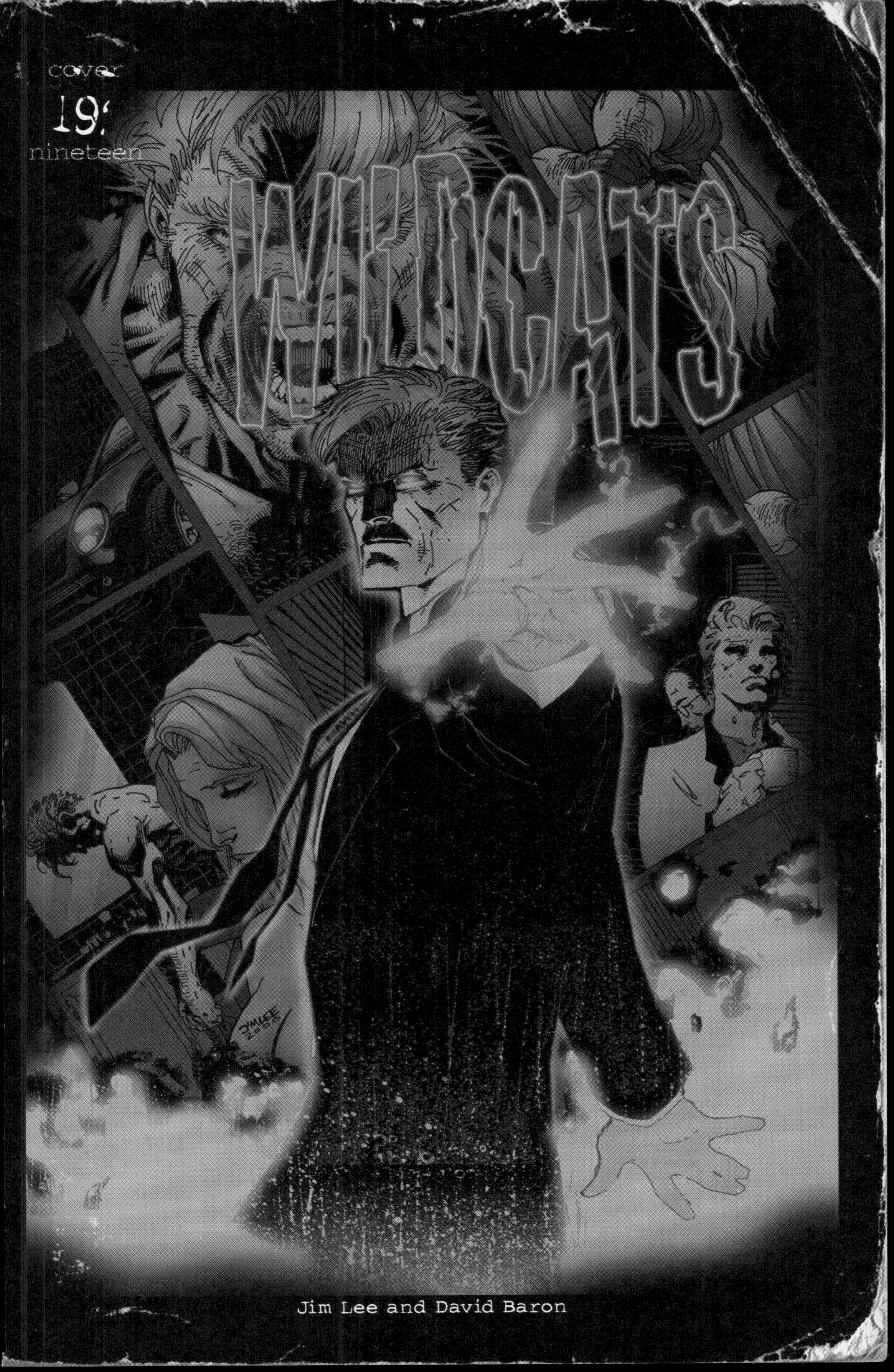
cover
19
nineteen
WILDCATS
Jim Lee and David Baron

Backlist

Look for these other great books from WildStorm and DC Comics:

WILDSTORM COLLECTIONS

The Authority: Relentless
Ellis/Hitch/Neary

The Authority:
Under New Management
Ellis/Millar/Hitch/Quitely

Crimson: Loyalty & Loss
Augustyn/Ramos/Hope

Crimson:
Heaven & Earth
Augustyn/Ramos/Hope

Crimson:
Earth Angel
Augustyn/Ramos/Hope

Deathblow:
Sinners and Saints
Choi/Lee/Sale/Scott

Danger Girl:
The Dangerous Collection
#1-3
Hartnell/Campbell/Garner

Divine Right:
Collected Edition #1-3
Lee/Williams

Gen^{13}
Choi/Lee/Campbell/Garner

Gen^{13}: #13 ABC
Choi/Lee/Campbell/Garner

Gen^{13}: Bootleg Vol. 1
Various writers and artists

Gen^{13}: Grunge the Movie
Warren

Gen^{13}: I Love New York
Arcudi/Frank/Smith

Gen^{13}: Interactive Plus
Various writers and artists

Gen^{13}: Starting Over
Choi/Lee/Campbell/Garner

Gen^{13}:
We'll Take Manhattan
Lobdell/Benes/Sibal

Kurt Busiek's Astro City:
Life in the Big City
Busiek/Anderson

Kurt Busiek's Astro City:
Confession
Busiek/Anderson/Blyberg

Kurt Busiek's Astro City:
Family Album
Busiek/Anderson/Blyberg

Kurt Busiek's Astro City:
Tarnished Angel
Busiek/Anderson/Blyberg

Leave It to Chance:
Shaman's Rain
Robinson/Smith

Leave It to Chance:
Trick or Threat
Robinson/Smith/Freeman

Wetworks: Rebirth
Portacio/Choi/Williams

Planetary/Authority:
Ruling the World
Ellis/Jimenez/Lanning

Planetary:
All Over the World
and Other Stories
Ellis/Cassaday

Planetary:
The Fourth Man
Ellis/Cassaday

StormWatch:
Force of Nature
Ellis/Raney/Elliott

StormWatch:
Lightning Strikes
Ellis/Raney/Lee/
Elliott/Williams

StormWatch:
Change or Die
Ellis/Raney/Jimenez

StormWatch:
A Finer World
Ellis/Hitch/Neary

WildC.A.T.s: Gang War
Moore/Various

WildC.A.T.s:
Gathering of Eagles
Claremont/Lee/Williams

WildC.A.T.s: Homecoming
Moore/Various

WildC.A.T.s/X-Men
Various writers and artists

Wildcats: Street Smart
Lobdell/Charest/Friend

Wildcats:
Vicious Circles
Casey/Phillips

STAR TREK COLLECTIONS

Star Trek: Voyager
False Colors
Archer/Moy/Carani

Star Trek: All of Me
Isabella & Ingersoll/
Lopresti/Emberlin

Star Trek:
The Next Generation
Embrace the Wolf
Golden & Sniegoski/
Hoover/Hubbs

Star Trek:
The Next Generation
Gorn Crisis
Anderson & Moesta/
Kordey

Star Trek: Voyager
Elite Force
Abnett & Lanning/
Moy/Carani

Star Trek: Voyager
Avalon Rising
Young & Young/Roach

Star Trek: New Frontier
Double Time
David/Collins/Roach

OTHER COLLECTIONS OF INTEREST

The Batman Adventures:
Mad Love
Dini/Timm

Batman:
The Dark Knight Returns
Miller/Janson/Varley

Batman: Faces
Wagner

Batman: The Killing Joke
Moore/Bolland/Higgins

Batman: Year One
Miller/Mazzucchelli/Lewis

JLA: New World Order
Morrison/Porter/Dell

JLA/ WildC.A.T.s
Morrison/Semeiks/Conrad

Kingdom Come
Waid/Ross

Ronin
Miller

For the nearest comics shop carrying collected editions and monthly titles from DC Comics, call 1-888-COMIC BOOK.